Emails to John:

Beyond Salvation

Sir M.J. Wasik

A very special thanks to the 'IX Group, especially John, who has put up with my ramblings for almost thirty years.

Contents

Foreword

No matter what field or genre, politics or religion, fiction or nonfiction, or even the medium of art it is recorded in, there is really only one story worth telling. It the story which speaks most directly to the heart of human existence, for it is the story of the struggle of the human heart. The true measure of success, is not found in such external factors as victory in war or business but in the overcoming those doubts, fears and pains which keeps us from living life. That keeps us from living a life worth living.

Do you understand the struggle of which I speak? To seek virtue even though vice is easier? To stick to the narrow Way even though the broad path promises to fulfill your desires? To face the pain, the uncertainty, the chaos, instead of running to the addictions we use to distract us? And what is the worth of victory if it was not won through pain? What is the price of wealth if it was not born from struggle? What is the worth of Life is it is not purchased with the Cross? Can there even be Life without barring our own cross?

For me, it started when I met John. I sometimes call him my first pupil, and that is true in a way. Looking back at it, I was never wiser than him, just more experienced He was young and arrogant, and I was a bit older and even more arrogant. He would be the first to give words to the nature of discipleship, that I was simply an older brother who experienced it first. God had different paths for our lives. Different callings, but the same focus. Both with that deep burning to be that person God would have us have so we both had questions in what that means.

As it turns out that my calling, my ministry is in finding those answers. That this book started twenty or so ago literally as emails to john, where I would be answering a question, he had asked on a phone call, or simply sharing something I had discovered for myself. Those emails are long gone as they were never really meant to be shared. But as time went on, other people joined who also felt like there was more to Faith than just 'getting into heaven'. I called it the 'IX Group because that was what I had labeled the folder I kept the emails in. From their it expanded into a newsletter, *The Way of the Inner-Life: beyond salvation*. As the name implies, I focus almost excessively on our hearts, our spirits, that which changes inside during sanctification, as we draw closer to God.

To put it plainly, there is no glory in victory, the glory is found in refusing to surrender. This we already know. One needs to face the chaos so that they can understand that there is no Ground, no stability outside of God. That all our well-constructed ideology, our dogmatic doctrine, our carefully crafted theology, are often just our way of avoiding the Truth, avoiding Christ. But it is not chaos which is our enemy for that is simply life. Nor is it all the religious stuff, for that can be good. Nor it is the temptations of all the distractions in the world which is the true struggle, for they are only an excuse, a way to avoid the struggle.

This book, and its companion *An Endless Road of Words*, is a collection of articles, emails and poems written, and now printed with for a specific group of people. Though it is my hope that some of it may be useful to you.

2

A Disposable Life

No joy found with what we see
Change the channel to fill our eyes
Loading our minds with the noise
Thinking belongs in the past

Another toy in our lives
Temporary happiness for sale
Throw it away when it gets dusty
Home is just a stop on the way to the trash

Enslaving in the name of freedom
Killing for the sake of convenience
When we are looking for a bargain,
Nothing is as cheap as a disposable life

Shrink wrapped hearts and plastic dreams
Living seems easy in a disposable world
No were to hide when we run from ourselves
Never seeing that life is not worth keeping 'til it's broken

The Cost of Grace

If I was going to raise my fist about anything at this moment it would be that attitude that salvation is free. That idea that Grace is cheap. I know that the theology of it is important in regards to the fact that no work of ours can earn salvation, and God gives Grace according to His Will rather than on merit. That is, I have no irritation at the theology of it, but I have to wonder why I hear it as often as I do, and spoken with such passion when I have never met anyone which has thought that you must earn your way into heaven through works. But then it is obvious that those who are so adamant on this point, some going as far as saying that James was wrong, are trying to justify their lack of works. That they are excusing their ingratitude towards God.

Something is not worth writing if it is not worthy to be written in blood. There is nothing worth saying if it is not worth ripping one's heart out to say. That which is free, that which costs nothing, is something which has no worth. If salvation was truly free then it would be of no value. For those who say that salvation is free, without cost, I can only respond by saying 'take another look at Christ, and Him crucified.' Look at what it cost God, and say again it was free. If I was worth millions and gave you a hundred dollars, you might be grateful, but would you not consider it a greater gift if I gave it to you even though it meant that I could not afford to eat for a while? So, considering that Christ gave up His life, I think we might want to show a bit more gratitude.

But the reason I do not raise up my fist is simply because I know what irritates me is not the gratitude you may or may not have but my own ingratitude. Being as intimate with the Cross as I am, I still am sitting here whining over the petty amount that Grace costs me. That what the suffering of Christ does cover, it bothers me to balk at the idea of covering that which is lacking in the Cross. It upsets me for I understand that the cost of Grace, what we must pay is to put aside our carnal desires so we may live a life of Charity. Or if you would, I am wise enough to understand that even the price, the death of our sinful side, is a benefit. And wise enough to understand how much Christ gave me so that I may pay so little. So, if knowing that even the price we must pay is for our benefit, then why do I still struggle?

Pain, horrible and terrible pain. There is no way to sugar coat that. I talk much about the wiliness to suffer because avoiding pain is very much part of the human condition which gets us in trouble. As much as I hate to admit it, I am but a human. So I struggle, as humans struggle to endure and accept the pain for the benefit of others, rather than to snarl and bite as an animal would. And that is the real cost of Grace, the real struggle and fight between flesh and spirit. Some will disagree, but if one is not willing to fight against the darkness in their own heart, if they are not willing to strive and struggle to beat down their flesh, they will see no progress in the Inner-Life.

Fasting, and all those lesser mortifications that are far more common are good, but there must be understanding that they are only a work, a method in which we use to fight against the flesh. That the real mortification is not about earning some sycophantic points, or earning favor by our sacrifices but about changing the nature of our heart. That our goal is to become a Christian, to become Christ-like. To increase the Grace which started at our salvation, and just as with salvation, the increase in Grace comes only to those who seek to be worthy of it.

Now, do not mistake my meaning. We cannot earn or be worthy of an increase in Grace any more than we can earn or be worthy of salvation. I am pointing out that the work required of us comes after the gift. When I had my conversion experience it was with much repenting and tears, but it was not until later did I really realize how unworthy I was of the Life God had given me. How much I was worthy of the death which Christ took to the Cross.

Salvation comes and then we are driven to, must try our best to live up to it, and the same way with increasing Grace. Every time God alters our heart in order to live a more perfect Life of Charity, there is always hardship, always a struggle to live according to that Grace. Work required of us to live up to, and in that, increase Faith, Hope and Charity.

I can write and preach about sacrifice until the End of the Age,

5

but all sacrifices, all works are for not if they are not born from mercy, from a heart of Charity. Mortification, such as fasting, is itself a nothing, simply a means in which to train ourselves so we may keep that vow of obedience, to do what is God would have us to do, no matter how much we think it is going to cost us. So that we know that though we sacrifice everything we have in obedience to the Will of God, we lose nothing, for the pearl we gain is worth far more than anything we may give up.

The Cost of Wisdom

Ecclesiastes 9.16-18

During my pagan years I still kept the Bible with me for one book, Ecclesiastes. More than any other book, I relate with its author. Now more than ever I can say it echoes my own heart. More to the point, what kept my interest in this book was the Preacher's words in the first chapter, 'for in much wisdom is much grief and he who increases knowledge increases sorrow." Or to put it in my own words, with wisdom comes pain.

What I could not answer was, what is it the author meant by wisdom? I was too modern for that. For wisdom is not knowing what to do, but what is right or wrong to do. This, my friends, is true wisdom. To see the world as it really is. At the heart of this, I must add, is to see the world as God sees it.

Our Lord told us that how we judge others we will be judged (Mathew 7). And this is the pebble in my shoe that keeps me striving for greater Grace. By what measure do I judge others? And the question for you is how do you judge others? Is a man more righteous in your sight if he wears a suit and speaks with thunder? Drives a nice car or is praised by other men? Indeed, do we praise him for living a righteous life? In the words of the preacher, 'this also is grasping for the wind'.

To make my point let me return to myself. I judge a person on only one thing. Are they seeking after God? Noble enough, after all, it is what wisdom seems to dictate. As I have written before, to know Elohim is our highest goal. Yet, is this how I want to be judged? Nay, for even if I rank highest among all people in seeking God, it would still fall short of the Glory of God. My only hope, as yours, is to be judged through the Blood of Jesus Christ. And this, my brothers, is how we must strive to judge others. Through Love and Forgiveness of such greatness for which our Lord allowed Himself to be nailed to a tree.

Conclusion: put aside your judgments so you may be able to listen to God's wisdom even if the words come from a poor and quiet man.

If You Are Lucky

You hurt.
You cry.
You do many things
Dark things
Evil things
To strike back at them
To strike at God
In hope that the pain goes away
At least for a little while

And if you are lucky
Really lucky
You find a friend
To offer a hand
To show compassion
To give understanding
To give their life

And if you are lucky
Really lucky
You find the strength
To face the pain
To face God
To forgive them
To forgive yourself

And if you are lucky
Really lucky
You kill the pain
Before it kills you
If you are lucky
Really lucky

A Cross of Swords

Let me start with a story, taking place in Japan long ago.

A lord was killed by an assassin, which is a great shame to the samurai whose Life was justified by the protection they gave their lord. So enters our hero, having just lost the justification for his Life, leaving him only two choices. The first, he could accept the shame of failure, end his existence which was no longer justified, a life that was now without purpose or meaning. But being our hero, he chose the second path, to find justification for his Life, a new purpose of his life. Which was to hunt down the person responsible for his lord's death, to bring the assassin to justice.

After many long years, and many trials, he was finally able to corner the assassin. The end of the story is upon us, the time for justice had arrived but just before our hero brings down the killing stroke the assassin spat in his face. This is an insult in any culture, but in feudal Japan, it is immoral in a way we in our culture have nothing to compare. People with any sense of decency, any at all, would simply not do it. In literary terms this could be seen as simply a way of showing that the assassin was truly a villain. Making it obvious that he deserved to die. So, in response to this great offence, our hero, the samurai, in anger, with the rage boiling inside, put his sword back into his belt and walked away.

The samurai in the story had an understanding which is lacking in today's world. That the application of force must never be personal, born from our own desires. While few of you will ever be in position which you must choose to be killed or be killed, to decide whether another will live or die, the Honor of this ideal still applies. While a true Warrior such as those in the military or Police, must take a more serious view as the force they use may be deadly, it applies just as much to us any time we use force.

The discipline of children or employees, when we preach, write, whether to use harsh or gentle words, or even as simple as voting, we are in essence applying force. And the question one must ask themselves before the application of force, am I doing this because it is

4

the right thing to do? Or am I doing it because I am angry, frustrated, wanting.

A Warrior of the Way does not pick up their Sword to defend themselves, but in the defense of others. We do not protect our own rights, but the rights of others. Every Warrior, in a real way must be as Christ on the Cross. Jesus, who had a legion of angels that would come and apply force on His behalf, but died none-the-less.

Indeed, while the world will not see it, every Warrior knows that the Cross is the symbol of their Way. To sacrifice one's own life, their dignity, even their Honor, for the sake of others, is the very heart of every true Warrior.

My Godmother

No connection of clan or kin,
No reason why she must,
She simply prayed for me.

I did not ask her to,
Or even suggested it,
She simply prayed for me.

My struggles and tribulations
She took onto herself,
She simply prayed for me.

No lectures of condemnation,
Or judgmental tones,
She simply prayed for me.

When I did not understand
Either the Cross or Charity,
She simply prayed for me.

Because of this I learned
What happens when people pray,
And gratitude for those who do.
And that is why I call her my Godmother.

Finding Joy in Trials

James 1

For Nkonye: Blessed are you when you seek the Lord in the trials you find in your youth, for then the troubles which come with age will not weigh on you as heavily. And in thanks for the Precious Gift our friendship has been to me.

Times of troubles come to all who live. Even though I have no need to tell you this, they are often marked by pain. Sometimes it is an irritation such as when our little sibling wants to play with us when we are busy, and sometimes they are that deep indescribable pain as if someone has a barbed hook deep in our heart and will not stop turning it.

I could easily give you advice on how to avoid such times or even how to survive them. As you have expressed a desire to deepen your Faith, I find that I should go further than that, if I can, to help you not only at such times to draw closer to God, but ultimately that you may gain the grace in which you can say honestly that you count it all joy when you meet trials.

I know that it seems like an impossible dream to have the same enjoyment of life while we are suffering that we find while we are not suffering. To give praise to the Lord, not simply in spite of trials but because of them, is an idea alien and opposed to our natural selves. Yet you are of an age at which you should know that we strive to live a life of grace, one which is beyond what we are capable of doing in our natural selves.

As you already know, it is not an easy path upon which you are embarking. The Grace to accomplish it will be given to you by God, yet you will find that it is hard work preparing your heart to live by that Grace. If it was left up to us, we would have a life of ease and pleasure. We were made for the Garden, and it is our desire to return to Eden -- which often leads us into sin. We are impatient and want our pleasures now, unwilling to wait until we are called home. Yet you must come to understand that the pains and troubles of this life are not something to be avoided, but instead should be welcomed for the benefits they are. You must use this time to learn to use everything to draw closer to God.

Trials Must Come
Mathew 13.20-21

There are those who will try to teach that if you have enough Faith, you will no longer face trials; that if you but believe enough, you will have all that you want. I, for one, give praise to Christ that He gives me what I need, and not what I want. Trials are something we need. It is through trials that we gain steadfastness, where we learn to focus on Jesus with a single-mindedness that leaves nothing else in our sight.

As you could tell me, sometimes the pain of our trials is of such intensity that we feel that it is beyond our ability to survive, even that the pain itself will kill us. This pain often stems from the feeling that life is out of control, which we are not getting from others what we need to survive.

There is some truth to this. As I have told you before, at one time or another we will all fail you, will not be there while you are in need -- everyone except for Christ. We find this out first-hand during trials. There is always the temptation during such times to turn away from God and find our own way out of them, to do it our way instead of His. This is why it is called a trial, for these tests show us where we are putting our Faith. It is where we seek our comfort from the pain that determines which is the god we worship. And it is by seeking the Living God in such times that we are freed from the idols we have in our lives.

This is the very reason we must go through trials and gain steadfastness. The point of the trials is not to become resistant to the pain, but to find our comfort in God. They are times during which, by seeking God in them, we learn to stop finding our peace in ourselves, others, or things. Instead, we learn to find peace in the only place which is everlasting, Jesus Christ.

(That is not to say that our Lord will not use other people, or things to help you with the trials; but no matter what form the help takes, it will always point you towards God. Those in your life who are truly sent to help you in your trials will not only help you feel better, but will also leave you with the knowledge that it was through Christ whom the help came.)

The Trial between Trials
Mathew 13.22

We cannot truly say that we have let steadfastness have its full effect unless we are seeking God as much, once the pain has left, as we did when the pain was there. For the benefit we gained from the trial will be quickly lost if we do not keep with our passionate prayers once the trial is over. Indeed, for some, happiness and pleasure are more of a test of Faith than the worst pain. It is easy to turn to God when we feel that we have no other choice but we need to learn to draw closer to Him when it does not seem that our life depends on it.

Too often, when we face the pains of life, we call out to God and get further frustrated that he does not seem to care. Yet Jesus is Faithful, and is always with us; but if we have not been able to draw joy from God when our hearts and minds are quiet, can we expect to find comfort in His presence when we have so much turmoil distracting us? And when God does eventually comfort us, do we then turn our back on Jesus until the next time we need a shot of happiness, treating the Lord like some sort of drug?

Saint Paul would liken the Christian life to a race, and told us to run to win. Yet, if we were to get up one morning and decide to run a marathon, we would not make it far and would collapse before the end. We could try every year and not get any farther. Not even just to win, but simply to finish. Armed with the knowledge we are not yet strong enough we would start running in between the marathons. We would have to push ourselves to get a little farther each day. And because we run more often, the running itself becomes easier and we could run farther with the same amount of effort. Maybe we would not be able to finish the next time we tried, but we would get much farther, and would know how much we have improved.

The trials can be seen as the marathon where we give it our all and end up on the ground, tired and in pain. If we simply go along with life as usual until the next trial comes our way, we will see only the same result. Yet, if we strive to draw closer to God in between trials, when the next trial comes, we find that it takes longer to be distracted from our focus on Jesus. We continue the cycle until we not only finish the race, but win, reaching that place where no trial is so hard that it can distract us from what is most important, our life in Christ.

Eyes on the Cross
1 peter 5.6-11

In facing the trials of life, as with everything else, we must first turn to Christ. For we must strive to find our comfort in God, and in this let us start with the Cross: spend time meditating on the suffering the Lord went through at Golgotha. For nothing we can go through can compare to the suffering which Jesus took upon himself that day. The whip and the nails, and more, for he took on all of our sufferings as well.

Jesus is our teacher as well as our God, and the Crucifixion is a lesson not only in suffering but in victory. For the blood and torture would be meaningless without Christ taking our sins to death with Him, and the empty grave proving it all. In the same way, our own suffering means little if we do not allow God's Grace to abound because of it. We could know a life of pain and poverty and not be the better for it. Suffering is not redemptive in itself, it only becomes an instrument of grace when it is linked with the Cross.

I have already told you when you are in pain to give it to God, to allow Christ to have it and do what He wants with it. So let us go to the next step and apply this to the cause of the pain. When another person treats you unfairly, think on this: our Lord did not deserve the whip to be brought down on his back, yet he accepted it out of love for us. Let your love abound, and when someone brings the whip of their tongue to bear on you, hold it not as a sin against them. In this, always strive to forgive more quickly, until you reach that point in which the forgiveness comes so easily and quickly that you have given it, even without thought, before they have even finished doing the wrong against you. As with Christ, you forgive them while you are still nailed to the cross.

You must strive to love, the spring in which forgiveness flows, so that even though the they still may harm you, the only pain you will feel will be from your desire to do what is best for them.

Eyes on Heaven
1 Peter 1.3-9

Let us now, and always, find peace in the Lord during times of trials. Let us focus our eyes on eternity, and realize that no matter how long we live, it is but the blinking of an eye compared to heaven. That suffering we face now is short beyond measure when we lay it next to the pleasure which we will have when we are called home. Indeed, can there be any greater hope than the Blessed Hope when we will see God face to face instead of through a dark glass?

So, we must learn to keep heaven in our view, and this is much of what we learn during trials. It is a difficult lesson to master, but we must understand that, just as pleasures passes away, so do pain and tears. You should not think that the pain you feel at this moment will last forever, for it often does not even last the week. Yet, even if it lasts a lifetime, it is not really a long time.

I know a man who, several years ago, developed constant pain in his hands and feet. Sometimes it is so mild he barely notices

11

it, other times it is so bad that he can barely walk or grip things. When it first started, he simply wanted it to go away, he did not want to live with it. As time went on, and he eventually faced that it was going to stay and was getting worse, he looked for a meaning in it. Like we often do, he wanted to know why he had to suffer such, going as far as saying those words which we have all thought: it was unfair. Facing the prospect that it will not go away, and will only worsen with age, he can now say with a shrug of the shoulders 'it will only last a little while; besides, it reminds me of the Nails.'

Pain will come to us all in various forms, but no matter the way, the enemy will try to use it to distract us from our focus on Christ. The reason is simple: if we fall into that trap of thinking that the pain is forever, it becomes unbearable. If we lose the Hope which is what God has promised us, then all we have left is the trouble of the now.

The reason we must find our Hope in God's promises of eternity is because tomorrow may be evil as well. For if we place our trust in what may happen tomorrow, we will find that, more than once, this trust will be unwarranted. We may go as far as to hate tomorrow for the evil it might bring. Yet, when we turn to the good which eternity will bring, it will not matter what good or evil tomorrow holds, nor even the troubles of today (and as the Lord said, Grace is enough), for the price becomes known to us as small compared to what we will receive.

So, strive to keep your hope fixed, not on the promises of this world, but on what our Lord has promised us, and eternity with Him.

Eyes on His Body
1 peter 3.8-18

It is not easy to live a life of joy when there are bombs falling to destroy you and your village. It is difficult to give your Lord thanks for your food when you do not know when or if you are going to eat again. Now, you and I may never face such a life, so our trials are not nearly as intense as we may think they are; yet that does not mean that they are not trials, or that the pain and frustration which we are feeling is without cause.

It is easy for one not in pain to point to those who have it worse than you, and say that you have no reason for your pain. Now it is true that no matter what you are going through, you could easily find others who have it far worse; but happiness of this kind is not finding peace in Jesus, it is promoting the pride that you are better than others. It is nothing less than evil to take pleasure in the pain of others, for if we have Charity then we suffer with the suffering of others and are comforted when others are comforted.

Yet, look again at those who are suffering a fate which makes your own look small. See those who in the midst of that turmoil are still placing their trust in God, and have found their peace in Christ. They are great examples to us, that they suffer worse than us, yet they do not let it trouble their hearts. Take comfort in theirs; for if Christ can give them such peace in their troubles, will not God give it to you in yours?

In the same way, there are those who suffer in ways which are not as severe as ours, but still their pain is just as real, just as bad as ours. Instead of saying that their suffering is less than ours so they have no right to their pain, let us instead find our own peace in the Lord so that they may find comfort in ours. Let us be an example to others, during our own trials, that there is a peace which God gives us in the midst of our troubles; that the Hope which Christ promised is more than wishful thinking, and is alive in our own hearts, as He lives in our hearts.

In His Hands
1 peter 2.18-25

Now all of this does not mean that you should not avoid trouble when you can do such. Many of the trials we find in life are caused by our own hands; but those in which we find ourselves because of our virtue, or simply by the virtue of being alive, let us strive to find

13

joy in them. In this, I must write about one more thing, for you now know what to do but you still lack the how. As I know you pray often, I will not have to tell you to do such. Let me instead add another thing to your prayers.

As you well know, we cannot accomplish what we have set out to do without the Grace of God and there is but one way to receive that Grace. Which is, giving control of our lives to Christ. God can do all things if we will let Him do it. It is the same as when I told you to give control of your pain to God. It is simply expanded to your entire life. For if you truly desire to find joy in trials, then that is what you must do.

We must be willing to trust God enough to allow Him to have control over everything. Finding the joy from trials requires you to spend those hours in prayers, and allow Christ to be in charge of it all. It may seem harsh, but the frustration and worries come from our not trusting Jesus enough to give him total control. That is, in truth, the key of finding the joy in any trial. For as I have said before, the fires which test our Faith do not harm our Faith, but only those parts which masquerade as Faith.

For all the pain and struggles are God's way of showing us what we have not yet given into his care. Use them to strive to give all of yourself to him. Even though the troubles of life will always come while we have these mortal bodies, once you have learned to trust God in all things, the trials are no longer something to worry about; they become simply a thing to do something about.

We are your neighbors

I have nowhere to go when the snow starts to fall
So, I huddle in the corner, in the places you will not go
Like a shadow in a mirror, a wisp of smoke in the rain
You turn your head and pretend not to see me shiver,
I am your neighbor, and I am in need.

My toothless grin and outstretched hand.
I meet you on the corners, and at the store fronts
Like a dog barking after dark, a phone ringing during dinner
You see me as only another annoyance in your life
I am your neighbor, and I am in need.

I have no bread to give to my children
So I sell myself, all I have left, so they can eat
Like uncombed hair, a stain on a shirt
You will not be seen with me, people might get the wrong idea
I am your neighbor and I am in need.

I am only seventeen and see no hope for the future
So, I put a needle in my arm to find a little pleasure
Like a dish in the sink, a flower bed in need of tending
You are too busy to help me with my pain before it kills me
I am your neighbor, and I am in need.

Do you give any thought to the Lord' words?
What you do not do for the least of Mine…
Give to all those who ask…
He who is without sin…
They shall know you belong to Me by your love…

We are your neighbors, and we are in need!

Finding your way

Sanctification is the meat in that shell of Christ as Way. If we look at the Cross for a moment, taking away all the theological metaphysics and even the Mystery, what we are left with is an invitation to a formal party. A grand party, with a feast, and singing and music, a worthy celebration for the King getting married. Everyone is invited, some have decided that they do not want to go, for various reasons. But that is not the focus, instead let us look at where we are when the invitation is presented to us. We are outside playing in the mud. So, there we are invited to a party in King's palace, standing there covered in mud, but still we have decided to go. But standing there, covered in mud we know that we are not ready to go, so we rush inside and take a shower.

So, we are standing there feeling good, after getting out of the shower. I mean even for a bohemian like myself that feeling of clean after a shower is a pleasant one. But then you learn the party is not for a while, and for some reason you look outside and see that mud puddle and you think fun. Maybe you resist for a while, after all you just got clean, but then you end up right back outside covered in mud. Feeling the icky sticky bad of the mud again, and feeling worse because you promised yourself you would not get muddy again. And this happens over and over again, long enough that your Inner-Life is alternates between getting muddy and clean. So much so, one could call it a habit, and so much so that we start saying that we are ready for the party when we are not covered in mud. We start getting the idea, we form the ideal of perfection as simply not covered in the mud, as not being 'sinful'. So much so, much of church culture today is focused on the mud, about all those people out there having fun in the mud, that if you can stay out of the mud then you are ready for the party. But look again.

We are standing with the mud washed off, but there is still grime underneath of our fingernails. Honestly now, do you want to be passing the mash potatoes with all that dirt under your fingernail? That might do when I am making myself a sandwich, but hardly when I will be a guest of the King. So, we clean the dirt out from our nails, and maybe we sit around waiting again, and have to clean our nails again. Have to deal with the same issue, the same venial sin over and over again.

Right, a dry season. We keep having to clean our nails over and over again, until we learn that we need a hair cut. And maybe we have to get our hair cut a dozen times until we learn to brush it. and then on to picking out our attire, pressing the cloths, trimming our nose hairs, and so on (let me stop before it really gets gross) until we learn that God is asking of us to simply continue to get ready for the party, and eventually help others get ready for the party as well.

It is important to understand, to remember what one knew at the beginning of the Inner-Life. Christ and Him crucified, Christ as the Way of the Inner-Life. That justification, accepting the invitation and allowing the Christ to wash away the mud is the first step, the most important step to be sure, but it is only the first step. That there is a lot of work, hardships of facing our pain, our shame, internally too much to do without Christ. Yes indeed much work involved so we may show up at that party celebrating the King's wedding as a spotless and perfect bride

**

Eli, Eli, lama sabachthina!?

It feels that way sometimes, does it not? That God has forsaken you? But you know that it is not so. That God is with you, always. So the fault must be in you. That you have turned your face away. That you have turned your focus onto a sin, or a desire, or a worry, a something instead of on Him. You know this, and this just makes you feel worse. It is just one more thing proving what a terrible person you are. How completely unworthy, worthless. Just more proof that that you are too weak, that you just cannot face the pain of the struggle.

It is Just that feeling which lets me know that one is on the right track. We all get distracted from God by and by. Sometimes it is not even sin. I could have been the task He set before you, which commonly happens to ministers. Or family, after all it is proper and good, and God's Will that one is dedicated to spouse and children above all else in this world. While I can only imagine, it just seems natural that there would be a struggle to maintain their focus on God when one must also keep their focus on the things of this world.

Indeed, I must say that there is no shame to be found in such struggles. No shame at all to be found in those times when you feel like you are drowning, gasping for that air which is the Spirit. I must go as far to say that there is no shame, no blame to be found even when what you struggle against is a sin. To be sure, Honor is not found in conquering but in the struggle, not in the victory but in the willingness of fight. St. Paul wrote for us to run the race to win it, and such is the attitude needed to the end. For while there is no shame in the struggle to win, there is shame in not struggling for the Victory.

Looking back at the last ten years, I can say that the times which I felt separated from God were far better than those times when I was separated but did not feel it. To be sure they were far more painful, but the pain was simply motivation to seek Him more earnestly. So much so I consider it a great blessing, the best Grace I have been given to acutely aware of how far I am be from God, even while being aware of Him. That knowing Life, I also long to know Him more.

**

When I was young, very young, I knew God. It was in that way in which I just knew that there was a God, over there, up there. Watching from heaven, a heaven I could almost point to in that inner, difficult-to-explain, way. In all my education the only thing which I could say that was really lacking was the teaching to seek God, to draw closer in that inner, difficult-to-explain, way to where

God is. Or if you would, I was never taught how to question my Faith. How to examine, to explore with part of my heart which knows there is a God.

This is why, of course, I spend much time talking and writing about it. It is that thing, that difficult-to-explain topic which is neglected more often than it is not. It is a hard subject because perceptions of it differ. Seeking God, drawing closer to Him, listening to the Spirit, keeping our focus on God, camping at the Cross, even having a relationship with Christ and knowing God are all terms used to describe more or less the same thing. If you have had the experience, and there is no mistaking it, then the term used becomes irrelevant. One knows the rose for a rose, and the name no longer affects the smell.

But what if you have no clue what I am talking about? What if you have never experienced that Great Mystery we call God? First, I would say, if it does not bother you, then do not let it bother you. If there is no whole, not feeling of an unanswered question, not feeling that you are looking for something which cannot be named, then there really is not a problem. That is, unless one has truly gone numb or completely cold, they will know when it is time, time to take it to the next level.

But there is the problem is it not, when we know it is time. When it has been past the time for weeks, months, even years. And when we are young, either physically or spiritually, it is easy to turn to the World, to our sins, our desires and obsessions, or worse, to our dogma and doctrine in order to try to fill that void, to scratch that itch, to sooth that ache. That is more or less what happened to me. But the World only promises but never fulfills, at least in the long run. I love philosophy, but the search for wisdom cannot replace the search for God, Wisdom cannot replace Christ, for one only finds it in Him.

Anyway, it can build up, make one feel unworthy. To which I can only shrug my shoulders, of course you are unworthy, as I am even as I write this. Such is the point of the Cross, and I am sure you must have heard this before. But think on this. St. Paul, when faced with the debates of theology of his day, was determined to know nothing except for Christ, and Him Crucified. It was not because they were unimportant, just unimportant compared to God.

That is, you may be under the belief that you must be perfect, or at least righteous before you can find or go to God. That is an upside-down pyramid. It is that belief, is it not, which is preventing you from going to God? So, I say spend some time knowing nothing, nothing of the past, believing nothing. Spend some time being still, where nothing exists except for God. and if you are not ready for that, spend some time when the only thing which is real is the search for God, that crying out for God. Spend the time seeking God, really spend the time doing it, and eventually you will understand. Draw closer to God and He will draw closer to you.

**

There is an image, of the Warrior going to war, and in a heroic act, an act of Honor, sacrifices themselves by throwing themselves on a grenade. We may dream of performing such, literally or metaphorically, sacrificing ourselves for the good of the whole. But such Warriors, the men and women who do such things, do not become a hero in that single act. Long before the sacrifice which they gained recognition, they lived as a hero, with Honor. They lived every day as a ministry.

You may never get that chance to throw yourself on a grenade for the sake of your comrades. You may never get that chance to make that obvious sacrifice which earns medals and praise from others. But what if you do? What if you get that moment in which your death will save the lives of many? That moment when you can save a soul by the sacrifice of your reputation? Would you be ready to sacrifice what you hold dear for the sake of Honor? Would you be ready to give even your Honor for the sake of Mercy? Are you ready?

There are those who say that one can tell an anointed by what they accomplished. There is some truth in this, because how we face death is important. However, how we die is based on character, and character is formed from the choices we make every day. We will never see that day we dream of, that day we can sacrifice in some glorious way, until we learn to see the sacrifices, the mercy needed of us in our daily lives.

We may dream of crusades and international ministries, mega-churches and auditoriums overflowing, of revival and renaissance, but all of that is meaningless if we are not living our daily lives in a way which is pleasing to God. Can we really say that we are doing the Will of God, if we accomplish what He would have us do, but in a way which is not His Will? What does it matter if all my words and works are for His sake, if my heart is far from Christ?

I have seen the great hopes of our time brake and shatter for no other reason than using the vision as an excuse not to live in the Heart of God. Quests failed, stripped from us for no other reason than we were so busy working, obsession on fulfilling it, to reach the top of the mountain that we failed to ask what would God have of me now, in this moment. A lesson I have had to learn more than once, and brought home to me again, made personal to me in my latest trips. A reminder not to lose the Way by focusing on where He is leading.

That is a lesson important for all ministers of the Word, but I think is relevant to everyone. At least, to everyone who dreams of being a Hero. It is those small none-lethal grenades which we need to be throwing ourselves on. That, to one another, to family and friends, coworkers and strangers, in which the sacrifices should be made. That those grenades, those struggles and stumbling blocks which we shrug our shoulders over, seem so small to us, should be the first we jump on. For that grenade which seems so small and petty to you, may very well be deadly to others.

The way that this all goes together, the point of it all, is that there is more Honor to be found in those small mercies, in the small sacrifices we do from Love in our daily lives, then in the great works done for our own gratification. That if one wants to be a Hero, that those who are Heroes, carry their cross every day, a living sacrifice to God, for spouse and children, for family and friends, for others. That it is not their gifts, their abilities and talents which is a measure of a Christian, but our Charity for one another.

As I am reminded once again, I remind you, that the question asked of us will not be how much we accomplished in this life, but how well we lived it. Do we live our life in a way pleasing to God, as a servant to Him and one another, or are we living it only for our own benefit, our own glory? And really that is the only real choice in life, one must either live it to His Glory, or for our own.

**

When it comes to meditative prayer, that deep spiritual thinking about the Way of God, the hardest thing is often knowing what it is we should be pondering. I used to worry about that. What it is I should be working on at this time. Is it humility? That one seems like it should be often. Faith? Hope? Charity? One of my favorites. Should it be one of the Mysteries? The Cross, the Resurrection or Incarnation, for example. Should it be scriptures, diving into the depth which is found there? That is always the fun of awakening into a bigger world, is it not?

I used to worry about it, but not anymore. Now I understand more how the Spirit rather than our thoughts are the cause. So I just let it happen. One such contemplative prayer, which I have not spent much time writing about, but one I have come to believe is very important, is the Love from God. We can understand well enough that God Loves us, has a great Love for everyone, but that is not the same thing as feeling Loved.

Of the ways that one must kill their God, to stop focusing on our own idea of God and to focus on God, I think God's Love may be one of the most important. That is, we know that God Loves us and we take comfort in that idea. But the idea of God's Love is just that, an idea, which means it can be changed, altered, corrupted by the what-if syndrome. But God's Love itself is perfect, eternal and to understand that, to truly know that, you have to have experienced it, feel it.

The reason I write this here, instead of making it an article of its own, is because I have observed that many, many times many of our sins are caused by an attempt to feel loved. The human heart has a need, not just a desire but a need to be loved, to feel loved. The desire to fulfill that need will motivate us to do many things. We may forsake Honor, our character, for the sake of feeling loved by another. Do things we would not normally do, accept treatment that we would not normally accept. That we will sin, or allow one to sin against us, for no other reason for a feeling, even the illusion of the feeling that we are loved.

Not as obvious, but just as true, we may even seek to be righteous, to have a strong character, only from a desire to love ourselves, or from the idea that God will only Love us when we are righteous. Thus, making His love dependent on our own righteousness, which leads us to the error of loving others, or ourselves, only when they are acting as they should, or at least as we think they should.

Very often we are motivated from the idea that we must do, or not do in order to be loved. But that is not really love, but an idea of love. That is, such as in romance, when one spouse feels the love of the other, that allows the other to relax, to not be afraid of losing that love for not being perfect. And as that love grows the understanding (not necessarily a knowing) that it is that feeling of love, that being loved is what the heart needs. And as love grows, all those little irritating things, those panty-hose issues (John's phrase) not only become nothing, but something you enjoy about the person. Enjoy because they are part of the person who is fulfilling your need.

We keep God's commandments because we love Him, so the more we love Him the better we are at doing His will. Harsh, true, but it seems to be then that we often look at that from the wrong view. That is, we see righteousness as proof of our love, instead of seeing it as something we do simply because we love. That we focus on improving our ability to follow the Law, instead of Christ. Focusing in increasing our love for Him, and for others, which motivates us to keep the Law, which frees us from that restrictive feeling of the Law.

And the point is, that it is much easier to love someone, if you can feel the love they have for you. I have been at this awhile, and have striven to have that love even for those who hate me, but I must say I still find it much easier to love those who love me. No work at all, right? So keep that in mind the next time the Spirit lets you decide what to ponder on, and try to not just believe that God Loves you, but feel that Love. That the more you can feel it, the more you experience it, the more you will feel that need of your heart fulfilled. The more that happens, the less you will spend seeking that need, seeking the illusion of that need fulfilled from other things.

Human Sacrifice

The price of being a Warrior is death. The cost of being a leader is the sacrifice of one's self. It is the love which motivates that sacrifice which has always been the very foundation of leadership. It is that attitude which is almost entirely missing in today's world, and in truth, the Church as well. We hate being reminded that the price of Life is death, that we avoid Life perfected, Christ and Him Crucified. We go to great lengths in using anything and everything, philosophy, theology, entertainment in our attempt to find something in which to replace the Cross. Few people would actually say that, there are few honest enough to admit that we simply do not want to pay the price.

I was watching a program in which Joseph Campbell was talking about how the old myths are no longer relevant in today's world. I am a fan of his work, and I understood his point, that the symbolism of the old stories is no longer modern. In a way, I agree, how many people really understand the importance of the High Priest ripping his robe, or that the religious trial of Christ was held at night? But do we need a new and modern story to replace the Cross? Thinking that a mere story, an expression of an ideal, can we truly replace Christ and Him crucified? It has been attempting just that which has caused the worst crimes in history, both inside and outside the Church.

It is universal knowledge, bore out in every People and time, that when there is sin, when there is something wrong, it can only be cleansed by blood, whether literally or metaphorically. While it is true that few, if any still practice a ritualized, religious spilling of blood in order to cleanse a spirit, the principle is still very much at the core of human existence. Metaphorically we, as individuals, as cultures and as humanity, still very much perform sacrifices, even human sacrifices, in order to cover our sins.

Take a look at any utopian philosophy, every attempt to

create a better world, you will find its proponents advocating the need for the blood of humans to replace the Blood of Christ. Sacrifice the unborn, sacrifice the innocent, sacrifice the guilty, sacrifice yourself and we will have a perfect world without having to prostate ourselves before the Cross. Maybe we hope that it can be accomplished, even though every attempt has been at best a failure, and at worst, a holocaust.

National Socialism is the most obvious example, because of its extremity. Where the purification of the Germanic communal spirit, the *Volk,* what we would call the People, was used as justification for genocide. That looking at the Nazi philosophy with an eye of redemptive theology, it is easy to see that they were trying to wash away their own sins with the blood of the Jews. They thought that if they had simply killed enough (all) the Jews, Gypsies and other undesirables that they would create the Kingdom of Heaven. That by labeling others as the problem, and by sacrificing the other, cutting the other out of the People, that it would cleanse, rid them of the darkness in their own hearts. But while the scapegoat-principle is obvious in its extremity, we are less likely see the comparison to our own actions because of that extremity.

It is well known that when you judge the Law as unjust in order to excuse your sin then you are placing yourself above the Law and equal to God. But do we not know when we judge others according to the Law, we are also placing ourselves over the Law, and thus equal with God? That when we condemn another under the Law, we condemn ourselves, as we are guilty under the Law. But as I am innocent, not according to the Law but according to the Cross, then how can I condemn another according to the Law, and not by the Cross? And if I am to judge according the Christ and Him Crucified, should then not the judgment I derive be one of healing, of reconciliation to God, rather than a cutting off from the People. That even when one must be cut away from the People, should not it be done with the view, the attitude and philosophy, of not simply to protect the People but with the goal of the healing of that person so that they may once again return to the People.

Does it not sadden the heart that Christ came to heal the sick, to bring the sinner back to God, to give Life to the Lifeless, to save the condemned, and we, the Church, His Body here on earth, is so quick to abandon those who need healing, forgiveness, Life, salvation? I can only conclude that it is because we forget, that no matter how holy we may think we are, we too are the ones in need of healing, of forgiveness, of Life and salvation. That we are in need of Christ, His Blood, His Sacrifice, every single day of our lives.

A Poor Knight's Observations

The law of average leadership: The average skill in which any society shows in leadership throughout its lifetime falls into a very small range compared to other societies, no matter what form of government they have.

The law of opposite sensations: When any sensation is prolonged, and then becomes absent, it will create the opposite sensation.

The law of applied intelligence: The lack of natural intelligence can be overcome by taking the time to apply the intelligence one does have to a situation, but no amount of natural intelligence can overcome not taking the time to apply it to the situation.

The law of faulty data: Dissect any mistake in logic, and one will find that the logic was rarely at fault but instead the data which was used in the equation.

The law of the moving denominator: No matter how low you move your expectation, the level of performance will always be slightly lower.

The law of cattle-prod activity: At any given time, what a person is giving the most energy to is that thing which is giving them the most pain.

The laws of degrading debates: The chance of finding a solution to an issue starts to decreases dramatically the moment it moves from a debate of the issue, and becomes a debate of opinions.

The law of democracy: Those that are chosen as leaders are those who are most willing to speak and remove any doubt that they are fools.

The law of tyranny: When obsession is mistaken for love, control becomes the mechanism of expression.

The law of wisdom: The great majority is the lovers of

their opinions, but it is hard to find anyone who has spent the time to form an opinion.

The law of emotion: Dissect each emotion and you will find that they are either a manifestation of Love or a lack there of.

The law of politics: One's politics are rarely what are actually best for the society, but what they perceive to be best for themselves.

The law of Honor: One is capable of knowing what they should do in a situation in direct proportion they have the will to do what they should do in a situation.

Like the Wind

Mathew 5.3

Change is a difficult thing to deal with. Change not only threatens our ability to control our environment, more importantly it threatens our well-constructed image of the world. It throws doubts on the future, and the past. We long for a world which is constant, which 'remains the same from the time our fathers' fell asleep'. It is human nature, a primal instinct, to exert control on our environment, and when that fails to ignore the reality of the universe is constant change, and create an illusion of control. Yet when our environment changes to the extent where our illusion is a danger to our survival, we have only two choices. To either hold onto the illusion as it pulls us down into destruction or let go completely and slip into that insanity of being like the Wind. A choice between the shackles which bind us to this world, and cutting those chains and living completely free. To have the freedom of the Wind.

Of course, I do not refer to such common freedom, that is the hall mark of modern ideology. True freedom is found in the heart. When you are truly free, you are such even when there are shackles on your limbs and a lash brought down on your back. When you have been granted the Grace of such freedom, there are no principalities or powers which can take it away from you. But there is a price to this freedom.

Of course, at the core of this is doing the will of God, or more accurate those things which hold us back from doing His will. Those of you who have dedicated yourself to seeking God and His will for your life know personally how hard it is at times. That it seems simply impossible, too hard, too painful. Those times in which when it seems that your cross is just too heavy to lift, let alone carry. This may seem harsh, but the truth of the matter is that the cross is not heavy at all, it is all the luggage you try to carry with the cross which weights us down. You cannot be moved by the Wind if you are still

30

holding onto a millstone.

Carrying our cross, our ministry, our calling, vocation or whatever you may call it, is the easiest thing to do in the world. Not because the work is easy, but because the part of it which is difficult is accomplished by Christ Himself. Because God carried the Cross, our crosses are light, so again, when you find that it seems heavy, ask yourself what are you carrying other than your cross. What is it that you want more than God?

It is a serious question, and a hard one to ask yourself. Even harder to have God show you. You might be surprised at the answer. Even considering my vow of poverty, the hardest thing for me to give up is ...my fear. More specifically, a fear of what I am capable of doing. With all the other fighting I have done, the hardest struggle has been against the fire which burns in my own heart. I had come to hate my spiritual strength more and more, came to see it as a corruption, a spreading virus left over from my days of darkness. At every turn I tried to put out the fire, and every turn my attempts would only make it stronger. Some of you do not have a clue what I am talking about, others have seen hints and glimpses of the fire, and those of you, who are dear to me, which may not understand what it is, have seen my struggle to keep it at bay. My fear is what may happen if I do not hide it in a box.

As I have written before, my vow of poverty has little to do with material possessions, it has everything to do with motive. It has to do with a singularity of focus on God and His will. Yet, let me make this clear that this is more than simply giving up distractions, it is living in a constant state of war. It is about the spiritual war, which everyone of us is in, whether we want to be or not, whether we believe in it or not.

The change in which I have been trying to align myself to, is one of going into my calling full time. And in that context, I must live completely on the generosity of others. The only thing which I can ask for, expect, is a place to sleep, and not necessarily indoors. You might find it odd that I would receive the Grace of Hope when

God was practically saying that there will be times when I will be wet, cold and hungry. To understand you must try to see it from my viewpoint. Eight years ago, I knelt and vowed my sword and my life in service of our Lord, Jesus the Christ. These years of being forged, tempered and sharpened have been filled with pain and hardship. All of it I endured, at times not well, but all with the knowledge that someday, that day which the Lord decides, I will be put to use. Even in every time I whined that it was too hard, there was too much pain, not any point to it, I never seriously gave a thought to ringing the bell. I am far too stubborn to give up.

I made a comment last year to a dear friend, that I spent the last eight years preparing myself for the future, it is now time for me to prepare others. I know that this is a bit weird coming from me, considering how much I focus on helping others. The truth is, that up until now I have only been able to help people survive in a world which is darkening. But I am tired of simply surviving, of losing ground to the enemy, tired of spilling my blood and life in blunted attacks. And I know that I am not alone in this.

But this is nothing new. This frustration has been compounded with the fact that we never had an answer to; what are we going to do about it? Well? Ok, I am not really looking for an answer, because I, after pleading for so long, have finally received one. My mind and spirit have been set in action once again. This will be the topics of my future emails. That is, I know what I need to do, but it is time for you to ask yourself what you need to do. Let me give this advice though. Do not be overly concern if the answer does not come quickly. You know as well as I do that God's timing makes little sense to us until after the event, and sometimes not even then.

It may seem that I have gotten way off the point, but I have not. Whenever God gives you Grace, there is a reason. For there to be freedom, there must be purpose. The Grace He gives you, is so you may have the ability to do what He asks of you. the question is never whether or not He gives us Grace, the question is always whether or not we accept it. If God gives you the order, He always gives you the ability to accomplish it. But it is not that simple, is it? For there are those times when no matter how hard we try, how hard we work, we fall far short of what we were supposed to do. Oh, I can go into all the different reasons this is such, which all boil down to the rejection of Grace, or in other words, trying to do it ourselves. But in truth, I must shrug my shoulders and say; so, what?

Do you believe that God did not know that you would fail? That you would stumble and sin again? See, God does not demand for us to be perfect (am I not I lucky?), He only demands that we try to be such. If God only accepted us when we were perfect, then there would never have been the Cross. Let us never forget that the Blood Christ shed, washes away such things, but let us also not forget the role of the Spirit, which leads us into perfection. If you want to be perfect it is simply a matter of allowing the Spirit to guide your every step. Allowing the Grace of God, to fill every moment of your life. I say simply, like it is an easy thing.

But maybe, just maybe it is so hard, because we try too hard. It is easy for me to say, for I have just come out of my 'trying too hard' phase. That is, the ability to let the Spirit lead you is also a Grace. I know that it seems a tautology that we need to be led by God in order to be able to be led by God, but that just the way it is. Do not mistake what I am saying, we must do our part, but our part is goes back to something I have said often, but seem to forget from time to time. That is allowing God to do what He pleases with our heart. And that is the essence and the point of being like the Wind. To give God free reign not only over our external lives, but over our hearts as well.

Leaders and Elders

Do you ever get the desire to strip off all vestiges of civilization and run with the wolves, to hunt, to howl? To race the wind, pushing with everything you have until you collapse? Do you ever have the urge bubble up from deep inside to throw yourself into a tornado just for the pleasure of the ride? Do you ever dream of being a great samurai facing an opponent, not even questioning whether you will win or loose, not caring about victory or defeat but finding pleasure in the fight itself? The question is, no matter how it manifests, do you feel that pull, that longing deep inside to live, to truly live?

Maybe not. Maybe you are too old, maybe you say that is for the young, any passion you had for life dried up a long time ago. But I do not see age as a factor. I know people twice my age who live a life of gusto, and I know people half my age who find no passion in life, who have given up. And I know, the majority that I meet, people who have a look in the eyes tells that they long to live, they long for passion, they long, for most of them something they cannot put into words. Their spirits scream out 'this cannot be all there is, there has to be more.'

Passion! Forget oil, forget electricity and defiantly forget money. Passion is the energy which truly runs a nation. Forget technology, forget information, what are these compared to the will to use them? It is passion that people seek. Not wealth, not glory, not power but passion, to feel alive, to be filled with life so abundantly that there are no more questions about the meaning of life, for you can feel what it means to be alive. If I could point to the sky, and crack open the heavens you would see passion perfected, the Resurrection. In that fleeting moment you would weep, for you would know what it means to be alive. And in that moment, you would weep because you would understand the cost for life, there is always a cost, the Cross.

Life is not possible without suffering, and suffering is

pointless unless it is redemptive, unless it brings life. From the beginning, life is not possible without suffering. The life you have today was bought for you by the sufferings of others and yourself. Your mother's suffering to carry and birth you, your parent's suffering to care and provide, your friends' wiliness to care and your suffering to endure and suffer for others. Suffering is the cost of life, the cost of passion. Without the Cross there could be no Resurrection, but without the Resurrection, the Cross would be pointless.

God allows, even wills us to suffer because it is by that suffering that we learn how to be alive, how to find joy in living, how we learn to use the life we have. Suffering, the wiliness to allow ourselves to suffer, does not only make those moments when we are not suffering a pleasure, it is also the cost of wisdom.

If I had to give a definition to wisdom, it would be the perfect balance between passion and intellect. It would be not only knowing how to act, but having the will to act. But the question is not how I define wisdom, but how a society defines it. All other social assumptions fall secondary to the nation's ideal of the concept we call wisdom. Morality or social norms, economics, culture, and public policy all derive from the wisdom that society has, how they define what is wise. And as the wisdom of a community flows not from its leader but from its elders, then that community's ideal of an elder is of vital importance.

Even with this understanding, I am ill equipped to describe what an elder should be, or even could be. I am like a man who has been trained in a profession to the point in which they can name and use each of the tools of their trade, and then goes to try to explain what it like to be a member of that profession. Or I am like one who, at seeing a figure far off in the distance, proceeds to gives a detailed description of that person. Life is like that. The future is like that. We look to the future and see what might happen, and even for those of us who can see what will happen, we never fully understand it until it does happen.

I could point to that elder I will be some day. I could try to describe the wisdom that he will have. I could even point out that for some reason, I will even have a different name. But the truth is, I would not be describing the future, I would be describing an image of the future created by the understanding of the now. Nor can I really speak of wisdom. It is funny that almost a life time as a philosopher, one who seeks to acquire wisdom, I understand it very little. Oh, I understand its nature, I can write for days examining it, but its application is an entirely different thing. Just as suffering is pointless unless it is redemptive, so is wisdom useless unless it is used to benefit the community. Which, in all honesty is where I am starting with my ideal of an elder, the first of the steps towards my future self.

The wisdom of an elder does not differ from others in either quality or quantity but in focus. A leader needs wisdom, they must be able to determine how to secure the welfare of the People, in the now, and they must have the wisdom to respect the wisdom of the elders. The elder's wisdom is focused less on the now, and more on the future. I do not mean that they must be prophets, what I mean is that they must be able to weigh, to balance the welfare of the People in the now with the welfare of the People in the future.

I could go on, and on, and on, but like I said I have only really begun to understand what this means, at what level this really needs to be at. I have only written what I have because for some of you, becoming an elder is not far off in the distance. Not that I am saying that my own wisdom is so great that I know what you need, only that I am a voice for my generation (and the younger if I can be so bold), and I can say what it is that we expect from you, what we need from you. I will never be able to write with the passion, the desire the force that is in my heart for this.

We do not need friends, or stars, or even for you to 'understand' us. What we need from you is your wisdom. If we have any hope of a better tomorrow, our work will have to be guided by you, your experience, and the wisdom that the sufferings of life have taught you. And as wrote in my journal this is a simple statement of fact, a cry of desperation, and a plea for mercy: We need elders!

Three Oaths of this Knight

Now I will be talking about the three oaths I have taken. Now when I say I have taken these oaths I do not mean I merely raised my hand and recited some words as when I joined the military. As much as my sense of duty bound me to that oath, these oaths were done with my whole being. That is, each oath was said in deep prayer and has radically affected my life. In truth, I did not even realize I was taking an oath until after I said them. I keep them posted and I pray about them each day. it has been hard work, as my ultimate goal is to never fail in them.

Obedience: Whatever You ask of me, I will do

I wrote to you several years ago that one is not born to be great but becomes great by embracing the greatness already inside them. That one is not born to be a Saint but becomes one by deciding never to say no to God again. When I gave my oath of obedience I imagined all sorts of things. Missionary work, martyrdom etc. It was hard for me to accept that what the Lord has asked of me the most was simply to listen to Him and learn. It has been a long road for me to learn the truth of Eckert's words when he said that the smallest work accomplished in God's will is greater then the greatest works accomplished outside of His will.

This oath has driven me the most and has been the easiest for me to keep. I have done well in it not because of my own will but because by following it I learned the truth of why we need Elohim. See, when the Lord tells us to go there, or to give something up it is not just because others need help or that we He does not want us to have something. It is because it is best for us as well. There is nothing in which God has us do, or not do that does not improve us, even if we are unable to see it.

Poverty: Everything I have belongs to You

Most of us Protestants do not want to believe that poverty is central to our Faith. Indeed, most think I am talking about physical possessions when I mention my oath of poverty. If this was the case with you, you are either too cynical or too attached to your possessions. What I mean by poverty has little to do with physical possessions. It is about attachment. In fact, when I first uttered these words, I was not even talking about possessions. That did not come until later. I was talking about everything I had. My strengths and my weaknesses. Heart, body and soul. See, I do not want to be able to say that everything I have I owe to God. I deepest desire is to have everything I have to be owned by God. I want everything in my life to be Holy.

There are those that will say 'you are holy because you gave up a lot.' To this I reply the way in which Eckert would. Even if you did not own the world but in your heart, you would give up the whole world if you owned it you shall be rewarded as if you had owned the world and gave it up. Our Lord told us that those with little, little is expected. Indeed, many of those greater than myself are those that had little to give but gave it all compared to the much I gave but still held back that little part for myself.

Again, let me say the oath of poverty is not about being poor it is about not loving what you have. Indeed, those who have the most wealth are those that need to follow this way the most. Let me also say though that for some this would mean being poor. Why? Because if one lacks the spiritual strength to give up things in their hearts it is better for them to give them up in the world. For what are those things compared to knowing God.

Now our Lord also said that He desires mercy not sacrifice which may seem to contradict my second oath but let me show you how they reconcile. I shall put it this way. If I have not given my honor to God then how can I show you mercy if you wrong me? How can I give you the help which God requires me to give you if what I must give you I have not first given it to God? Indeed, the second oath has become precious to me because it has helped me with my pride. For what every help I have given you, in whatever form it has taken, you can give the Glory to God freely for it was his to give, not mine.

Servitude: Whatever you give to me I will give to others
Which leads us naturally into my third, or the oath of servitude. I have always helped people when I could but this only became an oath last Easter Holy Week. It has been a hard one and it had filled my prayers for the last couple of months for it has taken on a meaning in which I had not expected. I want to be is someone it is true to say that others are better because they knew me. That was the movement of my heart for this oath.

This is also why I preach about Love so much. See, no matter how much we give or help others if we are not doing it out of Love then we are only doing it for ourselves. Now I will not go as far as to say that I have been perfect in this over the last year. In fact, I will say I have acted as much (if not more) out of my own will as I have out of God's Love. If I was perfect at keeping my convictions the moment, I made them I would already be what I seek to be.

Now on to the deeper meaning for me. When I say I have been praying about it I mean that I have prayed about little else. This had not been my choice for everything I pray about something else this is what the Spirit presses on me. With everything which I have shared over the past years there is one thing I have always held back. One thing that I would never give. That is God. I am not talking about witnessing what I am talking about is God and His Love.

This is hard to explain so you will have to bear with me. Since my conversion God has poured Himself, His Love, into my heart and I always held this as being precious. Too precious. I have kept it to myself and measured it out in doses. What I am working on now is not just loving with God's love but being a vessel in which it pours out of. Let me say this another way so there can be no misunderstanding. I do not want to be a clear glass in which others sees God clearly. I do not even want to be there. To be a person where whatever I do to help another, they know it was not me but our Lord. That it is not I who loves them but God.

His Kingdom Come

Luke 22.42

Too often I hear people pray for things which are not Elohim's Will. Let me tell you I do not mean from the pagans but from you and me. Now you may be thinking to yourself that you do not do such but hear me out and you may be convicted yet. In this, let me share my own that you may more fully understand what I mean. It was just this weekend when I sat in the middle of my stairs without the strength to go up or down. I sat there in a tearful prayer. I had but a single request -if was Your Will, take away my pain. The Lord came to me and asked 'and if it is My Will that you should feel this pain 'til the end of your days?' (It seems that Elohim always uses a question to convict me.) Well, what could I say? There was no way I could break my first oath for something as petty as pain.

For even though I was saying "if it is Your will", I was really meaning 'just take away the pain'. Each time I said "Your Will be done" it was only to feed my vanity. I prayed that phrase because it is my first oath: not my will but Yours. It was not because I really wanted His Will. I had placed my will above His. What was shown to me was that my will must be replaced by His. For if it the Lord's Will that I should be in pain and I really desired His Will then I would rejoice in my pain.

I was going to leave it at that but so not to leave it unresolved, let me leave you with hope. There are those who will tell you that it is not God's will for you to suffer. To this I say, Elohim does not harm his children but sometimes we need the pain to help us grow. If it is the Lord's Will for me to suffer far worse pain, to be inflicted with terrible deformities, to be scorned by my fellow humans then, as His will, it is what is best for me. For as I told you before, God is not motivated by His power over us but by His Love for us. Just as in this Love, He will give us the strength to not only survive such tribulations but rejoice when such times come.

Also let me make a distinction. I am not saying that you should not pray to be rid of such things. If your heart is troubled, pray. What I am saying, hear and understand, do not pray from your selfish desire. For if your desire is truly for His will and if it is His Will that you suffer then how can you pray against it. You should, as James put it, consider it pure joy. If this seems harsh it is only because of your immature Faith. You consider only your carnal self and give no thought to the benefit to your soul. For with the Christ's suffering on the cross, not for His benefit but for ours, how can you, we, I complain for any pain Elohim allows for my benefit.

Now this is not only limited to our low threshold for pain. It applies just the same to our search for virtue. For If you pray for an increase in patience but have no desire for it then you pray in vain. Instead pray for the desire to be patience. Do not pray to know God's Will until you have the desire to do it. For I may know His will in every moment but if I do not desire it then the cost will be too high. Indeed, again we return to love, for if you love Him you will do His will. Why? Because your desire will be for Him, and to fulfill that desire no cross is too heavy.

Conclusion: in your prayers and in your actions seek to deepen your desire for God because it is only through this Love can you know God's will.

Love Is Greater than Miracles

Ephesians 3.14-21

The desire for signs and miracles is a common thread in the Church today and is one of the reasons for the trouble we are in. For have you ever thought that if we could just perform the miracles the apostles did as recorded in Acts you could do great things for the Lord? Ever wonder why we do not see them or if we do, they almost always come to naught? The answer is simply that we do not have Love.

During my pagan years I learned the nature of power and many of its so-called secrets. I am no stranger to spiritual power and I will share with you one of those things that I learned early in my Walk. Power is nothing. Absolutely nothing. In the words of the preacher - it is chasing the wind. Why? To paraphrase Saint Paul, I could preach to all people and nations and perform signs and wonders greater than our Lord's, but if I do not have Love I am nothing.

Let me make it plain. Love is greater than miracles. God's Love is the spring in which miracles flow. For it is from His Love that he gives us what we need. It is the reason for which the Christ came and was crucified (John 3) and is the example we must follow (Ephesians 5). All of the Lord's miracles combined does not compare to the Love He showed on the Cross. Indeed, each miracle He did, He did because of Love.

It is why so many are turning to pagan masters for guidance. It is a great scandal that they show more love than us. Why is the enemy of the Truth being the ones that are heaping the coals upon heads instead of us? As we strive for our miracles, we fail to show the Love that we must. It should not, does not, have to be this way - for even a small portion of the Creator's Love is greater than is possible by all the love of the created.

Conclusion: Seek not signs or miracles but seek God, for the Love He gives you is greater than anything else you could get.

The Love of God

As I moved out of dealing with my pride of not needing others to preparing to taking my Charity to the next level, I have come to truly understand for the first time Eckert's words 'the eye in which I see God is the eye in which He sees me'. When I examined my love for others, I found a defect in my love for God. I had to turn that eye towards my Faith, and ask myself some serious questions.

Do I serve God in order to know more fully His glory? Nay, I know His glory because I serve Him, and I serve because I love Him. So, the question that must be faced is, why and how do I love God? As with most of my writings I am not talking of the physical things we do but the condition of our heart. Simply what is the nature of the love I have for Him.

Once I was willing to face what God was showing me, I felt ashamed. I have written before about the purity of love, and here I find my own love tarnished. Having failed to hear my own warning, I thought my love for God had reached its apex. I am failing in achieving true Charity because I have not yet achieved true Faith. I love the Lord because of His glory, because of His perfection, because He is God. As great as this love is it is not perfect.

Let me go back and start in the beginning. When we first come to the Faith, we love God for all the things that He has done for us. He gave us His Son and died on the cross for us. He created an entire universe just so we could have life. As we mature, we go beyond this. After all, to love one simply for what they have done for us, or because they loved us first is not perfect love. (Mathew 5)

Coming to know His glory it is not hard to love God for simply being God. He never betrays us, never makes mistakes, and is the Truth. In His perfection, God is more than worthy of our love. This love is great and powerful, yet to love one for the sake of who they are is not pure love. For if it was, then who could expect God to love them. Because God does love us, we know what pure love

45

is.

It was by comparing my love for God to His love for me that I saw how I fell short. God loves me no matter how evil or vile I may be. This is pure love, unconditional love. We should love God, who is worthy of such love, in the same manner. Perfect love does not have a reason, it simply is. Such love is a mystery that should be pondered. It is easy to explain when it comes to you and me for we are not worthy. One would think a pure love of God would be easy for he is worthy. Yet, still I fall short.

Charity and Faith always go hand in hand. It is through the uniting with God in this perfect love that we can share His love for others. Thus, having pure love for each other. To drive the point home, I will reveal a weakness of mine. Forgiveness comes easy to me. I can easily bare any abuse against me except for one. Those that efficiently attack me do not do it directly but target those around me. To say I am protective is an understatement. God has trained me my entire life to be a stronghold. To allow my back to take the whip when others are too week to take it. (When all else fails blame it on Lumpy.)

This in itself is not my weakness; God has made me strong enough to deal with this. No, my weakness is how I deal with the evildoer. It is too easy to let the wrath overpower the love. Too easy to deal with them out of my anger rater then show them the pure love that God has them. This is especially true for those that claim to have the Truth but do not. When it is the ones doing the harm, that are the very ones that have been given he charge to protect, feed and nurture the young in the Faith, I am overwhelmed by God's anger. I will make the problem here clear. God's righteous anger against such people is tempered by His perfect love. Mine is not. Until I have untied with Him in this pure love, I have no business exercising His wrath.

I said before if we look at our weaknesses, we will also find our strengths. I wish I could say that it was my desire to do His will that has stayed my hand. Alas, it was my weakness that has prevented me from disobeying. It is the collateral damage in such wars that prevent me from waging them. I have seen this first hand. I cannot risk doing harm to those that I am fighting to protect.

My gift of discernment allows me to see the weakness in others that needs to be protected, but it also makes it easy to crush my enemies. To do such though would be like them. Until I learn to fight such battles with not only the power that Spirit gives me but the love as well, I must be content with defense. (Or as mother often says - choose your battles.)

Ok, ok, back to the point. I know that this may seem harsh but our love for God cannot depend on His love for us. Does His love for us depend on how much we love Him? No, to His Glory, God's love is pure and perfect. It is in His perfect love that He has given me what I need to perfect my love for Him. That is, I could never possibly have this pure love for God or others. The more I allow Christ to live in me (the more I die to myself), the more I am able to love with God's perfect love. Not only other people but also to God. Let me say that there is also a progression in this. We cannot hope to love God and each other with perfect love in the beginning. As with any relationship our love increases as time progresses.

Summary: Being imperfect creatures we cannot love perfectly on our own. As we mature in our Faith, we must strive to be an unblemished mirror reflecting God's perfect love. Striving not only to love each other as He does but also to love God with perfect love. How glorious it will be to have Christ so fully in our hearts to be able to say – The love in which I love God is the love in which He loves me.

Oh Captain! My Captain!

Something with me has either gone incredibly and horribly wrong, or incredibly and wonderfully right. Looking over my writings, examining my mood and thought process I finally figured it out. That is, it has been almost two weeks now and I have yet to exit the Mystery of the Cross. I am living in the Sabbath, that day between the Crucifixion and the Resurrection. Which makes me laugh, even as I cry out in anguish 'Oh Captain! My Captain!' I cry out to God for mercy in the same breath which praises Him for the Mercy.

I used to worry about a Cross focus. You know paying so much attention to the Cross that one forgets the empty tomb. Indeed, I once read an article that tried to make the case that mystical tradition, or the death-of-self theology as the writer called it, apparently not being versed in church history, was a demonic doctrine. I took it seriously, not because of the writer's biblical argument, as it was obviously twisted, but as he showed how it could be harmful to people. After much thought and prayer about it, at least six months' worth, I came to the conclusion that the person was correct. What the Cross teaches is in fact very harmful, a stumbling block and offense, for anyone who does not have a direct communion with God.

Without the Spirit of God as your guide, in whichever way you experience that, then you will have no idea what it is that you need to sacrifice, and what it is that you need to foster. You will not, cannot know the cross you must bear unless it is God telling you. Without the Spirit active in our Inner-Life, then we cannot really say that Christ is the Captain of our lives. There are those who say belief is enough, but then I must ask, belief in what? Right beliefs are an answer, but then who has the authority to say what is the right belief? Who can say what Christ meant when He said woe to them who are offended because of Him? Who has the authority to declare what St. Paul meant when he said that he took into his flesh that which was lacking in the suffering of Christ?

I once got in trouble because I said that whether or not God wants you to go to this or that church is more important than whether or not you agree with what that church is teaching. I only made it worse when I was challenged on it by replying that if you are not mature enough to know where God wants you to be you then are not mature enough to be judging the words of a pastor. Do not mistake what I am saying, there are a great number of pastors who need to be slapped around, figuratively speaking. But this whole ideal of wandering around until one finds a teacher that they agree with is nonsense. There is not a sin in this world you cannot find some teacher which will tell you it is not a sin. Or if it is more to your liking, you can find a pastor which will rant and rave on a sin you do not have so you can feel like the ones you do have are not worth worrying about.

We spend all this time arguing which tradition is the right one, when the real argument is who has the authority to say what God is saying. And I could easily claim such authority, as I have authority in such matters beyond the understandings of most. Yet, having that authority, I also have the understanding that it only exists so that I may help guide others in discovering what God is saying to them. To be sure it would be much easier, for me and for them, if I were just to say 'thus says the Lord' but it is not the better way.

Not a popular view, I know. The tyrant wants their power, and the masses want their tyrant. And do not think that my view is not completely without selfishness. For God does not give authority without responsibility and I am but human. I am not God, nor perfect as God is perfect. So, knowing myself to be a human and not God, I know that if I got in the habit of declaring what is and is not God's Will for someone, I would lose sight of that simple fact that sometimes I am wrong. Nor is this without Charity, for my desire is for people to know what God's Will is for them, and God is much better at knowing His Will then I am.

The point of all this, is that a question which we should ask ourselves frequently is who or what is our Captain, our Lord, our God. That which gives orders to the ship of our Life is our captain. For some that is an ideology, using a set of beliefs of what is right and wrong as a guide. Some use an ideal, which I have done far too often, heading towards a goal to dictate how they change their hearts. Some do not even think about it, chasing after each new desire like a ship tossed about in a storm. Still, some rely on others to tell them what they must do, children never wanting to grow teeth. Whichever way you go, if it is working for you, I can only shrug my shoulders. I can only say what God has told me, that it is a better way when we allow God to be our Captain. That it is a much better way indeed, when we open our hearts to the Grace, the conviction, guidance and comfort in which the Spirit of God is trying to bestow on us.

The Nature of Love

It is highly probable that there is no topic written about, or more misrepresented than that of love. From the treaties of Plato, The Art of Courtly Love by Capellanus, to the hundreds of modern books, we have no sacristy of resources. Most of these tomes deal the acquiring, the byproducts of and the actions of love. As you know me, I desire knowledge in the basest aspect of an item. So, I set my spirit and mind to understand love. Traditionally love is broken into four kinds. But when I examined these four, I found that they are superficial distinctions. Not different loves, but different areas in which we love. It will become clear what I mean by this and how the love is not different, just a part of the whole. In order to honestly look at love I had to strip away my own preconceptions about love. This was much harder than it has been in other areas, but let me share with you what I have discovered so far. As with everything, love follows the Rule of Three. I will first discuss these three parts and then write a bit about how they unite into love.

Desire: we should start with the most common component of love. There are none who can honestly say that they have not been affected by desire. Desire can easily be defined as what we want to receive from the object of our love. It can easily be seen that desire is generated from the body for even the most enlightened person still has a body which needs nutrition. As our bodies require sustenance, we desire food. Now, we do not develop love for food, even though we use the term often, for the other aspects of love is not present. We desire after many things in which we do not share the other aspects of love. There is nothing wrong with this except in regards to other people. It is a great shame of the modern society that we often see others as things which we desire very much like a piece of fruit. Still that is not to say that desire is bad. I know that runs counter to philosophy which shows that desire is the root of our suffering, but you must also remember that the human state is one of suffering. In order for there to be love there must be desire. Whether this is the carnal desire between husband and wife or the ultraistic desire of the Lord for the elevation of our souls, it is still desire.

Charity: this is the aspect of love that is concerned with giving the other what they need. Considering how much I write about Love you may find it hard to believe that Charity was the hardest for me to understand. Indeed, it is even hard now for me to find the words to describe it. On the surface it seems just to be a desire. Just a nobler one. It is easy to misunderstand the difference between Charity and the desire to do what is best for others. The difference is in which way the action flows. The desire to help others is for the good feeling we receive from helping others. We feel better about ourselves because of what we do for others. But Charity itself requires nothing in return. Charity is about only those things we can give without any concern for what we will get in return.

Unity: unity is the part of love which binds us together. Even with items there is a basal unity. For when eat we take the food and make it a part of us. It is the goal of such desire, not to merely eat but to make the food a part of us. Unity is the part of love that is a great mystery and is why all are equal in love. For the more unity there is in our love the more we see the other as ourselves. We become one body so how can I elevate myself above you if we are both united with the Body of our Lord. When I first looked at unity I thought it only a byproduct of love for it does become strengthened by desire and Charity. However, unity does not grow stronger because of what is given or received, as these do not cause it to grow, but because we feel comfortable to unite with the other. Indeed, a husband and wife are (should be) able to give and received freely from each other because they are united as one flesh. Just as it should be with the Church. As we are united to the Lord, we are one flesh with his Body. It is through this unity that we are (should be) able to give our blood and life for our fellow human.

Love: putting all three concepts together we have that thing

52

called love. The nature of our love does not change from one person in our life to the next. What changes the most is what it is we desire from the various people. You expect more from your spouse than you do from me, just as you desire more from me than from a stranger. Harsher philosophers will tell you that desire has no place with Charity. I even though before I looked into the subject that they were counter indicated. But there are times that what people need from us is for us to need them. Indeed, it is often the hardest part of Charity to receive from another, even when it is not for your benefit but for theirs. Now, if you desire to be holy you must strengthen your Charity for all people and align your desire to do what they need from you. Now, it may just be the romantic in me, but it is unity which makes love so desirable. It is hard for me to write about without becoming melancholy for it is what my heart has longed for ever since I can remember. If the truth be known, it is why Faith is so strong. For none has satisfied my desire for unity as the Lord has. It is also the source of my pain for there is so little to be found in His Body. (But I will devote a whole email to this). Unity's place in love exists so that we may know the other two aspects. With unity we know what the other needs from us and how much we can ask from them. It elevates our charities and restrains our desires. It is, if you will, the matrix that the other two work within.

Conclusion: we need desire, Charity and unity for a thing to be called love. For desire without Charity is obsession, desire without unity is lust. Unity without Charity and desire will not last long.

Overcoming Sin

Luke 6.27-28

I can count the amount of time I have wanted to write this email in years. No not only do I desire to write it I must write it. And never before has it been such a prayerful fight to get the words out.

I run across so many people that are struggling with sin, and I have never really been able to help. When I say struggle, I do not mean they are simply sinning but that they are fighting, and fighting hard to rid themselves of a reoccurring sin in their lives. We do all the things the experts tell us and at times we thing we have won, but, boom, there it is again. You may relate to this, or you may relate to it after I am finished. I could use many examples but as usual I will use myself.

I broke my fast yesterday. Why? The simple answer is I am weak. As is usual in such times, I was full of remorse afterwards and prayed about being weak. God's response was plainly: that is the point. This almost made me laugh for this was not the first time I have learned this lesson. See, I am a bit odd in how I run from God, I do it by seeking Him. I know this may seem contradictory so let me take you back to the days before I broke my fast.

Now, I spent most of my time praying, mostly just for the strength to endure. Physically I was doing well, I was not even hungry and I had more energy than I normally do when I eat. But emotionally I was declining fast. All those things which are heavy on my heart in my prayers became cursing. My normal prayers for Sudan which always contain tears left me a weeping puddle on the ground. All the elitism and bigotry in the Church was like sandpaper rubbing me raw and all the apathy in the Body for the pain of our fellow Christians was, well, rough. It was just too much for me to bear. So, I do what I always do when I need to escape such things, I took a bath.

During my baths I alternate my time between reading a

novel, reading a text and just thinking, when I get bored with one, I switch to another. This time I started with a novel, and as I went to switch it out with the text (The Collected Works of Saint Teresa of Avila) I knew I needed to keep reading the novel. That there was something coming up I needed to read. Not being in the patient mood I skimmed the pages in almost a panic. Luckily it was Dune and what I needed to read had been highlighted by mother. I knew that that was it before I even read the words, but reading it, it did not make sense to me. It was basically saying that we fail when we try our hardest.

I quit my bath and spent the rest of the night praying. What it meant did not come and I fell asleep frustrated. I woke up the next day feeling a bit better. I was still frustrated but at least I was not focused on all the other stuff. I went down stairs to do the 'morning thing' and then went into the kitchen to make sure the cats had food. That's when I broke. Almost before I realized what was happening I had already eaten two tortilla. Now, even though I did not get to examine what happened then until after I prayed for understanding let me explain it here. See, I was not hungry. Not at all. I was not saying to myself that it would be nice to eat or even struggling with it. the compulsion came from a source much deeper than my body.

Some of you might know what I am talking about. When you are struggling against a sin, sometimes there is no real desire for the sin, that is you do not succumb from any great passion, but use the sin to satisfy a deeper desire. It is well known that we use sin a quick fix for the pain of our hearts. We use it like a pain killer, a medicine which is addictive and slowly kills us. It is a popular thought that once you are 'saved' all those wounds go away, but if that was truly the case there would be no need to preach for all Christians would be great Saints and the world would already be heaven.

We can fight all we want against a sin, and even if we succeed in riding ourselves of it, the reason we are sinning is still there. So, either the sin will return or another will pop up in its place. But what about these wounds that are causing us so much pain? It is commonly taught that these are caused by those who have offended us in the past. Indeed, I would have written just that up until yesterday. See, that explains why you have the wound, but it does not explain why you still have it.

When God told me 'that is the point' it was only the words I heard with my mind, but like so many times, what was said to my spirit was more important, but that does not mean they were not linked. The lesson for my mind was humility. The lesson for my heart was forgiveness. One does not exist without the other and neither comes to life without love.

The wounds we bear today on our hearts are there because have not forgiven those who have placed them there in the past. We hold onto them to justify, either consciously or subconsciously, our current behavior. We point and say, 'see, I have been wronged, I have the right to be mad. See how they have hurt me, I have the right to your pity.' Maybe we say we forgive but withhold it in our hearts so we can secretly feel superior to those who have done us wrong. See, when I say, (what am I talking about), when the Lord says that we must give up everything for him, that includes these wounds.

Considering how painful they are, you think this would be easy. If you have found it so than you are fortunate indeed, for the rest of us it is a struggle. The reason I said that humility and forgiveness in linked is because when you refuse to forgive someone you are judging that person. You are in essence saying that they are not good enough to be forgiven. That it would not be fair. Do I really need to say that if God used this standard than none would be saved? That if life was fair none would escape damnation.

In fact, humility is one of the reasons it is hard to forgive. For forgiving someone who did you wrong, you must place them above you. You have to say that it does not matter at all that you hurt me, I am still your servant. It takes the kind of self-sacrifice which allowed Jesus the Christ to utter the first Word from the Cross. "Father forgive them…' Indeed, that is our goal on the Path of Holiness, to forgive them, while they are doing us wrong.

56

The humility aspect is not so easy to see when the person who you need to forgive is yourself. But the truth is it takes far more pride to not forgive yourself than it does not to forgive others. Why, because you are saying God is wrong. Have you repented? Yes? God has forgiven you, then why do you think you know better than our Lord? Or do think that you are so great that you are capable of committing such a horrid sin that Christ's blood cannot cleanse it?

In forgiving yourself, it is sometimes the feeling of being unworthy. That is, you have been running from God for one reason or another. Did not like what He is saying. Maybe it is a sin. Whatever it is, we can sometimes feel, well, unclean. Like when we were children and did something wrong. We were afraid of disappointing our parents so did not want to tell them about it. We are afraid that God is going to scold us. This is not so much us not forgiving ourselves but not accepting God's forgiveness. I am no stranger to this, as I am sure some of you are neither. I have no real advice you have not heard at least several times before. The God who can raise and crush nations, is also the God who's touch is as gentle as a lover.

The point of all this is when we find ourselves facing the same sin over and over again, and no matter how hard we try we cannot seem to shake it. Then it is time for us to be asking God why we are sinning rather than for him to remove it. We will often find that it is caused by a deeper sin which we are trying to hide with the one we are trying to rid ourselves of. Oh, yes, it is a sin not to forgive. Did our Lord not tell us to turn the other cheek, as he did when the Temple guard struck him? Does it really matter if the slap was emotional?

The Pain of Love

John 14.23

Over a decade ago I penned in my journal that 'It is not my love for the person that causes pain but my desire of the object.' As correct as this statement is it is also wrong. There is a pain in love that far exceeds anything I have known in any basal desire. For love is a desire, not a desire to have, but the desire for what is best for that person.

In this love we share not only the joys of the person but their struggles as well. Every time that they are harmed, we are harmed. It was a hard teaching when our Lord told us to love our enemies. To love the person that is harming you to the point that your heart sinks for the harm they do themselves by harming you. To forgive them while you are nailed to their cross. A hard teaching, but one that must be kept.

That is why the Church is in the condition that we are in. Our sin is not that we have failed to defend our Faith, but that we have not loved enough. The only way to show the world God's Love is to have it shining from our own hearts.

Love is a difficult thing and you must count the cost. For to love with God's Love is to weep with God's pain. Indeed, His pain is so great over just one person that refuses to turn to Him that all of heaven rejoices when they finally do. (Luke 15).

Yet, as not to unduly burden you, do not seek after the pain or become dishearten if you do not feel as deep as I. God portions such gifts to each according to their office and calling. Seek after Him alone, and you will find joy in anything he gives you, even the pain.

And I do call it a gift for it has tempered me beyond all the other fires. For knowing how much pain I feel when others will not return to Him and knowing that what I feel is not even a speck of dust in the universe compared to His pain how can I add to his pain.

For if I love our Lord I will keep his word.

Conclusion: no matter how much pain it brings always strive to reflect God's Love. For if you act out of God's Love, no matter what you do, it will be a great thing.

Thinking Thoughts

Many years ago, when I was a young lad,
Life was simple and I was thinking those young lad thoughts that
young lads think
Of candy and ways to stay up late.

Years passed and I was a teenager,
With those teenage thoughts that teenagers think
Of girls, schools and parties

More years went by and I was a man,
Complete with manly thoughts that men think
Of women, work and why does my friends have better cars then me.

Some time later and then I was middle aged,
Full of those thoughts that the middle age think.
Of business, bills, and my receding hairline.

So many years have passed and I was an old man
With only those thoughts that the old can think
Of dentures, God and how my life went by so quick.

Just a little time later and now I am dead
Thinking those thoughts only dead men can think.
But you will have to think those thoughts for yourself.

Justification

Luke 18.9-14

Now the question was 'why do we remember the good acts we perform for others more then we remember the ones done for us?" In a way I will be answering that today. I cannot fully answer it for it speaks of motivation and there are too many for the length I would like to keep this so I will be only dealing with the main issue.

In my last email I only hinted on the answer, or at least where we start with answering this, or any question. I will start here on the definition of a 'good act' or what I will call Charity for the ease of writing. Now, let us settle on a definition of 'an act performed solely for the benefit of another.' I will progress assuming that we can agree on this definition.

I have said that the question speaks of motivation because that is what we must judge our hearts about. The very reason we are performing the good act in the first place. I mean that our motivation is what determines whether or not a good act is a act of Charity or simply a form of business. Now I am sure we can agree that if you give a loaf of bread in exchange for a dollar bill, we would call this business and not Charity. Now, what if I give you a loaf of bread in exchange of you thinking well of me? Would I not also be buying something with the bread? Why not look at this deeper. What if I give you a loaf of bread because I want to think well of myself? Because I want that warm fuzzy inside from doing good. Again, it is not Charity but hire and salary. Thus, we can easily see why what is motivating us to give will decide whether or not what we do is Charity.

Let me give you an example. Many think that Charity has to be great acts of feeding the poor or the like but let me keep it closer to reality. Many of you have children. Now over the years you have fed your children. I mean, you have physically prepared them meals, sat them down and even made them eat those nasty vegetables that are good for them. Even on those days where you are so tired you do not want to get up, you still do it. Why? Why may seem like a silly thing to ask but I will ask it again. Why?

As they cannot feed themselves, do you not feed them out of love? This, my friends, is the motivation of true Charity. If the good act is motivated by anything else then it is not Charity. To stress this point let me say that it very painful for parents which are not able to do this for their children. This is the greatest pain of poverty. Not knowing when your next meal may come is hard but it is nothing compared to not knowing how you are going to get the next meal for your children.

Love is the greatest gift which a parent can give their children which all others pale in comparison. It is also unfortunately lacking in many of our families today. But that is an email for another day. Let us illustrate how motivation is key by removing love and replacing it with justification. We instantly get a parent which is feeding their child in order to be a 'good parent'. Instead of giving the children what they need they give them what a 'good parent' is supposed to give them. In the extreme of such cases the parent is stressed more by a child not behaving like a child of a good parent then they are from the pain which causes such behavior.

Let me say this clearly, Charity must be motivated by love. Can you see how this is related to all areas of our life? To your spouse, friends, coworkers? To that person help change a tire?

Now examining our own motivations (for it is judging our own hearts rather than those of others in which I speak) we may say that we act out of love because we feel bad for the other person. Yet, even in this we must be careful for, the question we must ask ourselves is 'are we helping them to relieve their pain or our own?' For those of us that are sensitive, it is easy for us to react from the pain then to act out of love. The problem with this is that instead of truly helping the person we get trapped in what is causing them pain. That is, we become a crutch for them instead of helping them become strong. If we love them, we will strive to heal the wound which is causing their pain instead of simply taking it away.

There is much more I wanted to say but as this is already longer than I wanted to make it I will leave you with this – if you find yourself upset because someone does not remember or is ungrateful for an act of Charity you have done for them, then most likely you were doing it for yourself. In this even, do not worry about doing good thing, simply love and you will not fail in doing what is truly needed?

For those of you which pay attention to such things you will have noticed that the first signature line on my email has changed from 'in service of the Emperor' to 'in your service'. The reason for this is hard to explain but at its heart is a lesson I received in humility. Or it would be better to say the lesson I am learning in humility.

As many of you know I spent a considerable about of energy trying to get a certain group of people to listen to what God was trying to tell them. It hurt me beyond words that they would not listen to me. But did you read what I just wrote – listen to me. I weep because I failed and I failed for one reason, and one reason only. My pride. Do not mistake what I am saying. They did not listen to God because of the stubbornness of their heart. But this is not about the lesson I am learning. See, I went into a meeting with one of them with the sole purpose of giving a message, which I did. However, because of secret desire, hidden from me in the back of my brain, of wanting to be the 'one' I failed to bring down the fire which what I am known for. You may be wondering what this has to do with justification. I was not justified enough in their eyes to be someone that could speak to them.

You know, this bothered me. Now, I am not going to blame my depression last year on them for I did it to myself. It was because I became acutely aware that I have nothing in which to justify myself in the eyes of men. I have none of those things which the church culture says makes a 'good Christian'. In fact, much of my depression was caused by me trying to rearrange my goal to becoming what I was expected from a Christian leader. Something I realized just this week was that this hidden motivation was the reason I went back to school. All the other reasons were secondary.

But I will tell you as secret. I am exactly how God wants me. (Of course, I do not mean that I am as holy as I could be.) something that I have just been coming to realize is that from the beginning Elohim was forging me into someone that has no justification except for Him. I have nothing to which I can point to say that I am justified, except for the Cross. Except the Cross.

This of course is nothing new. It is, after all, the basic precept of Christianity. Then tell me why do we so often hear the patronizing tone when we talk of non-Christians. If you doubt this happens wholesale, we could elicit the testimonies of the heathens in this group to tell us how they have been treated as less then human because they do not believe. But let us not wait for them, and let me tell you that I have been told more than one that I could not possibly know God, simply because I do not go to church. And if you do not think yourself guilty of this think of some group or person which has made the news because of their activities such as that fellow that sued to get the pledge out of the schools or having that judge remove the ten commandments out of his court room, prayers out of school, etc. If we see such people as our enemies, we are saying that we are better than them.

Do we honestly believe that because we are Christians, God loves us more? The verse is: God so loved the world that He gave His only begotten Son that whoever believes may be saved. It does not say - God so loved those that would believe that He sent his Son to save them. Look at it this way. If I were offer each of you an expensive watch and some of you accepted them and some did not would that mean that I would love those that took the watches more? Would it mean that those that took the watches were better than those who did not? You may be able to tell time better but you would not be a better person because of it. This however was not the point of the change.

The lesson I learned last year was one the hardest I have gone through. At the core of it was simply on how to give. This may seem odd for those which have known me a while for I am a generous fellow but stay with me and you will understand. The things I have given have meant very little to me. The prize which I have held most precious is myself. As you know I have been working on loving others with God's love, but this is not enough. What Elohim told me was that I need to love you with my own heart. See, it is relatively easy for me to love in the spiritual sense, but I have been for a very long time emotionally detached. I will not go into the reasons for this because that is the past and I am talking about the now.

See, I am not talking about liking people, for I am fond of a great many of you. Fondness is based on familiarity and similar interests. I am talking about loving people, and loving them before I even meet them. that is, instead of just loving them with God's love but to also love them as He does. The detail is a minor one but an important one. This, of course, is not a new teaching but simply a deepening of an old one for me.

Some might say that God's love should be sufficient but would your children agree if you told them that you do not love them but it is alright because God does? How would it affect you if your spouse told you such? Understand that this goes much deeper then just making people feel good. I speak of the heart of ministry and, indeed, Christianity.

We have heard it said that God hates the sin but loves the sinner . . . but do you, do you? How about when you are the victim of the sin? It is the longing of my heart to be able to answer with a resounding 'I do, I do' instead of the almost that we (I) live in.

The change in the line of my email represents a change in the direction of my life. It came from a question which I ask often. Why do I serve the Lord? That is – what is my motivation? See, it is a common problem in ministry that we can get so caught up in doing God's will we harm the very people we are supposed to be helping. That is, we are so busy trying to help the poor that we do not see the person in need standing next to us.

Let me conclude by saying that salvation is a byproduct of the Cross not the point. The point is that he loved us enough to shed His blood, so let us love one another as He loved us (John 13)

Sacrifice of Will

Philippians 3.7-14

The question is why must we give up our will to God? Let me state it more strongly, why must we sacrifice our own will in order to be Christian? Let me answer boldly as I am commanded. It takes more than saying or even believing Jesus is Lord to be saved, He has to be, in fact, not just in ideal, but our Lord. The act of conversion itself is a sacrifice of the will. That is, He must be not only our savior but our master. Indeed, coming to understand this is what causes many of us to run from God for the first time.

We call these dry seasons many things. Being lukewarm, backsliding, growing cold, whatever we call it or whatever form it takes, it is simply times we are running from God. It seems silly that once tasting the sweetness of God that we would want to avoid Him, but we still do. It is not something we readily admit, especially when we are doing it. We are embarrassed by it, and to make matters worse, our spiritual advisors often take the wrong approach. They will point to some sin in your life and tell you if you give that up, then God will return to you. I cannot stress how wrong that it.

Let me say that another way, so you will not mistake what I mean. This is dangerously wrong unless the Holy Spirit is guiding the person to point to what you are hanging on to. (Indeed, how glorious this is and I pray for the day when this is common.) Dry seasons are not caused by an increase of sin in our lives, but rather the increase of sin in our lives is caused by running from Him, who gives us the strength to resist temptation. In fact, some become 'holier' during dry seasons, at least from outward appearances. They put on the clothes of holiness so no one will know. It is this embarrassment which I want to speak about first.

I am not so holy that I do not still feel that embarrassment. A couple of weekends ago John and myself had our first conversation in a very long time. We have talked, but not in the way in which we strike at each other's heart. Why? He has been my friend and pupil for over ten years now, the closeness of this means we cannot hide from the other. So, when I am running from God I avoid him, when he runs from God he avoids me. We do not even talk when both of us are running.

The embarrassment is natural. That is, we know that we are doing something wrong. For me, I would much rather admit a most horrific sin than admit that I am running from God. It is something I should, nay, must change about myself. I can only write this because I am coming out of a dry season (as you can tell by me starting to write emails again). The unwillingness to admit that we are in such a time only prolongs it.

For some, the embarrassment is worse because, even though it is rarely said, it is the mindset of much of the Church that once you have your conversion you should never experience a dry season. That is true, you should not. However, in this, as with most things, there is a big difference between what should be and what actually happens. I am sure that there are a few that never experience this, but for the rest of it is a normal part of maturing in our Faith.

Yes, I did just say that. These dry sessions are part of the process of maturing in the Faith. Or if I can rephrase it, what causes them is the normal part of maturing. To illustrate let me take you back to shortly after conversion. Now I must qualify this by saying I am speaking of a true conversion, not simply an emotional one, and by this, I mean that when the person comes to the realization of the reality of Christ, not just simply trying to avoid hell or gets swept away in the passion of the moment. Now, a little while after conversion, maybe hours, days, months, we come to realize the meaning of Jesus is Lord. That is, He must be our Master not just our Savior. To put it in my own experience this is the moment God asks 'will you serve Me?" This is the time we usually run for the first time. For some this takes the form of being lukewarm for others it is what we call backsliding. For some it is only a dry season which is short for others it is a very long time. For me, I ran long and hard.

68

It would take me over ten years before I could or I should say, I would say 'whatever you ask of me, I will do."

This is often complicated by such things as a scandal in the church, or from burn-out from someone so young in the Faith being asked to do so much, or maybe the group around teaching by example that lukewarm is the way a Christian life is supposed to be. Even though we use these as excuses, they are not, for after all this question is God asking 'do you follow Me, or them'. This first dry season comes to an end the moment, whether it is instant or takes a lifetime, when we finally willing to knell our will to His.

The point of this, and how it answers the question is our free will is nothing else than our dominion over ourselves. I heard a preacher say once that the difference between animals and humans was that animals were born to be slaves and humans were born to be free. But to this I must respond that the only difference is that humans are able to choose who they are slaves to. That is, you can either be a slave to sin or a slave of God. There is no middle ground. But why is it so important to give up our will, to make Jesus the Lord of all of our will, of everything in our life.

It is like thus. God created the world and the Garden for our enjoyment. Like the fruit of the Tree of Knowledge this pleasure has its limits. That is we are allowed to enjoy but not beyond were it is healthy for us. See, Adam and Eve was still allowed to enjoy the fruit, they could look at it and marvel at its beauty all day long. They could have written songs, danced dances, and put on plays all dedicated to the beauty of the tree and its fruit. The tree and its fruit were there for their enjoyment, but within limits God set for their own protection. The same way for the enjoyments of the world. God created it for our enjoyment, everything from the smell of flowers to sex, but within the limits of what is healthy for us. Just as Adam and Eve would go beyond the healthy limits, so do we. The difference however, is that where they only had one harmful thing in their environment, we have more than be counted. And it is our nature, original sin if you will, to take our pleasure a bit too far, to let them have control over us.

It is also a matter of degrees. At our conversion we have made Jesus our Lord, but if we are honest with ourselves, or even if we are not but listen to God, we know this does not necessarily means that we have made Him Lord of everything in our life. I am sure there are a few, who kneel to God and never get up, but for the rest of us, it is not that simple.

Oswald Chambers wrote in his My Utmost for His Highest (September 2, Barbour Publishing) in speaking about our Lord's teaching 'His purpose is not the development of man; His purpose is to make a man exactly like himself, and the characteristic of the Son of God is self-expenditure." That daily devotion was called the Sacrament of Sacrifice, and it speaks well to what happens when we sacrifice. Maturing in the Faith does not mean we become more knowledgeable, or more virtues. These flow from maturity but is not being mature. I can study for countless hours, and I can change all my behavior but unless they are flowing from Grace they are only false fruits. That is not to say that we should not strive to be better in such areas, only that without God we are not truly changing our hearts.

Maturing in the Faith does not mean that we have increased, in fact, just the opposite. Maturing in the Faith means that we decrease so Christ can increase in us. When we turn over our will less of us, less of our sinful nature remains. It is replaced by Christ. When we are immature in our Faith, God is our Lord generally and our Lord in only a certain area. Each time we sacrifice our lordship (our will) over one of those areas to Him, he becomes the Lord of it and in that area Christ lives in us.

The Path of Holiness can be summed up by constantly searching for those areas which we are still claiming Lordship over and turning them over to Christ. And in this, as I always do, I must point out that it is by far more beneficial to have God point out what be sacrificed, for our natural selves will give up everything in order not to give up what we should.

Signs and Wonders

Mathew 24.3-26

On whether or not we have reached the End of the Age I have no insight but what we do know for sure is that there is a great number of false prophets who have made their way into our Body. So versed are they in deceiving that our Lord warned us three times in this chapter alone. I do not want you to be ignorant that you may fall prey to one of them. Indeed, it is my prayer and deepest desire that you become stronger than I; so, if someday I fail you, will be there to exhort me, but this you already know.

Many will not believe that not all of those who exhibit gifts are from the Lord. So unaccustomed are they to the use of God's Gifts that they will blindly follow any who shows such power. They say to themselves 'because this person knows the secrets of my heart they must be of God.' Yet, our own Lord told us that the false christs and false prophets will show great signs and wonders and will mislead us if they can. These sons and daughters of disobedience have come with counterfeit gifts to elevate themselves.

I have told you before that power which is not from God brings only destruction, and sometimes the wolves look like sheep or even worse, the shepherds. Like the prophet Hananiah they will preach a peace in the name of the Lord when in reality, it is rebellion against God. These false prophets, like Hananiah, preach the Christ with their mouths but listen to voices of deceiving spirits, or worse, the stubbornness of their own heart (Jeremiah 16). Not every prophecy that comes true is of the Lord, but every prophecy of the Lord will come to pass.

You may never be called to battle against false prophets but you will undoubtedly come across them in your calling. It is not enough that you are not fooled by their show of wonders and miracles; you must not be lulled by their false fruits as well. Test them the same way I have told you to judge me. If they preach God's love but do not manifest it, then they would be false in their Faith and not worthy of Him or you.

I would be neglectful in my duties to you if I did not leave you with this last piece of advice. Follow only God and His plan for your life and you will have no fear of being led astray; for the more you know God the easier it is to recognize what is not His (2 Peter 1).

Conclusion: do not give credit to signs and wonders for they are the ways in which the false prophets try to win the hearts of the elect. Do not follow those who give the appearance of love but puff themselves up in the eyes of men. As our Lord said, 'you will know them by their fruits'.

Towers of Illusion

Building your tower
In the valley of shadows
Neatly packaged fantasy
To lay your foundation

Hiding in the dark
Of an empty heart
The Light only burns
When you live in a cave

Living in a past of illusions
Brings the pain of the future
Wishing for what could have been
Never seeing what should be.

Trapped in a current
A river under ice
Freedom never found
Until we drown.

Putting your faith in a pulpit
Finding the answers you want
By ignoring the Word
From above

Enlightenment by the numbers
Salvation by the sound bite
But one is never set free
By clinging to their life

Sins of Conscience

I always start my weakly meditation by examining my life over the past week. A practice I started a decade ago and do it daily when I am more active. This week I realized a sin that I need to apologize to Bryan about. I have decided to do so publicly because it gives me a chance to talk about two things that I have been meaning to get to.

You (even Bryan) may be wondering what the sin is. Very simply I was argumentative. I am sure he remembers it but may not have thought much of it considering it was over in less then a minute. It wa s not that I disagreed with what he said just the incompleteness of it. Normally I would have just said a comment and he would have said something like 'good point.' However, because if was feeling combative I turned it into an argument. Because I felt like arguing I did not make my point.

Now, this is always bad. Again, there is no purpose in chasing wind unless your purpose is to chase wind. The reason to debate is to find the truth of the matter, not to win. For me, however, this is a sin of conscience and is the first thing I want to talk about, that is Sins of Conscience. Now, I define this as the things we are being convicted about. Technically these would be any sin but I want to focus on the sins that do not lead to death. I know that many do not believe in conviction and some teach thus but to this I say with all the authority of my office that one that does not know conviction does not know the full glory of the Spirit. Those that do not have one more thing to work on are far greater than me (and I far greater than I will ever be).

But if the wages of sin are death, how can there be sins that do not lead to death? Simply they are those that do not destroy or prevent our Faith. My combative nature is a good example of this. When we are heathens or new in the Faith we deal with the 'death' sins for these are counter to the Law, which is written on our spirit. Because of our nature we must choose between these sins and death or God and life. Our own conscience (if we are listening) will convict us of them and even the great pagan masters agree that they are harmful.

However, the sins that do not lead to death are 'little' sins we do not often see them as such. I saw my argumentative behavior as philosophically wrong long before I realized the sin. In truth, my combative nature is only a byproduct of the issue I am dealing with. That is my pride, which is a better example.

This is the second time I have had to deal with pride. The pride that leads to death is one that tells us we do not need God. Believe it or not this is uncommon and what seems like it is usually fear or anger. I did not have to deal with this pride simply because of my insecurity. Because of this, I was willing to draw close to God and so my training progressed quickly. Because of my natural talents and the Gifts, I were given the first time I had to deal with pride would be easily recognized. That is the feeling I was better than others. The example of how this does not lead to death – this pride will not prevent us from knowing God but must be overcome before we claim our office. Until we conquer this pride we cannot truly love and thus have no right to minister. It does not stop of from having Faith, it prevents us from being great in our Faith. Anyone can be stricken with this pride but I have found it more common with those who are called to help people and those that are granted insight into our Faith.

Dealing with this pride was relatively easy for me. It was just a matter of finding a trait (or traits) in the person I admire and sometimes envy. John's charm, Bryan's passion are strengths I do not have at their levels and thus cannot say I am better. For those who strengths are the same of mine I needed God's help. I am sure this is one of the reasons why He gave me the ability to see people, as they could be, their potential if you will. A good example is Nate who in many regards is a younger me, with similar strengths and weakness, and he will go quite far once he decides which way to run. I am not saying that this is the best way to deal with this pride if you come to struggle with it, it is simply the way I did.

You may wonder how I struggle with pride and insecurity at the same time. Before I continue, let us deal with this now. To put it simply, my insecurity is not based of the fear that I am weak just that I am not strong enough. In fact it was trying to rid myself of this that pushed my pride over the top. This insecurity is at the root of why I push myself so hard. Why I do not give up. No matter how great I am I can be better. Looking back at my youth and coming to realize that they were telling me the truth when they said 'you're not living up to your potential', I vowed that I would. That was a decade ago and I have come far. But even now I can see times that I could have done better, should have done better. So even though I am great, I will always feel that I can be greater. In truth I have to deal with the feeling of unworthiness every time I grow.

Now onto my current pride. I had spent so much energy on making myself strong and when I turned my training over to God, I reached levels that not even I thought were possible, nothing could stop me. Indeed, so fast I was running that when I hit this wall of this pride, I bounced off broken and bloody. So great was my fear of dealing with it that it took me almost a year to admit something was wrong, and almost another half to dig deep enough into myself to reach the dept the entire problem. The nature of my pride? Well, to say it plainly, the feeling that I do not need other people. After all, what can I go against that is too strong for me and God to deal with? What would others have to do with my growth? I have never been inspired by preachers, been years since I found a teacher that could teach me and never had a problem large enough that I needed help.

I can now look upon the vision with happiness but the little understanding I had of it horrified me. So much in fact, that I refused to dwell on it for almost six months. However, it was enough to throw me into one of my fits. All that time I spent tearing myself apart brick by brick. Examining each nook and cranny for defects. Six months with only a short brake for an obsession (I find it hard to control such things in my weakened state). This was by the worst and most painful fits I have had since high school. Before I could deal with the pride, I had to deal with all the wounds that kept me from dealing with the issues that prevented me from dealing with the pride. Reopening any wound is painful but these went back to early childhood.

Having flushed out the infections I have sutured them back up and am in the process of replacing the bricks and mortar. Before now it has always been easier to rebuild then to tear down. In fact, I have always found it much harder to figure out what the problem is then it is to deal with it once it is found. I hope it is the same way this time.

It has already been two months and I have seen very little progress besides finally admitting to myself that I do need other people. That I will never be any greater then I am right now without them. I may be being too hard on myself for I am dealing not only with the habit of the pride but the other habits hindering me as well. Such as my mistrust. I have a hard time trusting myself, for I find it much too easy to take advantage of people. Even though it has been a long time since I have it is a constant fear that I will relapse into this behavior of my youth. Even greater is my mistrust of others.

It is hard for me to allow people far enough in to call them a friend, and the intimacy needed for a spouse scares the hell out of me. I have a long history of having those people I pull close to me having one of two reactions. They either become awed or afraid of me. Everyone except for John who could not make up his mind between fear and awe and was having too much fun to pay attention and Nate who was becoming afraid but refused to let it go past respect. (A fact I tried to explain to Lee without insulting him but I think I failed) in my younger years I never minded such behavior for it made it easy to get what I wanted out of them, but I never realized how much this hurt me. Now, it is hard for me to look in people's eyes and see such. I am a beast but I am neither a god nor a monster.

Now how to deal with this pride I do not yet know. Before I can break through the wall of my pride I must first tackle my insecurity. I must allow people in before I can discern the matter in which I need them. Otherwise, I run the risk of needing them for their use rather than for them. That is not to say I have not made some progress. I have come to realize that I am unable to have fun without others. I mean I can have fun but I am talking of that giggling till you cry and can't breathe kind of fun. Even though I can admit that I need that unity that can only be found in marriage I still cannot tell you why.

The point of all this is that even though this pride was always sin it did not stop me from growing closer to God. I am unsure if I did not deal with it now whether or not it would lead to death. That is for greater prophets then me to figure out, I am not willing to take the chance. It is time to deal with these sins once we are convicted of them. This is not reason to fret though. In His Love, He never convicts us until we are ready to deal with it, sometimes it is as easy as turning to him, other times we must rely on our brothers.

(I am in no way implying that God is not strong enough to deal with this without others, what I am saying is that I am not strong enough to overcome this without others. that because of the very nature of the pride I would never fully deal with this without the very people I must need.)

I have often said that if a teaching seems too harsh or not harsh enough then it is usually missing something. This one is way too gentle, and it is the second half of 'if you love God you will no longer sin', which can be too harsh. This one alone leads to 'I do not feel convicted therefore it is not sin' even when we are in denial (such as I spent a year). To be harsh with those that have not been convicted on an issue can itself be a pride issue (I have dealt with this, why haven't you). I am not saying that the apostles should stop preaching, the teachers stop teaching, the judges stop exhorting or the prophets stop speaking words on it. Nay, the Spirit will often use others when we will not listen to Him. If we are silent the rocks will cry out.

I must say that there are sins of conscience that are not sins

78

in themselves. Again, I will use me as an example. As some of you know I spent over eight years as a vegetarian and even now, several years later I will rarely eat pork. The reason for this is that in my childhood I was so horrified at a pig's squealing when we killed it for food that I was plagued by nightmares of it years later. I have personally killed chickens and this never bothered me. I just stopped eating pork and became a vegetarian some time latter. Frankly, it is healthier to eat meat, just not in the great quantities that us Americans eat it in. (An argumentative statement that I will deal with later.) Now, is it a sin to eat pig? No, for we are free of such earthly regulations because of our Faith. My avoidance of pig and latter all meat was not the sin of eating meat but a way of running from other sins. For me, and many like me, giving up meat was a way that I tried to prove my own holiness. Somehow, it is believed that being a vegetarian is more enlightened then eating meat. This is simply not true but is far off the issue and as I said before I will deal with this latter.

I have tried several times to eat pig again but it has given me such an upset stomach that I have regretted it. I could never say that you must give up pig, in fact, there can be no doubt that it would be a sin if I did, as this runs counter to the truth. I must proclaim that there are things that we must give up that are not sins because the weakness of others (1 Cor. 8) but what these things are I will not tell you. It would be easy to burden you with heavy yokes that bare you down instead of freeing you. Shall we give up all things until all we have left is breathing? Some teach eating meat is a sin, others being a vegetarian a sin. What shall we do, eat nothing? There must be a line. The Spirit is clear on this - Do not fret over every little thing for when you are convicted you will have the strength to deal with it (that is not to say it is always easy.) And to as how much to give up, again listen to God, only He can draw that line.

Now as what to do with another that you see that has a sin not leading to death. Should you tell them? The teaching on this is simple. If God tells you to then do. If He does not then pray for the person, (1 john 5) for if you confront them before they are ready they will hate you and run from it. As to our own sins I have found it helpful to hear what people are saying about us. The old saying is true - by the time our behavior becomes bad enough for us to notice it has become bad indeed. I have found it much better to find a friend that you trust and has the courage to tell you things about yourself. This has the best of both worlds for it is easier to listen when it comes from someone you know loves you and you find out much quicker than relying on gossip. And as I often say I would much rather talk with a man that tells me the truth then one that makes me feel good.

Conclusion: Let me simply conclude by summing the teaching into a simple phrase- That when we live by the Spirit, we are dead to sin and the world is no longer in us, as we mature in our Faith we give up more and more of our sinful natures until we are completely dead to ourselves.

Return to Eden

Over the years Elohim has showed me many things but few things have rattled my world like what I am about to share with you. not only did it answer of philosophical question that I have been asking for a very long time it also shattered what was left of my illusions about society. Now I will talk about original sin and what it means to us. There is some argument about this concept but I will not be dealing with these. Like always I am making a point not trying to set down dogma.

If you will, travel back with me to the Garden of Eden. The pure pleasure that Adam and Eve knew the delights which you and I do not have imagination enough for. Still the joy was greater for they were face to face with God. They were made for the garden and the garden was made for them. This was the very life that Adam and Eve were created for.

The events that caused what I call the First Fall or the Great Fall is well known to all of us. What I want to draw your attention to is what God showed to me of what was going on in the hearts of the first two. Imagine if you would, the sorrow that Adam and Eve was going through. After all, they had been made for the garden. Through their sin they had lost it but more than this they lost it for their children as well. How they longed to return to the Garden. And they passed this to their children. For their children were the flesh of their flesh, a flesh that was made for the garden. Their children longed for the garden that they had only known through the eyes of their parents. And their children's children would long for it.

Indeed, all born of human flesh longs to return to the garden in which we were made. Every person longs for this even if they do not know it. This longing which I have labeled the Garden Instinct is the driving force of civilization. Everything we strive to create is our attempt to return to the garden. I will go into this with greater depth when I write it up in philosophical terms but every civilization built or revolted against was based on trying to create a new garden. Even the pagans and heathens do this, of course because they could not call it Eden, they call it utopia. Still the principle is the same. Indeed, the drive of this instinct is so great Jesus the Christ had to be nailed to the Cross for us to overcome it.

The reason I write about this today is because the main reason God showed me this was how it is relevant to the Church and us today. See there is a great movement in the Church today away from God and towards a return to the garden. It goes hand in had with what I wrote before about vision but let me digress.

Open your eyes and look. Far too many now when they preach or teach are promising a better life. They say if we do this or that then we will have revival, if we but do this then the Church will be great. They work hard, and teach others to work hard towards the goal of a vision rather then towards God. They gain their followers because they are promising a return to the Garden. I was shocked on how wide spread this is.

Indeed, even I am tempted to say – seek diligently after God and you will have the garden. Even though there is some truth to this I have been specifically warned against it. Why? Because we must seek God, period. I have written to you before that if you seek heaven you will not find it but if you seek God you will have heaven and much more. Who are we to ask for a reward for doing our duty? What a petty thing we make of Elohim in our hearts when we use Him such.

The point of all this is that you must make sure that when you are teaching and preaching that you are pointing them towards God. We must take great care that we are preaching God and not preaching the use of Elohim to return to the garden. If the Lord gives us Eden in our hearts so much the better, but it cannot be why we serve or teach others to serve.

Tending our soil

We all understand scripture according to our own Traditions, preconceptions, and so on. And so, each of us are going to understand scripture differently. I, of course, have that lens of the mystical Tradition, seeing everything in terms of that relationship with God. That being the case, my take on the parable of the seeds and soil is about that certain virtue called humility. We have a tendency to think of humility only in terms of our opinion of ourselves, the opposite of hubris.

That it true, but is only humility on a Sunday School level, for it is also not thinking of oneself at all. But that is only required for Heroic Charity, and is given according to calling and purpose. But there is an aspect of humility, which is less then heroic but more than a vaccine against pride. One which is required for any growth in the Inner-Life.

I once heard a sermon about how humility basically means to be like dirt. It made me laugh, as it was obvious the preacher knew nothing about gardening. That is the word root-origin is correct but there is a difference between humus and dirt. That if we were to use word origin as a key, then humility would be being good soil, full of all that organic material which makes for healthy plant growth.

Whatever we want to call it, humility or some other word, the garden of our soul still needs tending, clearing the thorns, removing the rocks, most importantly adding that organic material, the humus. We can do much of work. It just takes a willingness to remove the thorns and rocks, that self-improvement aspect people often talk about with religion, and for some the only point of religion. But…however, that is removing the bad stuff, and does nothing to improve the soil of our soul.

Is that not why we say no work can save us, for it is only God, and God alone, which can bring the heart alive? Christ is Life. That transformed heart, that soft soul, that soil full of humus

83

which will produce a healthy and fruitful plant. We can spend all the time we want ripping out thorns (vice) and removing stones (sin), but it is allowing God to improve the soil of our soul, which is going to determine the bounty of the harvest

Blessings

Some of you know about my three vows. I have not written about them in a while because I have not paid much attention to them. Not in the neglect of duty, but simply that they do not chafe anymore. I fulfill them without thought now. But a month or so ago I was having one of those 'I want' episodes, which basically means I wasted a week planning. I say wasted, because at the end of the week I simply deleted the file. Not because it was a poor plan, but because it just seemed to me a violation of my third vow, that what God gives to me, I will give to others.

God asked for my vows, but did not command. They are mine, for me to live up to, to decide what they mean. Or rather, they are not rules but lessons. A few years ago, I would have had no problem with my plan, but in that time, I have developed a deeper understanding what it is that God has given me. Which I can sum up by saying that I am nothing, so I have nothing which has not been given to me. I made the decision a long time ago that it would violate my vows, violate my Honor, to expect a return on my wisdom. That was, in fact a hard thing. It is not about monetary compensation, as a worker is due their pay, but about glory. About that expectation that others would grow, or just pay attention to what I had to say.

But it is not a hard thing for to spend most of my time in prayer and contemplation, to spend my time trying to gain the solutions to problems which arise in the Inner-Life of others, without expecting anything in return. I have enough Faith in God, and in people. I have seen the Spirit at work enough to know that if I am ever at a point where I am truly in need that I will be taken care of. There has, of course that dream of making a living on my fiction. But that is off the table for now, because of my reluctance to be noticed. But the point though, is that it is hard to boast when everything I have, these hands, my heart, everything I am, has been a gift of God.

I have just reached a point where I am more and more seeing what I am calling the Constant Miracle. More and more of my time is being spent aware of every moment, every beat of my heart, ever breath, every morsel of food in my mouth, everything outside and inside me as a gift from God, a Grace. As I have told you before simplicity, has little to do with poverty. I think it often goes hand in hand, because it typically takes poverty in order to learn it, or at least it did for me.

It is easier to squeeze a camel through a small little door that a person can barely get through, then a rich person to enter the kingdom of heaven. Why? Is it because money is such an evil that just handling it contaminates your soul? Or that in order to be saved, to be part of the Body of Christ, you must be poor? Those might be true, but I have yet to see anything which would make me agree with that. It is simply because those with an abundance of wealth have the hardest time understanding Christ, and Him crucified. That is, it is hard for one to understand the need for God, the need for Charity when you can rely on money to get your needs fulfilled.

Think about it. Your car breaks down, you hire a mechanic. You get sick, you hire a doctor. Life is about loss and gain, hire and salary. I work with my hands. I get paid for that work. Where is God in that? But this is not pointed at the rich, but all of us, our own such views. That is, when we are in need, and the need is fulfilled by the Charity of another, it is easier to see the Hand of God in it. But what about the needs fulfilled by our own hands? If you want to be perfect, as God is perfect, try looking at those needs you provide yourself, with that same kind of heart of praise you would if a stranger walked up an gave it to you in the Name of the Lord. Not because God gave you what you had, but rather all you have is because you are living the life He would have you live.

Forgiveness

With your words and deeds
You have inflicted
My heart with a pain
Which will not leave

In all the world
You were the one
who was supposed to love me,
Without condition, without fail

I have searched over the years
Wondering why you have treated me
Worse than any stranger
Instead of one of your own

Since you forsook me
For your own petty desires
Where else was I to turn
To fill the need of my soul

In all my attempts
To rid myself of this pain
I have created a wound
Far greater then the one you gave me.

I have hated you so long
For what you have done to me
That there is nothing left
But the anger in my thoughts

As I turn to ask you why
I see clearly that your selfish desire
Was to quite the pain in your own heart,
To find the love you never had.

It has not taken away the pain
But it has rid me of the anger
For you are not an enemy
But kindred in the pain.

I pray to God now
That He may fill the hole in your heart
With the love you never felt
As He has done for me.

The God of Now

Modern language reflects modern thought. Following the Descartes model, we start from the position of self, with the I. I think. I believe. I am. It naturally follows in such a system then that we would define the 'I', by what we think, what we believe. So much so, that we will draw far more of our self-image from the conclusion we drew of our experiences, then of on the experiences themselves. That what we think, our opinions and beliefs, take on more of an importance than the experiences we have. We will deny or reshape our memories of an experience, so they will fit better into our definition of the self.

One must always remember, especially before opening one's mouth, that Christianity is far more then belief. If one must have Faith to believe then Faith cannot be belief. It must be more then just an intellectual consent, approval and acceptance of tradition, scriptures, doctrine and dogma. Faith is the key which opens the treasure chest of tradition. Faith is the proof which makes belief possible. More than a noun, an active verb, Faith describes an experience. An experience which is both public and private, shared by both the individual and the Church.

This experience we call Faith cannot truly be put into words. That face to face with God, that communion, that kenosis found in Christ, that Life found in the Spirit, these are all words that are only understood if one has had the experience in which the words represent. Knowing all the right words, the theories, ideas and ideals, are simply meaningless without the experience.

The Faith I have today is not based on philosophical exercises or derived from intellectual studies into God but on experience. The Faith of the now is based on the experiences of the past. That, if you will notice, that each time you have increase in Faith it has been because of an experience, a moment when you noticed the greatness of God. A moment in which Scripture comes alive, or a moment your eyes were further opened to the miracle of

Life.

As such, it seems to me, that our Faith of tomorrow, if it will be different than today, must be born from the experience of the now. Which it also seems to me, the best way in which to grow our Faith, is to have more experience. And as one cannot forsake God for the sake of experience, it seems to me that the best means to go about this is to seek to have a constant experience of God, that constant awareness of God, with us. In the here, and in the now.

The Will to Love

Charity is most obviously a verb. Theological virtue which gives actions to our Faith. In fact, as Saint Paul points out, without Charity, we are dead. A bit of a hint on the whole Christ is Life thing, but if I had to define Charity it would be God's Love actively flowing through a person's heart.

That makes sense, does it not? That Charity being a theological Virtue, one which can only be given by the Spirit of God that it would be something beyond morality, beyond what the human heart can dream of regarding right and wrong. And is that not what limits Charity? Like with Faith, do not we decide what is an act of divine Love and what is not, before we even get into a situation. Is that not the debate which seems to be tearing the Church further apart is exactly what it means to Love?

And just like Faith, people draw their lines. They say you must believe this or that. I say that if one does not have the Light of God shining from your heart, if it is not the Love of Christ as found coming from the Cross, then it does not matter what you believe. Because as an individual, as a human we are limited. Our knowledge, feeling and understanding are limited. And thus our capability to do what is Charitable, to Love, is limited without the help of God.

And that, if you have Charity, you already know. If love, human love can be a model then there is a desire, a desire to what is best for the beloved. For our children, for our spouses, for our friends. That we strive to be better, more like God so that we may always do what is best for others. and…and is this not why the heart of Charity is prayer? (Did you see that coming?)

Even though I do not like to admit it, being but human, I simply do not know what is the best. Good, alright, but not best. Are you sick? My heart would like you to be better, but it might be best that you continue in your illness. You may need that struggle to draw closer to God, to place more trust in Him. or maybe it would be better for a swift and complete recovery.

So in such a case, we pray. Sometimes God lets us know what His Will is, other times not. Either way we put it in God's hands, we pray for His Will be done. Because we know that what ever God's Will is, is what is best. That God's Will, the desires of Christ are perfect because it is based on His perfect Love. And so in this regard, Charity can be seen as following God's Will, because God's Love is flowing from us.

Or if you prefer a more dogmatic statement. Charity is actively following God's Will because God's Love is flowing through us.

The Continuing Story of Lumpy

THE END
Lost in a world that does not care
I hide, confused, scared and alone
Where are my people, where do I belong
Every look feeds the wound that will not heal

No hope for a life of my own
Inability to express myself with words
Makes me depend on silence
No one listens, no one understands

Through a sharp and bitter tear
I see your face, as I turn and walk away
You yell to my heart
'Come close to me, came to me here'

ENOUGH
One kiss, that's all it took and I was falling,
Falling into what I thought was love
(Love, what an alien concept to me)
More pain from the wound that will not heal

New life, new hope
Same problem, same pain
New words, new ears
No one listens, no one understands

One too many laughs from the heartless
One too many sneers from the ignorant
I have no more tears to cry,
For I have no more love to give

THE VOID

Angels in rags, demons in gold
I have my roses and sold the thorns
All is forced to my will, except . . .
The wound that will not heal

Another lie, another fantasy
The way of the warrior is more then death
I hear you calling to my heart
I will not listen, I will not understand

Strong back and sharp mind
Rot comes from a decaying soul
All my power comes to not
For I am in the thralls of death

NAME ONLY

A word given, a word kept
A second chance found in a brother
The only pain that a hug cannot remove
Is from the wound that will not heal

Pure in thought, actions controlled
Truth in belief but not in spirit
Living only by the law brings only death
I still don't listen, I still don't understand

No fire, no light
Polished words from a tarnished heart
Counted the cost I will not pay
Easier just to play the game

FIRESTORM
A warning, a promise, a decision
The path is clear
Give up all for you
Even my wound that will not heal

My stick is yours, you are my master
Your face is my life
Mercy not sacrifices
I am listening, I am understanding

A lake of tears for what they have done
A knife in my heart for what I have done
All my pain, all my suffering
Does not compare to what you've endured for me

THE BEGAINING
Eyes that cry, eyes that burn
Strength found in my weakness
Your glory will be victorious
Even over their wounds that will not heal

I pray in the falling rain
Through the love and so much pain
Will they want, will they demand
Will they listen and understand

The hedge is gone, the fire comes
Purifying the gold, destroying the rest
No longer I, no longer parts
No longer our vision, but you

Thy Will Be Done

Whether in an official or unofficial capacity, whether we speak or write, every time we say 'thus is the Way of God', we are naming ourselves a Master, a teacher of others. We like to say we are only expressing an opinion, which is sometimes true, but other times we are in fact acting the teacher. Every time we express that opinion in order to guide another, convince another, show another, we acting as a teacher.

We do not like to think that way, after all, we all know that teachers are held to a higher standard, that those, such as myself 'shall receive a stricter judgment'. And those who have been anointed, trained by God to guide others in His Way, in Christ, know full well what I am talking about. Maybe even knew, or know the fear of it, as I have, driving them to make sure every word is perfect, that they are perfect in their expression, as God is perfect.

I do not know, maybe these great masses of would-be teachers will be shielded by their ignorance. But this I do know, that those who are their Masters, will not be so lucky. The ones who send them as an army out to convince and convert, rather than to go forth and be the light of the world. I understand that I am stepping on the toes of many of your traditions, but I am beyond caring. Not all are apostles, not all are teachers, preachers, prophets or evangelists. The question is not whether or not you should be a witness to the Resurrected Christ, of course you should. The question is, how should you go about being that witness?

Have you ever had a chance to see an evangelist, one who is truly anointed to bring people into the Church, at work? It is a thing of beauty, of an awe of God, to see them, to see the passion, the Love for the person in front of them. It is a Love which no human can have, unless God has put it there. It was, in truth, one which I envied, and one that I have a church-born guilt for not having, until God gave me my own Love, for my own purpose. But this is not about

96

me, for I am nothing.

What would Jesus do? That is an easy one, He would go to the Cross and die for our sins. He preached, He healed, did many great works, but all that was secondary to the Cross. Even the resurrection was secondary, proof given for the forgiveness of sins and the resurrection of the dead. The point being, that Christ could have avoided the Cross, spent His life preaching, working, could have even written a wonderful body of work, but He saw that the greatest work He could do was upon the Cross. That His Glory was not found in fulfilling what society, or his disciples, thought He should do, but in fulfilling the Will of the Father.

But what would the Cross be without the Resurrection? Would it matter to us that some dude died on a cross, if proof had not been given to its importance? More relevant to the point in hand, how convincing is it to say that 'Jesus saves' when the only difference between saved and unsaved is what we believe? How effective can we be when the world looks at the Church and sees only a different system of thought, instead of hearts transformed?

For the average Follower of the Way, that does not mean much. Do not mistake what I am saying, there is only one Way, only one Body so we are all interdependent. That, is there is a need for more individuals to go above and beyond, to seek to be perfect as God is perfect, but when the average Follower, stumbles, has an affair, blows up in anger, whatever, while it surely reflects poorly on the Church, it is not a scandal. That is, it does not teach, or create the idea that it is acceptable, to the degree that those whose public life is further reaching. How strict one is going to be judged on their shortcomings in morality and virtue, how strict they must be with themselves, is directly related to how those shortcomings affect other people.

But we already know this, do we not? That is why we are in such a crisis of clergy, both in number and quality. Because when it is God who trains us, the first thing He hits us with is that responsibility. We know full well where that line is, that line which we must live up to. It is a hard thing to bear. It is a great fear, a constant question. Will I be strong enough to endure the pain? The question which has kept you from taking that step into your own ministry, your own purpose. Made even worse by seeing those who we admire fall or simply grow cold.

Let me share with you my primary understanding so far from meditating the Mystery of the Cross this season of lent. That the pain of our cross is simply too much, a life too hard for us no matter how strong we are. That in fact, the only area, the only thing in which a Bond-Servant needs to be strong in is their ability to say 'Yes, God'. That when you feel the nails of temptation in your hands and feet, when you feel the hatred on your back like a scourge, the only strength you need is to look up to God and say 'Thy will be done'. Master that, and all things become possible.

Three Characteristics of Leadership

Upon meditating on Sun Tzu's the Art of War and more specifically his five factors which one must master to ensure success, my mind and spirit wondered not on how to master these five, but on the meaning of them. Indeed, what I found was what I now call the three characteristics of leadership.

Too often we think of leadership as a set of skills that we must acquire, but in this as in all things I look at it from its spiritual aspects. These characteristics that I will speak of are not behavior but the condition of the heart and mind. To be a true leader one must have and nurture these three characteristics.

Love: love is by far the most important in the leader. What I mean by this is that a true leader cares more about the welfare of those who follow them than the goal. In fact, the goal is only as important as it is beneficial to the group achieving the goal. In business the goal is important to the followers because if the goal is not achieved the business fails and they are harmed. One would think that our Lord's Body would produce many more true leaders considering that love is such an important aspect of our Faith. Even more so because we have the ability to manifest God's Love and the heathens do not. Yet, this is most often what is lacking in our modern leadership. I do understand this well, having fallen prey to it more than once myself. It is easy to forsake those helping you reach a goal for the goal itself. A true leader must always remember that they are there to serve those who follow them. (Mark 10:45) They always have greater love for those they lead than for the goal.

Ability: when I say ability most people think I mean the ability to perform certain tasks. Now, that type of ability is important. One must know how to read reports and such. What I am really talking about is the higher ability of taking ourselves out of the situation and taking command. That is to remain calm even under attack, to be able to step back and see life as a chess board. In

99

modern terms this means to see the real 'big picture' and not to react because of the stress they are under personally. Too often what keeps a leader from becoming a true leader is that they emotionalize those things which should be logically decided and they logically decide those things which should be emotionalized. Now if one has love, they will know those things in which emotion should play a part. (Luke 22:42)

Purity: a true leader must lead not only in physical things but in spiritual things as well. They, above all, must manifest a pure heart. Any of the various vices will destroy the leader faster than a poison. For the leader stands up and places themselves as the example for all those who follow them. If you stand up and say 'greed is good' (either in words or behavior) then do not become surprised when those who follow you only care for what they can get from the group. If you do not manifest love, then how can you expect those leaders under you to do such? This goes far beyond 'not doing anything wrong'. One must strive after doing what is right. A true leader will not stand by and allow any harm to come to those who follow them. They will fight until death to keep the wolves away. They must chastise without anger and be honest enough to step aside if a better leader comes along. (John 16: 7- 11)

Conclusion: these are the three characteristics of a true leader: Love, Ability, and Purity. There can be no substitute, and without all three of them one is only a pretender to the throne.

Twice Starved

There is a rather common teaching that fasting supercharges our prayers. Need a little extra something extra, do a fast. I do not know about that, as things are much different for me. Maybe it is only me, my life, and my Life has always been a bit odd. But for me, the beginning of a fast is always a time of feeling disconnected, a feeling of God pulling away. That is the reason why I do fast. That a fast is a way in which to have a hardship which separates me from God. A way to be twice starved. Without food, and without God.

Fasting is not an easy thing, at least not for me. Oh, the hunger of the first couple of days is a small thing now that I have experience, but that day comes the hunger starts to eat at me, consumes my mind. That is, the time comes that I am not simply hungry but am truly starving, there is no feeling of being spiritual, but only the pain. I do not know what it is like for you but usually on the fifth day and beyond there is nothing left but the hunger.

I know, in this world of fast food and easy enlightenment seeking to suffer, seeking to place oneself in a position in which the pain drowns out all our thoughts makes me a bit odd. But not as odd as one thinks. For that happens a lot to us in life, does it not? Money, job stress, wayward children, bills, relationships, life is full of pains which separate us from God, or at least makes us feel like we are separated from God. Robs us of that Peace. That life is full of times in which we become twice starved.

I have learned a lot from fasting, about myself, about human nature. It is why I fast, why I recommend fasting, because there is no better way, no safer way to learn to hunger more for God then for food. To desire God more then you want things. No safer way to learn to find your Peace in God. That learning to push aside the desire for food, so I am free to desire God during a fast, has helped in pushing away the stress of life. I have learned to better focus on God in my prayers, rather than the need or want that I am praying about.

Seek ye first the Kingdom and everything else falls into place. We do not live by bread alone but by the Word. It might just be me, but I have learned, that on that day during the fast when God returns in full force, when my soul is feed, the hunger of the body seems like a small thing. That all the problems of life do seem like starvation, when I am not twice starved…do you understand?

Simplicity is better than Gold

Romans 8

There have been many times when the self-pity of ministry has set in. That in the tone of woe-is-me there has been the desire to give up. That I have whined and complained by the sacrifices and payments I have made. All that silliness that plagues our emotions until Love grows to the point where there are no more sacrifices. I have long outgrown immature tantrums of how Life is unfair. I no longer fill any sorrow for the path of my own life. But now it seems, that I must face the temptation to give up, to give up, to say 'I have done enough, let someone else pick up the burden.'

Knowing one is tempted makes it easier to resist. As also knowing that much of it is simply the stresses of our present circumstances which bring on such feelings, makes them easier to endure. Most of all, it is easy to continue on because the work itself, the burden and yoke are light. Doing God's will is easy enough, it is surviving while doing it which is difficult for me. As I am supposed to be working on stability, I am not off to a very good start. Can you say crash and burn? It is not that I have to somehow come up with about two thousand five hundred dollars, it is the fact that it is worrying me to the point of fatigue which is the problem. You know that whole Mathew 6.24+ thing. It is not that my current struggle is important to you, as you have your own, but it is my state of mind which is relevant to what I am going to write.

Some time ago I was reading a modern and well-known theologian. (More known for his part in a fictional series then his theology.) He wrote that the reason that St. Paul worked as a tent-maker was out of Pride. Or to make this more personal, that it is only Pride in which I have hauled blocks, cleaned toilets, bussed tables and worked maintenance is because of pride. Basically, saying that it is Pride which motivates us who work very hard to keep money and ministry as two separate things. While I could easily say that taking those jobs was not about pride, it is my habit to give some thought to opposing views.

I do very much believe that it is Pride to not accept help when we are in need. To reject food when we are hungry, a cloak when we are cold. To ignore advice when we are in need of correction. It is not a pride which I am unaccustomed, wanting to be the one giving instead of the one receiving. It has also clearly pride when I have refused to reveal my own hardships and struggles in the past. But with the exception of the advice thing from time to time, I have out grown this. Now I am not above accepting a post card with a penny taped to it. Humility, in this regard, in this is rather easy once you have experienced real hunger, and real cold. And having been there, and without guaranty that I will not be again, I have lost my taste for the laminations of hardship and for once want to taste the sweet fruit of joy which wisdom can also bring. Or I should put it as a question. Must I be well fed and air conditioned before I find praise for the things God has done for me?

Though it may have very well have been Pride, my hubris which is why I always live my life on the edge of collapse. Maybe, most likely, if I had gone a more common route in my ministry, I would have missed out on much of its benefits. I would have had a salary, a stable life. I would have admiration, as titillating as that is to my ego, I would not have that is which is far more precious to me...friends.

I would much rather have my Godmother praying for me then money. That fellowship, real friends who have your back in your struggle to grow, is worth more than any amount of gold. That even though I have become poor in material things doing God's will, it has been more then worth it, I have been repaid a hundred fold by the kind of people in my life. Those who can be truly be called friend.

I talk about giving up, use hyperboles to make my points, but I can no more stop writing then I could stop breathing. I must think and ponder, write and talk of the Way of God because I have no other choice. I keep going out of a sense of duty, and out of a since of love. I keep going most of all, because there is really nothing which compares to, is as awesome, or as important as God in our lives. This we know, but where is our drive, were is our passion? Where is the excitement? Must we be well fed and air-conditioned before we can praise God for what He has done for us? Can we truthfully say that no struggle, no hardship, no pain can separate us from our love for God?

I find no scripture that condemns me for praying for a miracle and fully expecting God to take care of me in my troubles. There is no condemnation for crying out to God when we are in pain, or in need. (James 1 and 5) But there is definitely something wrong in allowing our sorrows for what we do not have to strip us of the joys in what we do. That as you Follow the Way, if you pay attention while you are living Life, you will notice that God does indeed give us many things far more precious then gold. The greatest of these, by far, is knowing Him. To be able to go to Him, to have Life, makes all others a pale-moon shadow by comparison. As such, this is the simplicity spoke of by the mystics of old: being in Christ is all we really need to rejoice.

What Time Do You Have?

Trapped by a dream of our own making
Living a life ruled only by fantasy
Nothing tastes sweet
Once the addiction has turned sour.

Warring against a feeling,
Which has never been named.
Struggling with ourselves,
We lose no matter which side wins.

Chasing after the future
As if it was a treasure,
Like trying to fight the air
Of a dreary afternoon.

We can have all we want
But become worse by the having.
The hardest poison to taste
Are those we feed ourselves.

Four fingers and a thumb,
Are they helping or fisted?
It is not always easy to tell,
When the hand is our own.

As the Preacher says
All is useless under the sun
So, let us turn from it
And find our use in the Son.

A call always there, a knock always at the door,
Maybe tomorrow it will be easier to answer.
Always asking for one more day to make the choice,
Even after the time has ran out.

Unity

Luke 17.7-10

I have heard it said that it is proper and good to feel joy for what you have done for the Lord. But to this I must respond that this is pride disguised. For what is the origin of this happiness? Nothing other than the fact that it has been I who has done the work. We should glory in nothing except that, through His Grace, we know the Lord (Jeremiah 9).

Now, do not mistake what I am saying. It is proper and good to feel joy that the Lord's work has been done. After all, all of creation rejoices when one lost is found. Does it really matter who was the one to show that lost person the Love of God? If we are truly acting out of Grace instead of our pride we would have as much joy over the Lord's work being accomplished when it has been others to do it. It is a prideful heart which feels its work is more important than the works of others.

This lesson is important to all Christians but is critical to the Faith of those called to a leadership ministry. If we let ourselves, it is easy to fall into the trap of believing the lie that because God has called us to make decisions that we are somehow more important than those who follow those orders. Or just as bad, the lie that just because we preach the Truth, we are better than those that do not yet have Him. The Pope is no more important to the Kingdom than a dishwasher working in a homeless shelter.

It is true that there are less leaders than workers but that is only because we need less leaders. If you are called to the duty of leading, preaching or teaching it is because of the Lord's Grace. Indeed, in such callings you must serve more, not be served more. You must be less than those you lead, preach and teach. Let me make this clear, I will accept nothing less from myself than always increasing my service to you, and I expect the same thing from you.

This is, of course, contrary to the world. My answer on how

it can be done is what I always give. Seek God, it is by His Grace we are saved, it is through God's Love that he increases our grace that we may show His Love to each other. It only when we are loving God and each other that we can truly say - we are brothers and equal heirs of the Father.

Conclusion: if we are to have true unity within the Church we must rid ourselves of our elitism and truly just serve each other with God's Grace and Love.

A View from the Cross

1 Corinthian 1.22-25

Those of you that have been with me for a while may have noticed that there was something missing in my email on forgiveness (Overcoming Sin). That is, what I was struggling with, what is it that I need to forgive. I did not speak of it, first, because it took me a day and a half to write what I did and I did not have enough energy. However, the stronger reason was because I would have to admit my calling. It would be solidifying the choice I needed to make. It would be me accepting the pain and struggle which is ahead of me. God had given me a choice. There was a way for me to escape, and that was the struggle. To choose between what was best for me and what was best for you.

Oh, it was very tempting to give up on the world and enter the life of a religious. It was even more so because God would have allowed it, that I would come to know a peace and joy in Him that even I did not think was possible. Why should I give that up for those who will attack me, or even worse, just not care? I bring this up because the struggle I was facing for almost a year was not a crisis of Faith, but one of Charity.

Now, it may seem like I am talking of things which have not yet happen. There is some truth in that, but that is not what I was struggling to forgive. It is what is happening now which is bringing my future about. I am talking about all the racism, elitism, and indifference in the church. I am talking about every leader who will not take their responsibility seriously. For every Christian who does not put the welfare of their Siblings of the Faith above their own.

Oh, I know how easy it could be to run from that responsibility. Even now I can feel the nails in my hands, and I cry out because I do not want this cup. But can you see why I fight so hard to increase my love? If you are not a good enough reason to sacrifice myself than what could be?

Can you see how being a living sacrifice to others, to be an example to imitate, scared, even still scares me? To say like Saint Paul 'you might have ten thousand instructors in Christ, yet you do not have many fathers ...therefore I urge you, imitate me'. Now, this is not much different than what I have always done. I have tried, and I think well, to present myself honestly enough that others say 'if lumpy can do it, then so can I'. But I have never stood up and said look at me. To lead is one thing, to be a leader is entirely different. It is that difference which frightens me, responsibility.

Sometimes I just run out of energy and this week was such a time. There were many times I just felt like giving up but today I met a young lady who reminded me why I fight. The pain in her heart screamed to me why I must never surrender no matter what it costs me. As Archbishop Fulton Sheen said once 'Christianity costs something, Grace is not cheap' and I add Love is the price we must pay. If you think that is easy, then you do not know Love.

Today I am drawing a line, showing you the goal. I will show you the view exactly as I see it. It is the view from the Cross. No, that is not a typo, it is from the Cross. See, my devotion centers around the Mystery of the Cross. This has been a great benefit for there is no greater example of God's Love for us than the Crucifixion. The more I matured in my Faith the more I felt Christ's Love for me in that moment, but the more I grieved over our Lord having to go through it. Over the last several years I have striven for just two things. To love God more and to love you more.

For you to fully understand what I will be saying what is next I must explain what the Mystery of the Cross means to me. Even though I misplaced it this weekend, I usually keep a crucifix in my pocket. Whenever I am going through something harsh, I will put my hand on it, or if it is really a hard time, I will take it out and look at it. why? Because it is my reassurance of God's Love. You may have favorite scriptures for this or maybe you look at all the ways which He has blessed you. For me, everything distills into the Cross. It is that Love coming from Christ on the Cross which makes my prayers a joy. The pleasure of basking in the light of God's Love is far greater than any other I have ever known in life. And the pain from just the minuscule amount I could handle of what Christ went through is more than all the suffering of my life combined. I am talking of far more than physical pain here. The spiritual pains which our Lord took on Himself makes the physical seem like a scratch. So great that even the smallest taste in which I have of it seem far beyond my ability to handle. Indeed, it is, for the lifetime of sins of even the most innocent of us is more than any of us could handle, that is the reason for the Cross after all.

I have shared this (even though would not have if I had a choice) so you will know that what I am about to say came with an understanding of what it meant. See, in my prayers last Saturday my love for God reached such a state that if I could, if it was only possible, I would have gone to the Cross to free Him from having to do it. In that moment I was united with Christ on the Cross in a way I never had before. The pain was still there but it was so overwhelmed by the Love that it was simply something to note. This in itself is nothing new for me. What was new for me was that the Love taking away the pain was not the Love for me but the Love for the world, that is, you. Honestly, the experience awed me.

I giggled off and on for hours after words and even though today was a day of tears, I have a joyful smile while I write about it. God has finally granted me something I have prayed for, for so long. More than loving you as Christ loved you, but Loving you with God's Love. Oh, do not mistake what I am saying and think I became a super-saint at the end of the prayer. This is one of those things for me which is far easier in prayer than in life. While I am praying, I would be willing to be crucified for any one of you, but this has yet to manifest in my actions. Indeed, I have sinned far worse this week than last for now I am guilty of not acting on that love.

That is why the pain of that young lady affected me so. Such people affect me, but the full reason would not be revealed to me until my prayers this evening. See, it hurts my heart that we live in a society which makes people with such pains common, even promotes the attitudes which causes them, and we, the church, do nothing about it. when I prayed about it and for this young lady the Lord responded with a single word. Hypocrite.

As painful as it is at times, I do enjoy the way that God can destroy all my defenses with a single thrust. All this week I have been guilty of what I hate most. I was not even trying. It was just easier to go on, business as usual. Once I got over my shock, I continued my prayers and tomorrow (well today) is a new day, and I have dedicated myself to the struggle of beating down my flesh and to be crucified for you, in action not only in prayer.

Now the reason I share this with you and why I say this is the line, the goal is not because I think that I have reached the top (far from it) but because we need to be crucified for each other. I, of course, do not mean that we go around dying for each other sins, but that we strive to always look out at the world from the Cross. That we love with Christ's Love no matter the cost, no matter how painful. Those we to must be a sacrifice on a cross, not to die but a living sacrifice for others. And also, I wanted to share the lesson that when God does increase your Charity, do not let your old habits get in the way of expressing it.

Weights and Measures

I have been struggling in my writing this month. It is for no other reason than I must apply what I have taught. That while I ask you 'what about Christ' I keep asking myself 'am I strong enough'? Pure enough? Humble enough? And the only answer I can give is laughter. Not because there is a lack of turmoil, but because my own hypocrisy always makes me laugh. That if I truly practiced what I preached, or maybe I should say if I practiced it as well as I preached it, I would not know turmoil, ever. I could give my body to the flames singing a lumpy song. But I am learning, improving, so maybe…someday.

To put it plainly that if you are following the Way, if you are letting God direct you completely, He will always take you to that place where you are not enough. It might not be throwing mountains around, it may not even seem all that grand, there just will be those times when it feels like God is asking more then you can do. I do not know how often you feel like that, but for me it has been constant since day one. I have argued with God, ran from God, tried not to give this or that up, and tried not to do this or that. All with the excuse that it is too hard, I am not strong enough, pure enough, humble enough.

So, I sit here caught between fantasies of power and the fear of the responsibility it brings. So I sit here struggling not to waist time with daydreams, or having my chest tighten up from the possibilities. So I sit here, laughing at my hypocrisy, for the moment I stopped asking about myself, and started asking myself. At that moment which I took my focus from what I need to do, and placed it where it belonged, on God, the turmoil melted away.

I am unsure what your tradition says about, but in my experience, both personally and with others, there is nothing which can seem large compared to God. That while all the problems, all the work is still there, it just does not seem like it is much to worry about. So, I say, seek God, keep your focus on God, and there is nothing which can rob you of your peace.

It is not that simple, is it? There must be more to it, otherwise we would all be throwing mountains around, would we not? But, in truth, in Truth, that is that simple. Always that simple, just not always easy. There is only One God, but there are countless things which we will use to distract ourselves from Him. There is only One Way, but countless excuses we can give as not to Follow Him.

Even that is simple on a fundamental level, for all the distraction and excuses are not reason for not Following the Way. No, not reasons but our attempt to justify ourselves for not listening and doing what the Spirit of God would have of us. An attempt to pardon our choice to have something more important then God.

But we should already know, there is no justification, of pardon except by Christ, and Him crucified.

What is Your Treasure
Mathew 6.19-34

I have been in a dark mood for some time and my normal practice had been unfruitful in revealing the cause. Indeed, even my prayers were of little avail for whatever God was telling me was the thing I was hiding from. The answer to the puzzle came from my anger towards some of the replies from my recent emails. It was not that anyone disagreed with me but that I was being praised. My first reaction was to respond 'does one give praise to the hammer for the skill of the smith'. As I have told you before, any strong reaction for either the negative or positive is a sign to look at your motivations. In doing so I found what I had been running from.

As you know I have been working towards a revival at where I work. Even though some progress has been made, it is frustrating that we have not seen it yet. But this was not the root of my depression. It was what Elohim was asking me. That is, am I serving the revival or the God that brings life? This has shown me once again how easy it is to worship the miracles while fooling ourselves that we are really praising the source of the miracles.

How many times have we sat and waited for God to bring a miracle to us so we may have greater Faith? How many times have we said 'if God would just tell me clearly what He wants of me or gives me a sign I would gladly do it'? Yet, no sign is clear enough and no miracle great enough. For look at the Israelites who while following a pillar of fire still the doubted the Most High or the Pharisees who saw the miracles of the Lord Himself, yet still would not follow him.

Conclusion: We must be forever diligent is seeking after God and God alone. That anytime we place what He gives us above Him we are guilty of idolatry. Our signs and miracles do not come because we are seeking them instead of the Living God. Indeed, they will not come until we are seeking only Him.

Proud to Call You Uncle

Deserving of the label of criminal
Put behind bars before I was born
You were still a man, still my uncle

Some say that people do not change
But you are proof that they are wrong
And the repentance which change takes

Knelt in prayer on concrete floors
Shadows of bars on words of freedom
You were an example to me of faith in hardship

My entire life you were labeled a criminal
I should have written this before it was too late
I have always been proud to call you uncle.

Struggles Against the Flesh

It seems to be the most common teaching that sin is some sort of cosmic balance sheet. That when I sin there is simply another tick put on the chalkboard next to my name, a debt that will not come due until I die. And according to this teaching, when we get saved, born again, or however one's Tradition may express it, an eraser is taken to the board and all the ticks disappear.

The teaching differ on what happens when we sin after receiving the Grace of Faith, but the questions and answer always center around salvation. Always with the view that God keeps a record of sin in heaven, but they do not really affect us in the here and now. Oh, to be sure, if I did some heinous act, one in which even those of carnal minds would call a sin, then we could agree that there is some damage done to my spirit, but not those little sins.

This is a good teaching, as far as it goes. But there is another view of sin. That sin is recorded not (only?) in heaven, but on our own hearts. That when I sin it hurts, it damages my heart. That a sin is a sin not simply because the Law forbids it, but is forbidden by God because it damages our heart, our spirit, or our soul, depending on how one defines such things. That when I sin, I do not have to wait for the Bema Seat but am harmed even in the here and now. That when I sin, or even when someone sins against me, a wound is formed on my heart. That the wages of sin is death, the death of our heart, a spiritual death.

While it should be well known to you, I will illustrate what this means by going back to the First Two (Genesis 3). There was Adam and Eve, as we call them, hanging out in the garden. With only one rule, do not eat from that one tree, or on that day you will die (2.17). Sounds easy enough, I mean it was not like they were starving. But along came the serpent, sin entered the world, and through sin, death and the rest is history as the saying goes. That, as some teach, there was no physical death until then. That may or not be the case, however it is interesting to note that that was the true part of the half-truth when the serpent said (in 3.3) 'you will surely not die.'

That is, for the carnal mind, to those who care only about the physical world, the serpent, or devils speak true when they say that the sin cannot harm us. You know, wear that protection, and no harm will come from having sex with whomever you want. That as long as you do not hit anyone, you can be filled with hate and bitterness. As long you will not physically die from sinning, so there is no such thing as sin. If you cannot feel the harm, then no harm must be present. That is, the serpent was the one telling the truth and God was the one who lied, if the death caused by sin, is not the death of our heart, our soul.

Oh, I know that people are basically good. Humans have a natural inclination to do what is kind, what is loving. But one does not have to be an expert observer to note that humans are basically evil as well. That we have a natural inclination to be selfish, to disregard others to get what we want, to sin. Let us be honest, and ask when was our first sin. When one disobeyed their parents? When we stole that candy off the table even though our mother said wait until after the meal? The first tantrum we threw when we did not get our way? But let me brutally cut away the argument, if humans were basically good, without also being basically evil, there would be no evil in the world.

As much as it might irritate the theologians I am not writing about original sin. I am not trying to show as we are born in sin, but that we sin from a very young age. We are born into a spiritual death (Romans 6.23) in which we are capable of doing harm to ourself, or to others without out even knowing we are doing wrong. While it is possible that St Paul was referring to a physical death (in Romans 5, and again in 8.6) sin kills us spiritually. That we are born atheists, as antichrists like to put it, and our sins very quickly kills our heart, kills our spirits. Original sin only explains why there is sin in the world, why we were born with the knowledge of evil along with of good. Only explains how the world became the way it is, the fact still remains that the world is a dark and threatening place but does not really answers the question of why we sin. Did not answer the question of why I sinned, and continue to sin.

However, sin begets sin, so with the dark and cold world is the best place to start. That, only a dead heart cannot see that we live in a world which attacks the heart. Even non-abusive parents cannot be perfect every moment, peers that bully or just pressure, those teenager years which are just insane with great happiness one moment and terrible sorrow the next. We live in a world in which by the time we come to age we have plenty of wounds and scars on our hearts. By the time we have grown to age we have a burning pain in your hearts, or we have a scab which we need to itch from time to time. But the world being as it is, explains why we develop such pain, but does not explain why would we do ourselves further harm, cause ourselves further pain by sinning?

The most common theological answer is that we have no choice. That without the Spirit of God, without the Cross, without being born again, we simply have no choice but to live in our sinful nature. That is certainly true, but the question still remains of why. Why do we continue to sin, though it causes us harm? Why do we not have any choice? After all, not too many people run around hitting themselves in the face with a large stick. At least they do not do it twice. So why would we have no choice but to commit sins, even knowing they are sins? Only a dead heart would not feel the pain of sin (1 Timothy 4, and Romans 1.18+), but why would we go through the pain required to kill the heart, in order just to sin? ...except in order to avoid a greater pain?

It is true when one says that the carnal mind, those without God has no choice but to sin. Even if they do not love their sin, they have nothing else to soothe the pain. There are some who come to age with pains caused by acts so horrid that they are repulsive even to the carnal mind. There are some who come to age with pains caused by acts so common, it is hard to recognize them as the cause.

There are those who come to age with a pain so intense that it feels like it alone could kill them. There are those whose pain is so mild, that it seems more like an itch. But regardless whether it feels like a burning pain, or just an itch that grows in intensity, we all have that inner stress in which we want to go away. And we find ways in which will make it go away…at least for a time. It always returns, no matter what we do, it returns and we do once again those things which will make it go away.

What one does depends greatly on their personality. Some people seek to soothe their pain with sex. That when the pain or itch appears, they become 'frustrated' until they can chase it away with sex. Others seek to satisfy themselves with wealth, going to the things they have collected to rid them of the pain. Still others find their comfort in food, in drink, in drugs. Some take refuge in being more educated, or being part of the 'beautiful people' part of the snob elite. As for me, my principle sin was to escape my pain by ambition, by accomplishment, by dreams of conquest.

While this shows that sin, almost all sin, is using good things in a disordered way, what I am pointing to is that the reason that we take something that is good and abuse it is because we are trying to compensate, trying to soothe a wound on our heart. That is, we may start down a road which is innocent at first. All we know is that this or that behavior takes away the pain or itch. So we do it, and we do it again when the pain or itch returns. That, every person I have spoken to who had once misused members of the opposite gender, and had overcome this, tell the story that they were trying to compensate for lack of love from a parent. That, my drive to achieve, at the cost of everyone around me, was due to my own feeling of inadequacy, of being unlovable.

And also, it is here where we see the trap. Compared to the pain that sin rids us of, the harm caused by the sin seems to be little. And it might be, but little by little, it kills that part of our heart which sees it as a sin, as harmful. This is why the majority seems to be 'good' and only a few degrade into 'evil' by the carnal mind's way of judging such things. Sin, such as my ambition, never truly satisfies that which is lacking. We are not able to find peace no matter how much we sin. I am never happy no matter what I achieved. That my friends were never happy, no matter how 'lucky' they were. This is because while sin satisfies the desires of the flesh, it cannot give us what our heart needs, the healing that our heart requires. So, we have to sin more, degrade into perversion. I had to accomplish more, become more ambitious, degrade into apathy, into a place where nothing, and no one mattered except my goals.

This also shows the short coming of the common views of sin that takes into account only the actions of the person. It sees sins as independent from the person. Does not take into account that our sins make it harder to resist sin, nor that the sins another does against us degrades us in the same way. We think only of changing our behavior, without addressing the pain which is the root of our sin. That outwardly this view saw me when my heart was dark, as one should be. Outwardly, I sin very little, but inwardly I was willing to lay waste to all love. That outwardly I was smiling, inwardly, I was in pain. That the all-too-common view is focused on ending the sin, instead of focusing on healing the cause of the sin. This is simply impossible without Christ, for in order to rid ourselves of that pain, in order to be healed we must go to God.

Unless we deal with why we are sinning, the carnal mind will account it important that we have changed our behavior. Unless our hearts are healed, without the Cross, we will simply change one sin for another in order to soothe the pain. Being of a carnal mind, I had no way of dealing with my pain, nothing else I could do but feed my pride, to harden my heart, until I could feel nothing at all. I say that I was in pain now, though when my heart was dark I did not see it that way. It had started as pain, but through sin, I had killed my heart. I no longer felt the pain, only an inner numbness. Though I am not an emotional person by nature, I felt nothing except an occasional burst of anger. I say my heart was dark, dead, because I could no longer see that I acted simply to soothe the pain.

That my old heart was greatly wounded, and in great pain, I can see clearly now, and in asking how my heart became tattered so, I could see that sin begets sin. Because there is sin in the world, because we live in a world in which harms our heart, because people sin against us. That we live in a world in which others, in avoiding the pain of their own hearts, causes wounds in the hearts of others. That others, because they were in pain, wounded me, and not knowing God, I had no choice but to seek carnal ways of dealing with this pain. Being of a carnal mind, I was in rebellion against God. That I would not, and according to St. Paul (in Romans 6.6-8), could not subject myself to the law of God.

Morality? Let us once and for all put aside that tired and worn idea that the carnal mind, the antichrists, cannot be moral. That while a nation needs a religious principle, the individual can be moral without one. Those without God can, and most often are very moral people because morality is defined by the group. Violations of social norms are also punished by the group. The carnal mind can be disciplined, can understand Honor, can be moral. Conscience is little more than the desire to avoid punishment and seek rewards, to seek pleasure and avoid pain. Our carnal mind, our wills decide our actions, and attitudes, on in terms of getting what it wants. That it will do what it can to scratch the itch, to soothe the pain of the heart. If to be moral is the means of doing this, then the carnal mind will be moral, will have Honor.

However, the carnal mind, no matter how well conditioned by logic, will not, cannot be subject to the Law. The Law is simply too harsh, too painful. It convicts us, but cannot save us. That when the Law enters our life we cannot avoid, cannot help but hide from our own pain. The carnal mind hates the light and loves the darkness, because the Law brings into focus, all the pain and deformities of our heart. That the carnal mind is moral, for it says in this morality it can say that it is beautiful, but when the Law comes, it sees itself as it is, scared and corrupted. That the Law is very much like psychoanalysis. As the primary purpose of psychoanalysis, and self-analysis, is to open our eyes, to see that and how our behavior and attitudes are causing us harm. That when used properly it shines a light on that fundamental truth; the wages of sin is death.

The difference, and why the carnal mind may use psychoanalysis as a means of avoiding the pain of the heart, is that it is still in charge. Our will still decides what we will see, and what we will label sin. The Law leaves us no such choice, it strikes directly showing us the wounds of our heart. Which is the reason in which the carnal mind will not, and cannot subject itself to the Law. It is because what we are calling the heart, is in fact where the Law is written (Romans 2.12+). The part of the heart in which the Law is written is the part in which is harmed by the sin. The Law in our hearts, challenges our carnal mind, refuses to except that our carnal mind is in charge. Therefore, as my heart was wounded, and in pain, I could not embrace the Law, without it causing pain. Without it causing a pain in which the carnal mind would seek after sin to soothe. Indeed, the carnal mind is the enemy of the Law for it seeks to kill it as the source of its pain. And as the Law is written on my heart, I had no choice but to kill the heart.

According to the Law, which both the heart and mind knows, in order for there to be an end of the pain there must be a sacrifice. In order for there to be forgiveness, purification, healing there must be death, there must be the shedding of blood (Hebrew 9.22). Even when unaware of this, we still know that either our carnal self, or our heart must die. Good and evil cannot coexist, and our knowledge of both embroils us in that struggle. As it is natural for us to seek to rid ourselves of pain, it is our nature to try to rid ourselves of this knowledge. And as the Law cannot be separated from the heart, in order to get rid of the knowledge which causes our pain, we must get rid or our heart. The greater the pain, the more we not only seek those sins to distract us from it, but the more we wage a war to kill our heart, to become heartless. There is simply no other path to take.

I repeat again that the carnal mind is the enemy of our hearts because it is our hearts which hold the knowledge of good and evil.

It is our hearts which contain the Law. Our carnal minds cannot accept this, for it considers itself the Law. It cannot except that it must subjugate itself to anything outside itself. We see justice only if our carnal mind, our will, our own desires determine what would or would not cause us pain. We consider the Law unfair, for it says if we sin, or when others sin against us, we will be in pain. Our carnal mind, or worldly self cannot accept that there is simply no other choice in the matter. The more power in which the carnal mind has, the more that the heart is dead, the more we will not accept that we do not determine our own law. The more deprived the mind, the greater the wounds of the heart, the more we will consider our desires, even our whims to be the Law.

Which is also why the carnal mind will not, cannot seek God. It is why the carnal mind cannot know Faith. Why the Cross is foolishness and an offense. For the carnal mind cannot accept that we are not God. The stronger the will, the more damaged the heart, the more one will seek to be a tyrant, will consider themselves a god. That with heart completely dead, one would exalt themselves above everything else, even above the Law, declare themselves to be God. (II Thessalonians 2).

I sinned, caused harm to myself and to others. I sinned in a vain attempt to stop the pain in my heart. I sinned for I would not accept that my fate was not mine to make, that I would not accept that I was not, could not be the god of my life. I sinned for all the reasons I have written here, but then came Christ into my life. I was born again, came to know God, saved, filled with the Spirit, or however your Tradition expresses receiving the Grace of Faith. That in that moment in which I knelt before Christ, and pledged my sword and life to God, my heart was healed. My heart became alive once more, and the Law, the knowledge of good and evil was active once more in my Life.

The Resurrection, the evidence of the fulfillment of the Promise of life eternal, cannot be over looked or forgotten, but it is the forgiveness of sin, the healing aspect of the Cross which is most relevant in the here and now. That when I was at the foot of the Cross, weeping in a way I have never known I was given a new heart, a new Life. That through the Cross my heart was healed (Isaiah 53.5), that with the Grace of Faith, we are given that Life in which the Lord spoke of (John 10.10), and thus life is grand, and there is no more sin, no more pain in our lives....Would it not be nice if that all too common teaching was true? That when we have Faith, we know only good and not evil. That we are no longer bound by the Law which says that when we sin, or other sins against us, it will cause us harm? But we still live in the world, in a cold and dark world where we must guard our hearts.

Unfortunately, such teachers who say that Faith is without cost, that leave out the struggles and hardships in which Faith brings, are no friends of ours. Our salvation carries no cost, none to us. Christ paid of our healing. He went to the Cross and bought our salvation. The Law of our hearts, Scripture and the Spirit of God all say that it is only by Grace, through Faith that we are saved (Ephesians 2). Those who would say otherwise, or worse teach otherwise, have not the Mind of Christ but speak form their carnal minds. For as I have noted, the carnal mind cannot tolerate anything given, to be indebted from the heart. Our carnal minds need to feel that they are justified, that they deserve what they receive, good or bad, for their own deeds and not from the deeds of others. It cannot accept that there is nothing we have done, or can do to deserve eternal life, for then there is nothing to boast, nothing in which our carnal mind can have hubris over.

There is a cost. For having found that narrow gate, we must walk that narrow path. That while we receive a new heart, a heart which has the new Law, the Law of the Spirit, the Law of Life, our carnal mind still wages war against our heart, still wants to live according to the Law of Death (Romans 6) We must work, fight back against our carnal mind, to keep our new heart safe, to keep it pure and healthy. We must seek to be righteous, not for heaven's sake for that comes from God, but to keep our Life, to keep our Faith alive (Mathew 7.15+). We must give up our old life, our carnal mind to Christ. This struggle, this war against flesh and spirit does not end when we receive the Grace of Faith. It is even possible to say that our hardships, our struggles, and even our pain increases. That though our hearts are new, and one may say perfected by the indwelling of the Spirit of God, our carnal mind is even fiercer. For now when we sin, or when we are sinned against, we have the Spirit of Christ keeping us from ignoring it, from simply finding any comfort for our pains in sin. That the cost we pay is having no choice but to follow God and His way.

When we are wounded by the world, when we feel the pain and the itch in our heart, we must now turn to God and His Will rather than reacting in the way it is our habit, our carnal way to react. When we are slapped the carnal mind says to slap back, the Spirit says to turn the other cheek. The flesh says to hold on to the pain until you have found justice, the Spirit says let go of the pain and forgive. The World says that our sins are not that harmful, the Spirit says to prostate yourself in front of the Cross and repent so you may be healed. That the cost of Following Christ is to wage war against the carnal mind, to transform our minds from carnal to spiritual (Romans 12.2).

I can easily say that my struggle in this has been far more difficult with Faith, for there is no real struggle before Grace. Those that know not God know not the struggle against sin. They know only the carnal mind attacking the heart. But those with Faith by our nature fight against the flesh. That the same thing which makes the struggle more difficult, is also that which makes it possible. Though there are those who teach otherwise, we as Christians, as those with the Grace of Faith, have in their hearts the Spirit of Christ (Galatians 4:5-7). That by the Spirit we are convicted, and by the Spirit we can put aside carnal things, and keep our mind focused on God. That by the Spirit, and by the Word of God, we can put to death our carnal mind. That we can use the strength of having God in our hearts, and the instructions of Scriptures to transform our carnal-minds and put on the Mind of Christ. That we train our minds for that race, to turn aside from sin, to live a life which is approved by Faith, approved by God. That like any discipline, it becomes easier as time goes on, as long as one disciplines themselves to do it.

The struggle against the flesh, against the carnal mind becomes easier as long one keeps struggling. The temptation to stop, to become complacent is can itself be seen as a struggle. To be sure, there are many examples to us of those give themselves over to their carnal mind, becoming depraved in their thinking, doing worse in their behavior than many of the antichrists. But such people are easy to spot, they rarely make any pretense that they are still fighting that struggle, so there is little danger of us in them unless we also become depraved in our thinking. That in order to become like them, not only must we quite in our struggle against the carnal mind, but we must also seek a life in which is not in accord with our Faith. They live in constant pain, for they always seek sin to soothe their heart, but cannot escape that they are the ones doing the harm to themselves. They have no choice to but to degrade into the worst lawlessness, for they must seek to kill their new heart completely. While any Faith still remains in them, they can find no peace from the convictions of the Word. Little by little they lose the understanding of the Cross, of forgiveness and repentance and have become as one in the world. They desperately try to lose their enlightenment, to become once again as if they had not the grace of Faith, and loose the Way to God (Hebrews 6).

The greater danger to us in the Faith is when we put on the outer-image that we still struggle against the flesh but our mind is far from spiritual things. When we put on the act that we are following Christ though our hearts are far from Him. That we may sing praises, and congratulate ourself on our Faith, all in the attempt to fool ourselves that we doing that what Faith approves. We will say our lips that we seek to overcome, but in our hearts, we say we do not sin. We may study Scripture days and night, but without understanding, and we may hear the Word, but do not do what we

127

hear. That we go to Scriptures so that our carnal mind may convince us that we have knowledge, instead of studying so that we may know God (Read John 5.38+). That the greatest danger of not continuing in this struggle is not that we will become 'great sinners' like those in the world, but that we will become just like the antichrists, that is, unrepentive for the sins we do have. We must all take heed that we do not become like them, dead, having Life only in name. For God would rather have us not care at all then to be one such as them (Revelations 3.14-22 of course).

And in the times, such as now, we even see those who want to have depraved minds, and still pretend that they follow the Way, that they are living a life according to Faith, approved by God. For as I said, the carnal mind must rebel against God, for it will not have any Law over it. Thus if the carnal mind can make Faith only about the rules, the rituals and the show, then it once again can be its on law. We do this every time we judge the Law, judging God's Way as we think it should be. Every time we go to Scriptures to prove our view, rather then having them form our view. And we must be guard against seeking out peers and teachers who agree with our view, with our rules. Seeking out peers and teachers that will agree that you have not really given up the struggle, that your sin is not a sin after all. But the Word of God burns as well as soothes, as the Spirit of God convicts as it heals. (John 16.5-15).

In this, keep in mind that we fail, we are always going to fail, we are always going to be a sinner, so the carnal mind is always going to be telling us that the fight is useless. Always telling us that we gain from discipline is not worth the hardship and pain of the training. Obviously, many, many times many, will follow their flesh and stop the struggle. Some will fall away from the Faith. Others stay within church culture as the lukewarm. And as we all fail, we all sin and fall short of the perfection which is God, all of us from time to time will fail in this. Thinking that we have arrived, that we have obtained some perfect state, or at least as perfect as a human can achieve. That as we keep in mind that all sin, that we are always

128

sinners, then we know that we are always in need of repentance. And as we are always in need of repentance, then the feeling that we have nothing to repent, in that deep down letting the Spirit of Christ heal us, then we are not struggling against our flesh at the moment.

Now, there are those who even teach this, that one can reach some level in discipline that they are no longer even tempted. Though I have never heard them come out and say this, it would follow that such a state would mean that we no longer need Christ, for we no longer would have the need to repent. If one no longer sins, then one no longer needs to seek the mercy of God. It is a teaching that I oppose, and advise you not to take heed to it. For even if such a state was true, how would you know that you had reached it, and not simply being fooled by your carnal mind. For there are many times when we slip in our discipline, that we feel like we have finally won, that we have nothing else to work on. We all fail, all are going to fail, though we are redeemed and counted righteous only through Faith, thought Christ and the Cross. As we remain sinners, only counted as righteous, there are times when we will sin, fail in this, by thinking that we are righteous in and of ourselves. That we have become so disciplined that we no longer need the righteousness accounted to us through Faith in Christ. That there are times that I have thought myself to be righteous, and then came the Word, to show me once more that I am a sinner.

The Law cannot save us. It can only convict us. We can find righteousness only through Faith in Christ. That no matter how perfect we are, or how unworthy we feel, we are no more justified, or sanctified by our works then those without Faith. We have been freed form the Law of Death, freed from being held captive by our sins. Christ on the Cross freed us from our sins, so in Faith our sins are no longer counted against us, so sins no longer matter. Not so we may sin, so that we may be free to work with a new heart, a healed heart in the Spirit. Saved from the Second Death, so we may be free to seek righteousness through Faith, instead through the Law. Given the new life, the Life, so that we may be free to put our worries about the wages of sin aside and go to God for mercy. We are saved so we may struggle against flesh, not from a selfish desire to be saved, but so there will be less sin in the world. Which is the wonder, the awe, and the beauty of the Cross, it allows us to repent, to continually go to God for strength in our struggle against the carnal mind. To be healed from the wounds our sins, and the sins of others, have caused on our hearts.

For the carnal mind cannot convince us that we are perfect, or at least enough that we do not need to repent, then it will try to convince us that the struggle is too hard, our sins to great, we are too weak. Indeed, there are many, many times many, who are in Faith, but live in sin for no other reason than they do not feel worthy to turn to God and pray for that mercy. But as there is no condemnation for those who have Faith, who are in Christ (Romans 8.1+), we do not need to, nor should we condemn ourselves. If God judges us through the Cross, through the Passion and Blood of Christ, then why do you then judge yourself according to the Law? Is this not your carnal mind, trying to prevent you from repenting? We were sinners, are sinners, and will continue to be sinners. There is simply no way in which that will change in our first life. As we must let Scripture determine our views, rather than using our views to twist Scripture, so to must we go to God as a sinner, as one unworthy of mercy, instead of the view that we need not mercy. That indeed, to know that one is a sinner is good, but not if we focus on it to the degree which keeps us from going to God for the strength needed in our struggle against the flesh.

I sought to be righteous, not for the sake of being righteous, but to protect my new heart. But longing to protect my new heart, I harmed it none-the-less. I do what I know I should not, and not do what I know I should. Though I know, and indeed, desire to do what is good, I still sin. That while my mind is on spiritual things, it still must wage battle against carnal things. In my longing I sin less today then yesterday, though no less a sinner today then I was yesterday. That though I may say that I have subdued, put to death my carnal mind, I must still do battle against carnal things. That even when we have transformed our minds, when we are of a spiritual mind, we cannot escape that within our flesh, there is still a desire to sin. That we do not yet lived in our resurrected forms but still in this body, and in this world. That until the Blessed Hope, the resurrection promised to us, we are going to have to deal with this (Romans 7.23+).

That working out our salvation, sanctification, growing in the Faith, drawing closer to God or however your tradition prefers to refer to becoming more Christ-like, is an active fight against the carnal mind. I know that there are those among you that teach that there are shortcuts in this. That there are special types of prayers you can use, certain methods in which we can learn to listen to our hearts. But all of these are for not, or worse leads us away from Christ if the carnal mind is not first subdued. That the carnal mind will seek to say that which is God is not, and that which is not of God is His voice. That even if such methods produce the ability to hear what God is saying, the carnal mind will then warp the message so our will takes its place above that of God. That indeed, this is clearly seen with Scripture, a far more reliable source of what God is saying then any one of us. It is not even uncommon now to find those who twist them to fit what it is that their carnal mind wants to be true instead of letting Scripture tell us.

Just as we must struggle to continue the struggle, so to we must struggle against sin. We must fight to do no evil. As I noted, we live in a world in which is dark and cold, which harms the heart. This does not change once we have Faith. Indeed, It could even be said that the world we live in actively seeks to harm a heart that knows God, that has Faith. The carnal mind hates the Light, namely Christ, because it loves its sin (John 3.19-20) and a heart that has Faith, shines the Light, Christ to the world (Mathew 5.14-15), and so the carnal mind hates a heart with Faith. Both our own carnal mind, and the world will seek to prevent, to wound our heart to prevent the Light from shining form us. It can be no other way, for our carnal mind and the world hates the Light, for the Spirit of Christ reveals our ways as sinful. And as I noted, our heart is healed, it now feels the pain of these wounds. As such, our carnal mind will seek to do those sins which will soothe this pain. So, we must always be on guard, to discipline ourselves not to do harm, to our own heart, or to the heart of others. That while this harm will come into our lives and the lives of others, we must always strive not to be the one who does the harm (Mathew 18.7).

For the converts, for those who God gave the Grace of Faith later in life rather than as a youth, will face this, will experience this first hand when that time comes when you start struggling once again with your old habits. That when we were in the world, when we knew not God, that when our hearts hurts, we would seek out the sins which would make us feel better. That is our old self, a habit in which we formed, and indeed, we did not even see them as sins then. But now, we know the truth because we know the Truth, namely Christ. When it first happens, life is grand, the Life is wonderful in that first love. But then the stresses of life start pilling on, and the cold and dark world pressed down on us, we start to feel that pain or itch again. In such times, there is that struggle not to fall into those old habits, to do those sins which we know will take away the pain for a while. Indeed, knowing that the itch or pain will go away if you just give into the sin makes the struggle all that more difficult.

That we converts can look back on our old life, a life in darkness and can see the harm which we did to ourselves, and to others, that while it is not necessary for us to ask forgiveness once again for those sins, it is when we come to understand repentance. For seeing more clearly the sinner we were, the harm we did, we understand to repent is to strive not to do that harm again. From the view that sin harms our heart, and to repent and to forgive others is how we start the struggle against it. There must be a great importance that every prophet and even the Lord preached that we must repent or we will perish. That repenting, going to Christ for the forgiveness of our sins, and seeking not to do that harm again was important in the beginning, and remains so every day in our lives. Just as Christ purchased for us our Salvation, so to has He paid the price for our sins. That the Cross forgives the sins that we commit as well as the ones that we committed before Faith. That without the constant healing which God works in our repentance, our sins will kill our heart little by little.

While those raised in Faith lack the past in which to make that comparison, neither have they developed the habits of the depraved mind of which the convert must struggle against. It would be a mistake to think that their struggle is easier. In a way it may be, if they have struggled since their youth, if they have never lost the drive to stay on the Narrow Path. But in a way, they also find the struggle harder, and many of them have felt the same pain from life. While for the convert, once there was no conviction, suddenly the Law was against us, others came to age knowing that many of their desires are opposed by Faith. For they sinned, harmed and been harmed, in full knowledge of the Law, but not knowing the death in which sin brings, not knowing the full effect of a dark heart, it is easier for their carnal mind to promote compromise. That as to do what Faith requires of us is to be enemies, or at least outcasts from the world. In order to be at peace with the world, and in those years when the youth lack the inner strength to deal with such loneliness, the more one is drawn to those compromises, to not be that fanatic which opposes the teachings of the world. And in such a setting, in those years when a youth in determining who they are as separate from their parents, they will often rebel against the Law, thinking that they are rebelling only against their parents.

As they have sinned, harmed and been harmed, in full knowledge of the Law, they sin again by judging themselves, or being judged as weak. Though they know that we all fail, we all sin, they have never been taught, or if taught never understood that just as one learns the alphabet before they can learn to read so to one must learn not to be ashamed, but to repent. Not to wallow in a guilt of their own carnal mind, but to express to God the remorse of the spiritual mind.

As I have noted that those of the carnal mind, those who know not God, is the enemy of the Law, an enemy of God. This is true even for those with Faith, for those who know God. Our own carnal minds are as much an enemy of God as the carnal minds of the antichrists. This is stressed in Scripture, especially by Paul, time and time again that we must transform our mind from the carnal to the spiritual. That it does not matter how pure, how righteous our heart is, because our carnal mind will seek to keep us from God, and from doing what is approved by Faith. And whether we are a convert or raised in Faith, it does this primarily by keeping us unrepentive for our sins. That whether we convince ourselves that our sin is approved, or at least allowed, or we refuse to go to God for our forgiveness, the healing of our heart, it is our carnal mind trying to stay in charge.

And regardless of the sin, or whether one is a convert or raised in Faith, depending on our personality, we will struggle with either seeking forgiveness, or giving forgiveness. I found forgiving others far easier then forgiving myself. That in my pride, and my arrogance, I expected people to be weak, to fail, but could not tolerate it in myself. That I expect others to sin, even against me, in my pride I would except nothing less than that I was strong enough not to sin. That in my pride I nullified the Cross, seeking to be made righteous by the Law. Even though my Faith, that indwelling of the Spirit of Christ, and Scripture spoke differently my carnal mind would not except that I was in need of continual forgiveness. Would not accept that I was, am not perfect as God is perfect. I, we often think that our own will is the answer in this struggle. And while we must discipline our will, our minds, to bend it to the Will of God, it is only by walking according the Spirit and not our carnal mind are we able to do this.

There are many ways which our carnal mind, our flesh will try to hinder our struggle against it, to prevent us from putting an end to sin in our life, or at least improving in not sinning. That the spiritual mind will bring us to a peace and joy in God which is impossible by following the flesh, does not matter for then we are not in charge. We must be led by the Spirit rather than our carnal desires (Galatians 5.16+). The nature of the carnal mind is that it determines what is good and evil only on the terms of us getting what we want. When we get what we like, that is good. When we get what we do not like, lose that which we do like, that is evil. The carnal mind can never see God's Will for our lives (read Hebrews 12).

But the more we struggle against sin, to have a spiritual mind, the more we come to see how sin harms us. The more we struggle, the more we discipline ourselves to seek God and His way, the easier it becomes to avoid sin. I fell many times into pride and arrogance, into dreams of conquest. Many times, I fell as my carnal mind's twisting it into a conquest for God. I fooled myself to thinking I could still conquer the world, as long as I did it in Christ's name. The more I fought to keep my mind on spiritual rather then carnal things the more I did Godly things in God's way. The more I learned that following Christ was doing God's Will according to God's Will instead of our own. In order to do God's Will I could not do it according to my will, or even work my will within His Will. The more I struggled, the more we struggle against following our own mind, the easier it is not to sin. Our carnal mind, as does the enemy, have many tricks. That repentance and forgiveness we do for our one sake, to allow God to heal our hearts, and thus we may think of sin only as doing evil. Because our carnal mind is opposed to the Law of Life, to the Spirit of God, it will also try to prevent us from seeing that doing no harm is not enough, but one must also do good.

One could even reject the Fall and original sin and still see that natural state of the world is entropy, decay...death. That the world is in darkness, and without the Light. But this is not the world's fault, the fault of the darkness, but because those with the Light, with Christ, do not share Him. Oh, we evangelize, we preach, we teach, we do many great works, but we must always ask ourselves are we doing this from Love, form the desire to heal, or simply because that is what the rules require of us? Do we preach against the heretics who preach that there is no more sin because they are wrong or because we have sorrow for the damage they are doing? Do we feed the poor because it is what we are supposed to do, or is because of our hunger for them to know the love God has for them even in their hardship? There are many, many times many, who think they are strong in Faith because the do no evil. They think only of their own salvation, their own pain, and care nothing for those around them. Loving only those who love them, loving only those who give them what they want. What their carnal mind desires.

So, the third struggle against the carnal mind is to do good. To love even those who would do us harm, who would sin against us. Even those who are unrepentive about it and would like to see our hearts grow dark again, that would take pleasure to see us in pain once again (Luke 6.35). There are those who teach that one must work up to this, that the struggle in this is not until you are matured. While there are things which is only understood by the mature, things in which only the wise know, there are no secrets that need to be gained in the Faith. One does not have to be a genius or a scholar to find the richness of the Faith. You, as a child of God, already have everything needed to put off the old carnal mind and to run your race. That we the Church, as Christians have the choice whether or not to sin, because we have the choice of either following our carnal mind, or to put on the mind of Christ. You do not need to mature before you start your struggles against sin, and one does not have to be mature before they start the struggle to live a life of love for others.

The struggle to love others as we love ourselves is simply another aspect of the struggle against the carnal mind. That they are all the same struggle, simply named and classified for the sake of understanding. That we sin because of the pain of our heart, and while we may decrease this by decreasing our own sins, we still live in a world which is a slave of sin. We will be continued to be harmed, to be slapped, and thus from the very beginning we must learn not to slap back, not to return sin for sin, to forgive the one slapping us. That from the very beginning we must learn to love in a way in which we ignore the sins done against us (I Peter 4.8).

The struggle to do good, to Love, is the struggle against the tendency of the carnal mind to make everything about us. There are many, many times many, who are pleased with themselves simply because they are not doing evil, that they are not sinning. But are we not also sinning when we do not love others, to love them as we would want to be loved? Or so there can be no mistake, as we need to be loved. For very often when we fall into obvious sin, time and time again, it is because we are keeping the focus on what it is we need, rather than on the needs of those around us. That is why I say that this struggle is one in the same with the other two, all part of the struggle against the flesh. Because just as the greater the pain, the greater the temptation to sin, so is the greater the temptation to focus on our pain, rather than the pain of those around us.

To love others as we love our self, but as many can attest to, it is hard to love others, when you do not love yourself. And this is why it is it is important, from the very beginning to struggle to love others. For it is our carnal mind which says that we must be perfect, to be beautiful, rich and witty to be worthy of love. But none of that really matters to our carnal mind, and the pains of our heart, for no matter how perfect we may be, we still will not feel worthy. It is only arrogance of the flesh to think such things have anything to do with love. It is a clear sign one has not learned that love is not based on worth. That as we struggle to love others, even our enemies, we learn more and more that love is love because it loves even when there is no reason to love. That when we struggle to love others, in spite of their imperfections, then we also learn to love ourselves, in spite of our imperfections. And the more we can love ourselves, the more we can love others.

But do not let the carnal mind fool you into thinking that

simply doing good works is the same thing as doing good, the same thing as loving. As I have noted before, the carnal mind will do what it can to be its own law, to seek to justify ourselves through the Law of Death, and through our works. That we must always be a guard about those thoughts which point to what we have done, what we accomplished as proof that we are justified, that we are righteous. To keep trying to justify ourselves, to be saved by the Law instead by righteousness through Faith (Romans 9.30+). We will try to develop that pride in which we judge ourselves, and others, by the works they are doing. To be sure if one has Faith, they will have works, but it will be works from Faith, rather than works to justify ourselves. Works which are doing the Word, rather than works which allows us pretend that we have the Word. Works we do from mercy, rather than from judgment (James 2.13+).

We must always be on guard lest we become like the Pharisee (in Luke 18.9-14), being grateful that we keep the Law better than others, that we have so many works to which we can point. Thinking that we please God more by our works then by Faith. But there will be many who did great works, even miracles but will be cast out because they did not do the Will of God. They do their works only so they could boast in what they have accomplished, only so they could be counted righteous and great among men, but did not build on the Rock, which is Christ (Mathew 7.21-27). We must always be on guard lest we become puffed up in pride, thinking that it is our works, rather than being a servant which is how greatness is determined, if one desires to be great, as greatness is what I preach, then one must learn that in the Kingdom, greatness is found in mercy, in Love, in doing what is best for others rather then doing for ourselves. Indeed, to be great in the Kingdom one must put aside all titles and pomp, all thoughts of self and think only with the Mind of Christ, as a servant of others (Luke 22.24+).

Just as the struggle to keep struggling, and the struggle against sin becomes easier as we continue to struggle, so does the struggle to do good, to love grows easier as we mature. For when our carnal mind is still strong, we think of love only in carnal ways, of giving and receiving pleasure, and the avoidance of pain. This is why many teachers, who count themselves mature, but lack the wisdom of God, think they show love by condoning sin, by preaching only forgiveness. As I have noted many times, that the Spirit convicts us as it heals us. The Word causes us pain when He exposes our sin, and the wound is revealed to us so that we may repent, so that we may seek the Mercy from God which heals us. And that is why there are many teachers, who count themselves mature but lack the wisdom of God. They think they show love by condemning sin, preaching only repentance. As I have noted many times, that the Spirit heals us as it convicts us. The pain caused by the Word is the fading pain of a wound healed, of hard work followed by the peace of finding God's Mercy.

Teachers of both types preach not the Word, for the Spirit of Christ is the Way to God, points us to God, His mercy, and His Law, which is Life. Love, regardless of our method of expression, reveals the love for God, and the Love of God. Which is the importance of struggling to do good, to love. For just as we need to learn the difference between those who are edifying us and those who are leading us into greater harm, we must learn how to edify others, and not to do them harm while trying to do them well.

All of this I learned as I struggled to be holy, to live only by Faith. I longed to protect my heart, and the hearts of others. I disciplined myself in Faith, and in Scripture. So should I not be free from sin? With such wisdom, why is it that I still sin? If I practice what I preach, if I make my camp at the foot of the Cross, seeking forgiveness, and to forgive, seeking to always act from the Love for others, rather than for my own welfare, why must I still be a sinner? Why must I always have less sin in my life then having a sinless life? For as I have disciplined myself to have a spiritual mind, I have not sinned those sins I once sinned, but I have sinned no less. For those things which were not a sin, or at least did not appear as a sin to me, suddenly because a sin which I was struggling against. And though I have beat down my carnal mind and subdued my pride, I still must contend with my body, and struggle against lust. Should I be like those who see themselves a sinless because I keep my body from sin though there is still the desire in me to sin? Should I count myself among the antichrists by saying that our thoughts and feelings cannot be disciplined in the same way that we discipline our bodies? Or should I agree with the Lord that I sin even when I desire that which is not mine (Mathew 5.28+)? So, I keep fighting, and can say no more except for you to do the same. To continue in the struggle, against the carnal mind, and the flesh, now and this day, and into the future, to preserve until the end, until the Blessed Hope.

Unifying Vision

1 John 1.3-4, John 13.34-35

What does the following have in common: Boycotting of Disney, fear of Pikachu, a constitutional amendment banning homosexual marriages and Churches picketing the Passion of Christ? They are all proof that Satan has distracted us from our true purpose.

I have already written about overcoming sin. This email continues this but links it to the path of holiness. See, I must point out a misunderstanding which is common today. We confuse holiness with righteousness. They do go hand in hand but not in a way which many people think. Too many people have the idea that righteousness leads to holiness when it is the other way around. That is, we mistakenly believe that because we sin less that we get closer to God, when in fact, it is only by getting closer to Him do we have the ability to stop sinning. (Do you see where I am going with this?)

See, what I am pointing out here is that we focus entirely too much on behavior instead of the nature of our hearts. We are just like the Pharisees which our lord accused of washing the outside of the cup and leaving the inside unclean. Now, do not in anyway, mistake what I am saying. Saint Augustine taught for us to 'love God and do what you will' and too many says he meant that behavior was not important. He was saying the same thing I am now. The same thing Saint John the Apostle was saying. The more you love God the less you will want to sin. But that is just it. That is where we are failing. We worry so much about changing our behavior, and even worse, care too much about changing the behavior of others that we loose sight of what is important. Changing the heart.

As I wrote a friend today the closer we get to God, the more unworthy we feel. Because the closer we get to the Light the more we are able to see our imperfections. But listen and understand, we know they are there because they are being burned away. Sometimes it is painful and takes a long time, and sometimes it is quick and painless but either way it is God's Glory which is purifying us not our own work. That is not to say that we do not have our part to play, indeed it often very hard to keep embracing God in His Light. And that is the point, our job, if you will excuse the term, is to hold on to God with everything we have. To keep our steps heading towards Him no matter how painful it becomes.

I know that some people do not want to face such things but the Church in America is in serious trouble. Let me make this plain. Before a revival would have been nice, now it is necessary for our survival. But let me say that revival is not the vision. The trap we fall into, the one I almost fell into is focusing on revival. Revival is not God's Will it is only the byproduct of His Will.

Now we can say getting closer to God is His will, but it is not our purpose. That is the how, not the why. See, Faith is the how, but Charity is the why. If the purpose of Christianity was only salvation, if it was only a matter of getting closer to God, than what is the point of staying alive? I mean, really, the world is a dark place and life is hard. Especially for those who are sensitive to the decay around us. That is the point, our purpose. God allows us to be filled with more of His light not so we can feel good but so we can lighten the world. We are the light of the world and if the world is dark it is not the world's fault but ours. If the world does not taste salty it is because we have lost our flavor.

Every philosopher, who takes such a label serious, comes to a time when they realize that they must put into practice all they have learned. It is the same with Faith. in our egocentric culture we too often focus on the Love we can get from God. But God does not give us his light just so we can feel good about ourselves, He gives it to us so we can share it with those who do not have it, to give it to each other. If you do not do good with what God gives you do not be surprised when He takes it away from you.

To be mature is to live by this simple statement, God first, everyone else second and ourselves last. Now, do not judge yourself too harshly on this. Such a life is our goal, but any goal worth striving for is hard to obtain. It is a matter of maturity. And in this to let me restate that we cannot measure our maturity by our righteousness, for (as many of you know) the more we mature the more we conscience we are of being a sinner. In fact, if you would like to know how to judge your maturity? You can determine the maturity of your Faith by how much Charity you have for your enemies. By how much love you give the person who hates you the most.

Yet to be honest, the Church, as a whole, has never done well in this. We do not even love our fellow Christians. We have always, being human, been caught up in the nature of our world. When our church culture is communal it is all about the safety of the Church, with a wiliness to destroy the Christian for the sake of that safety. And those of us who, especially in this time, are individualistic, see only the the love of the individual and often forsake the Church for the sake of the Christian. Being human we have trouble in politics, in religion and in our everyday life, balancing the love for the People and loving the person.

On the mount our Lord asked what benefit we would have if we loved only those who loved us. After all, almost everyone does this. The problem is we are not even doing this. See, I believe that a great number of Christians are trying to get closer to God, that they try to take the Faith serious, they are just neglecting the Charity. In that way that I often neglect Hope. That they cry out to God to increase their Faith only to have their prayers unfruitful. I think they just do not realize that you cannot have Faith without Charity. The Lord told us that loving each other is like loving God, and Saint James taught that Faith without Charity is dead.

I am focusing here on the Love which should be easiest for us. That is, our love for our fellow Christians. A Love which is lacking in the Church. See, Charity is a love not based on familiarity but on loving God. To have Charity is to love nature for it reflects God's Glory, and especially to Love humans for we are made in His image. That is why I say it should be easier for us, as Christians, for we know God, have the image of God in our hearts by the Spirit of Christ. And in loving God, how easy it should be to Love such a person who has been transformed (if even a little) into a walking image of Christ.

I call it a vision on unity, and understanding based on my meditations of the header verse. But it does not take much wisdom, Godly insight, to know that the Lord told us that the world would know that we belonged to Him, because we Love each other enough to sacrifice ourselves to one another. To love each other, as He loves us is the very definition of Charity. The Scriptures are clear enough that my heathen and atheist friends know it. That they ask how are they to take Christianity seriously when they see only spitefulness and hypocrisy in the Church? It is not a valid excuse for them, and while we cannot expect them to understand our view on sin, or agree with the need for Charity, but they do understand love as a motivation. I make it clear that my Faith is the source of my Charity, but they see it only as something about me, that I am different. We need to love one another, as Christ loves us, so the world knows that it is not just a 'special' few who love but that it is the normal state of the Church.

And that, my friends, is why I called this email the Unifying Vision. You see, no matter what your calling is, no matter how great or small a vision God gives you, at the core of it is Charity. That no matter the Calling, Vision, Gifts, the purpose is to Love. You can tell when someone is following a vision instead of God when they are sacrificing to achieve a goal, instead of giving themselves to others. That one thing I have learned already are that shepherds according to His heart do not separate themselves from the sheep but are the ones who walk among them. After all, did not the Lord tell use all that those who are the greatest in the Kingdom are those who are willing to humble themselves and be the servant?

Now let me return to how this relates to overcoming sin. In my last email I said that forgiveness and humility go hand in hand and Love is the source of both. The root of all sin is the lack of Love.

Either a lack of love for God (Faith) or the lack of love for others (Charity). I once wrote that I have a problem with both arrogance and a low self-esteem. This may seem like a paradox to some people, but if I was going to describe myself in a word it would be paradox. And a paradox is only a cue to look deeper. Now the truth of why both of these can exist at the same time is because both are rooted in being egocentric. That is, the feeling that we are worthless and the feeling we are better than everyone else comes from focusing on ourselves. See, as I have said countless times, whenever God asks something of us, we are helped just as much as we help others. And in this case, the more I focus on the needs of others the less I care about my own wants. The more Charity I have the more I am willing to forget about my own troubles, because there are plenty of troubles of others which I can help with.

Now listen and learn, the lack of Charity is often the reason why all the support systems fail us. We can go to countless bible studies and worship services but our problems do not go away. But when you start to poor out to others the Love God has given you, that your problems will seem to fade. Even if they do not go away, you will just come to realize who petty they are compared to what you already have from God.

In no way am I preaching that Charity is the answer to feeling good. Again, this is simply a byproduct. Indeed, increasing Charity can be as hard, and as painful, as growing in our Faith. A man who I admire much and has been a great example for me in Charity will admit that there are times which he finds it hard to care. We are running a race, and to make matters worse, we have an enemy which waits upon the path we run placing boulders to climb over and planting thorn bushes to tear our metaphoric flesh. and if we are running to win, we are pushing ourselves to our limits, and sometimes even harder, and we grow tired. There is no shame in this. They are just times in which we have to pause for a moment and refocus on our goal (God).

I am unsure if I have written before on the connection

between Faith and Charity before so I will finish with it here. I do not remember which Saint it was who said that in order to increase your love for God then love others more, and to increase your love for others than love God more. As I have said before Charity is God's love flowing out of us for others. That is when you love God you will love others, and because you love others you will seek after God in order you can do better for those you love. the more you love others the more you seek after God, the more you Seek after God, the more your love for others will grow. It is a most wonderful cycle. One that once you have gotten into, you have to fight very hard to leave it, and if you let it, it will take you much farther than you can even imagine.

I will leave you with my translation of Verse 18 of the Toe Te Ching.

When God is forgotten
We have only laws for Charity and Justice
But do not have them in our hearts
This leads to great hypocrisy.
Only when there is no love in the family
We need to preach on duty and devotion
Only when the nation is in darkness and disorder
We need to preach on loyalty and virtue.

A Tym for war, A Tym for peace

Occasionally I will bring up Tym, the threads of fate, but almost always in passing. It is because people get weird when you start talking about the spiritual river in which we swim, and worse many, too many become obsessed on knowing where it is going. That of course is the danger, the trap I fell in which was the primary cause of my dark years. To know the future is to be able to gain control, but to know the future one losses control. This is a warning to all who would try to see what is on the other side of the mountain of the now. The human spirit cannot do it. One cannot see the future. We must be shown. Which means one either sees the future reflected in God, or the future the darkness would create, which brings me to the point.

Most of you will not be tempted by the future, you have a hard enough time just seeing the now. That is a good thing in my opinion, because you will have an easier time then I did with living what I am about to write. We, in the Church, talk much about Tym, about fate. We talk about callings and when we do, we are talking about the future, the fate in which God wants for us. This is a mistake, an incomplete understanding, if you would. Many are called, but few are chosen.

I ran across a youth, who more or less God said would be a preacher. His pastor made a show about it, which would have irritated me except I agreed. But with my mouth, it was not long before I got in trouble. I have not given it much thought since then, but recently I just got a wakeup call that what I had said was simply wisdom beyond that what I had at the time.

That is, when the question of how the youth was to become a preacher, the answers being thrown around was about seminary and such. Out of nowhere (well not out of nowhere but the subtle aspect of the Spirit was lost on me when I was younger) I had a thought, and spoke the thought. I said, that no matter what this youth did they were going to be a preacher, the only question was whether or not they were going to preach God.

That thing we often call a calling, from one view can be said to be nothing more than us becoming aware, or God showing us, our nature. Who it is in us to be. That new person that we are in Christ, the Gifts He has given us and such. See, the question is not whether or not you will become such or such, it is whether or not you do it in a way pleasing to God.

A preacher is going to preach, whether they preach God or simply their own ego. An evangelist is going to evangelize, bring people into their way of life, be it a Godly life or one of sin. A prophet will tell you the direction one should go, it is just a matter of whether it is towards Christ or towards destruction.

I have some skill with words. I have pointed out that my words are nothing but that does not mean that there is not power in them. I have that way of talking, and to a lesser extent writing in a way which touches the human heart. That is hardly new for me, at least the speaking part. I took great pride during my dark years in this ability.

The real change has not been my improvement in this, as there has been that, but that it is important for me that I order my words in such a way, not so they are a benefit to me, but that they may be pleasing and a glory to God. That which each passing day I see my abilities, my Giftings, everything I can do, everything that I am, as a Sacred Trust. One which exists not only for my own sake, but so God's name may be glorified.

That right there is the improvement which we should always strive for. That whether we are raising the dead or washing dishes, working or playing, fighting for safety, or for peace, that we do such in a way which brings Glory to God. And as to be expected, I must say, I know no way to do that without seeking Him, always.

Could it be?

Idols on the television
Saying we are not responsible,
If our predictions don't come true.
You just lack the faith to be blessed.
Could it be - we would rather deceive than pick up the Cross?

Preachers giving love to everyone,
Except for our own children,
And giving a bit too much
To our neighbor's wives.
Could it be - we have forsaken our first love?

White washed tombs sitting in our seats
Agreeing with the sermon each Sunday
Things need to change; more life is what we need
So, we put on a new coat of paint.
Could it be - we are not as our name applies?

Wearing faith as we would a new suit
Is like the emperor's new clothes.
Fooling only the other people
Who pretend to be clothed.
Could it be - our tongues confess what we do not believe?

Could it be, just maybe, could it be,
That our lives would be better, just a bit,
If we asked God what He thought of our lives,
And let Him show us which road is best?
Could it be - we are meant to live a life of Faith and Charity!?

Into High Adventure

James 1

'Far better it is to dare mighty things, to win glorious triumphs even though checkered by failure, then to rank with those timid spirits who neither enjoy nor suffer much because they live in the gray twilight that knows neither victory nor defeat.'- Theodore Roosevelt, 26th President of the United States, Noble Peace Prize and Medal of Honor winner.

I am off again on the road of High Adventure. I will be going offline tomorrow. With no idea when or if I will have easy access to the internet I write with some since of finality. Writing with that trepidation of a warrior-poet who has spent time in rest, in healing and now must once again throw themselves into the breach. Once again face those trials, those struggles and conflicts in which there are simply two choices. Success or death. And that is something we are missing today.

Forget all of the temptations of society, the decadence of entertainment, the lure of the senses. These are trifles compared to the complicity in our Faith that a soft and leisurely life may produce. Carnal desires and worldly concerns are nothing more then distractions unless we excuse, seek to justify, or ignore them. They are not a threat until that day we stop treating them as threatening, when we stop fighting against our old-self. Indeed, we are dead to sin not because we sin no more, but by Faith, by the Cross we have been given the ability to struggle against sin. As I have said and written many times, we fail in our struggle against sin not when we fall, but when we refuse to get up again. When we become complacent in our Faith, and our Life.

We fail to fight not from being cowards, rarely that, but because we lack the proper vision. Or better stated, our complacency is because our vision too worldly, too vulgar, too common. Our Life is mediocre, not because we are not great enough, but because our vision, or ideal is not grand enough. We are pleased when our sermons are entertaining, a good alternative to that latest TV series *The Sinful Life*. Our goal has become a comfortable life of small groups and Sunday brunches. Our vision has degraded into the view that bible studies are living the Christian life instead of simply equipping us to live that Life. We have forgotten that the sanctuary of the Church exists not to make our life pleasing, but to provide a safe place to grow, to become strong enough to be that light of the world.

I want more than a mediocre Faith. I want everything that God is willing to give. I want to do everything God would have me do. I want to be sanctified by as much Fire as I can survive. I want to be that person Christ would have me be. And I want....not to pay the price. I want to do those easy things which God wants of me, but do not want to do those hard things which God asks to be done. Yet, how is doing only those things we want to do any different then what those without Faith do.

As I know from experience, it is easy enough to get carried away with such feelings. Both the depths of pleasure and the heights of pain are the products of poor sight. From judging our own lives from the improper vision. It is easy enough, as I know from experience, to mistake true vision with the tasks in front of us, the purpose we must fulfill, or the things which God has shown us. To start defining ourselves, judging ourselves by tasks we have done, the demons that we have cast out, instead of by our Faith, by belonging to Him.

The only proper vision, the only true vision is Jesus the Christ. A life of High Adventure is having our footsteps following the Way, regardless of where He leads. When our sight is not fixed on the hardships and pleasures of life, but when our vision is filled with Christ. That is to say....there is no High Adventure in our life without prayer. We can read scripture day and night. Go to church three days a week. We can give our money and time for the aid of others. But we can do all this, as still be missing the Truth. We can do all this and not even have the grace of salvation. Indeed, we may even do all this in a vain attempt at earning our salvation.

Knowing this, knowing that as our Life comes from God, is it not reasonable that the enjoyment, excitement and even maturing of our Life can only come from God as well? We may not like it, we like doing things the way we like doing things. Christ expects us to follow Him, instead of plotting our own course.

To conclude this matter, as it is time to end this. There are times in our race when all pleasures of this world seem like ash in our mouths and we wonder what went wrong. Sometimes this is because we have allowed our hardships to strip the joy of our Life from us, other times it is because God has hidden that joy from us, other times it is because we are trying to find that joy somewhere other than Christ. Regardless, they are times which remind us how fleeting life is, and how important Life is. A reminder that our Life is found nowhere except in Christ and so for us there is nowhere else for us to go to feel alive, to have that High Adventure except to Christ.

Thornless Roses

Naturally I feel no attachments so I feel guilt only when I violate my internal law: There is no failure, only success or death. Without God actively convicting me, I have never felt remorse for the wrongs I have committed, only for the goals I have failed to achieve. No sympathy for the death I have witnessed, only regret that they died against my will. That with all my abilities events transpire beyond my control. Outside of the Christ I have no understanding of repentance, because without the Spirit I have no understanding of sin. Morality, right and wrong, gain and loss, are all measured by how they affect the achievement of the goal. All my actions are determined by my goal, and I am capable of doing anything to achieve it...and do not fool yourself into believing that you are any different.

Of course, goal is just the word we use to make our desires more respectable. A word we use to imply that we have some measure of dedication to fulfilling that desire. Resolution used to be a stronger word, back when a person's word meant something, but that is neither hither nor thither. I have spent many years pondering goals on a philosophical level, which is fitting for a philosophical writer. Over the last year I have pondered whether writing is the best way in which to achieve my goals. Or is it simply that writing is the best I have, the only thing I have, but that is neither then or now. It is not the method of our art which is really all that important, nor even how good we are at expressing ourselves. It is precisely my goal which puts me at odds with the modern church culture. My goal, and if I may be so bold as to say our goal, is not to win the hearts and minds of the masses but to help in the sanctification of each other, the Faithful, the Church, His Body.

Colossians 2: Beware lest anyone cheat you through philosophy and empty deceit, according to the tradition of men, according to the basic principles of the world, and not according to Christ...these things indeed have an appearance of wisdom in self-imposed religion, false humility, and neglect of body, but are of no value against the indulgence of the flesh.

I used to dance naked in the midnight rain until the coming of the dawn. Once tasting the burning dryness of a mouth full of ashes, I now toil throughout the long and lonely night waiting for a glory to come with the returning Son. Happiness is the goal of all philosophy, even Christian philosophy. Discontent is the motivation for all that we do. No one asks the meaning of life unless they first become unhappy with life, until they gain some understanding that there must be more then what they are living. No one puts themselves through the work and struggles of creativity unless they first grown discontent with the art in which the world already has. No one repents, truly repents unless they are convicted, until they are unhappy and discontented by their sins. So, as the goal of philosophy is to that path, to gain the wisdom in which we can order our lives to bring happiness, the first question is not all that deep but simply; what makes you happy?

Lest you think I have suddenly become a post-modern hedonist, let me forsake my normal habits of pages of artful tripe and get straight to the point. Stress is the internal measure of the distance between the world as it is, and the world as how we want it to be. The deference between what we want and what we have. We become frustrated because of desires unfulfilled. We become frustrated because our natural inclination to start with the wrong question. We begin by asking ourselves how to gain what it is we want. Indeed, in our hedonistic culture we are taught that the first and only real question is what we must do in order to fulfill our desires. When the first question should be is this a proper desire. As God pointed out during the Sermon on the Mount, judgment does not start with our actions but with our hearts.

It is one of those forgotten pillars of our Faith that our flesh will not be judged and purified until the End of the Age, but our souls are being judged and sanctified now. Forgotten? Forgotten by whom? The church of the masses to be sure, but certainly not the Church invisible? Though we differ in perception, for each of us the Grace of Faith, that Faith which saves is a crown of thorns placed upon our heads. Thorns pressed into our flesh, each one striking into a sin, each one striking into a vice. Each one a desire not yet purified. Each one such a struggle and pain to pull out...or at least it seems that way.

1 Timothy 4: Do not neglect the gift that is in you...Meditate on these things; give yourself entirely to them, that your progress may be evident to all. Take head to yourself and to the doctrine. Continue in them. For in doing this you will save both yourself and those who hear you.

The temptations, the dire hardships, the thorns of Life, sometime seem harsh, do they not? In them we gain a glimpse of what will be, having our works judged as if by fire. Each with Faith will be sanctified, purified, some of it now, some of it then. As such, we have to ask what is the point. Why put ourselves through the hardship and struggles of the thorns? My response has always been rude by answering with a question. Do we have a choice in the matter?

Sanctification is such a normal aspect of our Faith that from the moment we are given the Grace of salvation we are either actively pursuing, or actively avoiding Him. It is such a universal working of the Spirit on one with Faith, our only choice is if we accept it or fight against Him. Whether we embrace the thorns or run around in a panic, looking like a monkey doing the party dance. Have you not noticed, though the hardships, struggles and tribulations may not be pleasing the times which are the most painful, the times which seems the harshest are the times in which you were fighting against God? That the thorns of Life which irritate us most are the ones which God is trying to remove but we are desperately trying to hold onto.

We have all experienced that at one point or another, that sin, that vice, that attitude or view in which we want to keep. Eventually we get tired of the fight, of the hardships brought by our own stubbornness and let God have His way. There is a part of us which knows that once God starts working to remove a thorn He does not give up. It will be removed even if it takes the rest of our lives. That is, early on we learn the futility of wrestling with God, though that does not mean we do not give it a try from time to time. This is hardly news, even if your own experiences had not taught you this, I have brought it up many times. I repeat it here only to give context.

I believe that God gives us a pre-conversion thorn, at desire for Faith, to be saved. To have no doubt that God is real. This is why so many mistake Faith with belief. One can believe without Faith, but for us Faith is the reason we know what we believe is true. But as St. James points out in his letter, Faith limited to only belief does not save. A Faith which saves is an active Faith. One which produces works. One which produces fruits, which multiplies the talents. It is a belief which changes our lives. It is a Faith in which the existence of God is just a matter-of-fact and we can rest assured in our justification by placing our trust in Christ and His work upon the Cross.

Rest assured in our justification...in Christ and His work upon the Cross. As you have experienced, very often when we talk about sanctification people get the impression we are talking about justification. Indeed, I have met more than a few legalists, who did think sanctification was earning salvation. Ironically, as sanctification, maturing in Faith is learning to trust God more and more, this starts with learning to trust God with our justification. Sanctification, having Christ as our Lord, is the means in which He removes the thorn of our doubts about justification.

I know, I know, I have always been rather analytical, which is why it has been difficult being a mystic. When I was asked about my salvation in the youth of my Faith, I would often say that it was none of my businesses. Did not know, did not care. The way I see it, even taking the resurrection out of the equation, what I have done is nothing compare to what God has done for me. But that is the beauty of sanctification, is it not?

That by maturing in the Faith, by trusting in God through those hardships and struggles, through those works He has us do even though they feel that they might kill us we learn. We learn the nature of God. That He does give us Grace, joy and peace, blessings so great there is no way we can say we earn them by our works. We learn that if we just hold on to our Faith, if we just hold onto our trust in Him our salvation is assured. And suddenly that thorn we were so afraid to let go of is removed, and transforms into a rose.

Ephesians 4: He Himself gave some to be apostles, some prophets, some evangelists, and some pastors and teachers, for the equipping of the saints for the work of the ministry, for the edifying of the body of Christ, until we all come to the unity of the Faith and the knowledge of the Son of God, to a perfect man, to the measure of the stature of the fullness of Christ.

Another thorn is sanctification itself. That when we are young, we mistake sanctification for the hardships, struggle and work which God uses to purify us. Indeed, in preparing to write this I pulled out and read some of my earliest writings. Back when I thought that sanctification was the method instead of being the Grace. Though I hate to put it such, back when I thought of humility as a cost of service instead of a reward of it. Things change, we get older, hopefully wiser and we learn that virtue really is its own reward.

There are many thorns in this Life which God works to turn into roses. Many vices He would turn into virtues. But I think if it was simply a matter of being a better person, if the only purpose of sanctification was our own purification it would be a thorn to far less people. When we are metaphoric children in the Faith, sanctification is about us. That is as it should be, we still have those two by fours in our eye. And it is fun being a babe in Christ, as we call it, or at least it was for me. A whole new world to explore. And prayer. Wow, prayer. For the first time it was real, it meant something. It no longer felt like I might as well be talking to my television. Anyway, things change, we get older, hopefully wiser and we get that glimpse that the purpose of philosophy may be happiness, but the purpose of sanctification is ministry.

Obviously, this is a time when we get into a lot of trouble. As a child we think only of pleasing God, to earn that pat on the head, but when we become youths, we start to see the affect we have on our peers, and the affect they have on us. Call it the thorn of Charity, if you would but we start to see the effect of our lives. Many people run from this, after all responsibility does not come easy in our self-centered pleasure-seeking culture. They simply do not want to pay the cost. What do you mean I am not allowed to simply command weak-willed individuals to do my bidding? Oops, I mean....

We all have different struggles depending on our personality, our pathology, our abilities and talents, our strengths and weaknesses. And the details change as we mature. For the past few years, I have had to deal with lust, in a way I never understood as a youth. But the youth of our Faith, regardless of the details center around a single question...whom do you serve? Whom do you follow? Who is your Lord? Obviously, that is always the question, but it starts shifting from the temptation to indulge our basal nature to the temptation to either abuse and/or avoid our calling. Ironically those who abuse there calling typically can only get away with it because of the ones which avoid theirs.

This is hardly news either. I have written long and hard about my struggle to be the hero God wants me to be instead of the tyrant I desire to be. I read people who say that we need another Luther or Spurgeon to rise up and lead a rebellion against the decayed and dead church of the masses. And the thought of standing up and saying here I am is titillating. I have the skill with words, or at least I am arrogant enough to think so. But here is the thing, is that not the problem? The people want someone else to grow for them, to take care of the struggles of their Faith for them instead of turning to God for themselves. Or for those of us in the other side, do we not want the control, the feeling of power in which such people give us.

If you go back up to the Scripture for this section you will notice that the work of the ministry belongs to the Church, the whole Church. It is not the clergy is in ministry and the rest of you play a supporting role. The opposite is true, is it not? The clergy, that list of titles or positions, are appointed or ordained by God to build up the Church, to raise up the young of the Faith so they may mature into productive adults in the ministry of the Church. But we cannot have that, now can we? If there were a bunch of mature laypeople running around it would ruin my whole ego-pride-high I got going on thinking I am all so more important than everyone else. Indeed, I might have to confess that though I may be an aid from time to time, your growth has had little to do with me and a whole lot due to the fact that you were willing to turn to God for your sanctification.

Which, at least for me, is a thorn transformed into a rose....

1 Corinthians 9: What is my reward then? That when I preach the Gospel, I may present the gospel of Christ without charge, that I may not abuse my authority in the gospel. For though I am free from all men, I have made myself a servant to all, that I might win the more.

Sometimes I get tired of writing the same thing over and over again. Sometimes I have to wonder what is the reason I am compelled and struggle so hard to find new words for such ancient ideas. If you have never felt like giving up the fight...if you have never asked what is the point...if you have never had that desire of standing up and shouting 'are you people willfully ignorant or just simply stupid!' If you have never felt like there is no chance of success no matter what you do then, to be blunt, you have never really tried to do anything.

It is somewhat difficult to come to terms with the fact that the thorns are always going to be here, always out numbering the roses. After all, a smile is only a fleeting moment in which the sweet fragrance of a rose allows us to forget the thorns. Maybe it is just me, a product of my calling, which feels the constant pressure of the thorns on my scalp. As unheroic as it sounds, sometimes the only thing which gets me through the day is dancing on my grave. As morbid as it sounds, I do very much look forward to my death as a child looks forward to Christmas. To be able to rest, to finally able to quite the field of battle with my Honor intact, is a reason to rejoice, is it not?

Post-depression life has been...interesting. I do not 'feel' my emotions any more than I did before, by I am aware of them now. I long for death no less than I did before, but now I also want to live. Without the candle flame, without that bleeding gash on my heart I have hard time maintaining an iron-will control on my internal process. The most interesting part is that somewhere through my struggles to learn how to live post-depression I have found that the crown of thorns is also a crown of roses. That somewhere during all of this, once I had accepted, truly accept that my words are nothing and they are all I have, I learned that my words are something.

From time to time, I used to envy the evangelist. Mostly, as with much of my 'used to' it was my pride, but in part it was simply because they often get to smell the rose of their labor. Sanctification, spiritual growth is rarely that obvious in the short run, and as I wrote above, more and more I had to face that my words really amount to nothing. But as I have given up everything else in order to write these words, they are all I have. So, that thorn came, as it does for all of us when we ask 'what's the point'.

The pride which devastates us the most is the pride in which we want to save the world, even if that world is only a group or a single person. That pride which the Enemy uses to change preachers into politicians and Saints into crusaders. It is that pride which says 'I am not going to work, or at least not work hard unless I can see the results.' And to be blunt, as you know I like being, it is that pride which wants to be the Giver of the Grace instead of simply a vehicle for the giving. Yes? We see someone in trouble, someone who needs Grace and we set out trying to give it to them. I mean, that is a good thing, born from Charity. But we always have to ask ourselves when they reject the Grace whether we are frustrated because of the sorrow we share through our love for them, or is because we think that they should be responding to what we do or say.

We all feel that frustration, feel that thorn pressing into us from time to time. Times in which we do not see the roses. Times when we do not see the point of struggling to remove a thorn or to help another with theirs. After all, there is only going to be another, and another and even then, another. To make matters worse, even though you rip out our heart, because you honestly and deeply want to help there are going to be those who despise and even abuse you because of it. At some point though, we have to accept just as we cannot force God to give Grace, neither can we force someone to accept it.

But what is the point? Why do we preach and teach? Why do we stay up all night in prayer? Why do we rip our hearts out in words and deeds? What reward is there in toiling through the lonely and dark night? Grace is the rose, and these are the means through which God gives Grace. Once we leave this corrupted flesh, we will have the roses without thorns, Grace without struggles. In this life, however, we are given both, because the thorns are what God gives us to know that He gives roses only to those who seek Him.

Which is what it all boils down to, returning to what I have said and written so often. We make it so hard, so complicated. Thrash around like a fish out of water or run around in a panic screaming like a half-dressed girl in a bad horror movie. Easier said than done, to be sure, but it really is that simple. Maybe it is just me, but I have never found a problem of the inner-life which was not solved by seeking Christ. I have found no turmoil which was not soothed by kneeling before the Lord and asking what will He have of me. I have had no struggle in which the solution was not to put my trust in God. And when you think about it, is not the Grace we have, to be able to do that, to trust and go to God, a crown of roses we wear today?

In His Glory

Hebrews 12: It is for discipline you endure; God deals with you as sons: for what son is there whom the father does not chasten? But if you are without chastening, of which all have become partakers, then you are illegitimate and not sons.

So, let me kick of the revolution with a question; are there three kind of Christians? It is a bit rhetorical, but one which needs to be addressed. From time to time, I get some blow back from my writings. The worst of these was when years ago, when I first came to realize that we are not really saved unless we have submitted to Christ as our Lord. That we are not assured of salvation until we bend our knee and take that oath to do whatever God asks of us. We come from different Traditions so we use different words. Born-again, regenerated, following Christ, relationship with Him, being moved by the Spirit, being nothing except alive in Christ. Obviously, this comes out in my talk about knighthood, our being a servant onto to the King, on which mine is based. Different words but the same truth, each of us who has Life by Grace through Faith in Christ has His Spirit working us towards our sanctification.

Though it is considered unkind to bring it up, belief itself is not enough for our salvation. Scripture, Tradition and our Lives all confirm that we are saved by Grace through Faith. The Grace is the revelation, the baptism by the Spirit of God, so when we take a close look we see Faith is more than believing but also trusting in Christ. That is, we know there are two types of Christians, the saved and unsaved. There are those who call themselves Christian because they believe but are not saved because their trust is in their belief and not in Christ. They believe themselves saved because they believe in the Cross, not because they have put their Faith in Him.

This has been a constant problem since Constantine. If the society is Christian, then the majority of people will believe simply because it is the cultural norm. As today we believe that individual rights are the highest importance when in the majority of cultures throughout history such a belief would be considered antisocial. Though it is not brought up much because it offends, it is found in the Church early enough to be recorded in Scripture that there are those who believe that Christ is Savior but do not put their Faith in Him. Those who claim to be His, may even do the 'religious thing', but do not have the Spirit of Christ within.

2 Corinthians 13: Examine yourselves as to whether you are in the Faith. Test yourselves. Do you know yourselves, that Jesus Christ is in you? – unless indeed you are disqualified.

That, of course forced me to ask if there are those saved who are not squires? Are their Christians in which are saved, have the Spirit, are in Christ, but will not have to submit to the Lordship of Christ in their lives? I am not talking about following the Law but about sanctification, maturing in the Faith. Whether or not everyone with Faith will come to a time when they must willing submit to the work the Spirit is doing on them? Or are there those whom God decides that their Faith in Christ for salvation is enough? Is it for some who the birth of a new creation, the regeneration, does not bring with it a need and desire for God's Will to be done? Or let me make it clearer, are those whom God justifies that He does not sanctify?

Obviously more rhetorical questions as I reject the idea that there is a third kind of Christian. Everyone whom God justifies He also sanctifies. If He is our Savior, He is our Lord, regardless of how good or bad a servant we may be. I am not even sure why there is an argument. A person who has Faith that saves simply wants Christ as their Lord. It is a mark that we have a Faith which saves that we long to obey. Not that we obey. but that we want to obey. If obedience was required, then who would be saved? Grace is enough, and indeed, it is all we need. But the Grace which allows us to trust Christ to save us from our sins for justification is also the same Grace which allows us to trust Christ to save us from our sins in sanctification.

2 Corinthians 3: We all...beholding as in a mirror the glory of the Lord, are being transformed into the same image from glory to glory, just as by the Spirit of the Lord

This is something we learn, have confirmed in the maturing of our election, from our sanctification. When we have the saving Grace, the Faith that saves, the Spirit of Christ is within us. And the Spirit works to transform us into Christians, into His Image. Sometimes this is wonderful and pleasing, sometimes it is not so much, as painful as training-stick, a switch as my Grandfather would have called it. There are times in which it seems like God is asking too much, the conviction the Spirit brings too harsh. There are times in which we feel that we need the sin God is commanding us to put aside. Or that the task He is sending us on will certainly kill us. Yet, as we matured, we have learned through those times that God is not an apathetic or cruel Father. That His chastening is for our own good. When God commands, we are better for the doing, or the not doing.

If we are honest, we have to admit that each of us, at one time or another, found that we were not happy with a commandment of God. In the youth of our Faith, it is easy to see sanctification, seeing the lordship of Christ as a negative, as a cost, as a sacrifice. In the youth of our Faith, it is often difficult to see the liberty which is found in being a slave of righteousness, the freedom which comes from being a slave of God. As we mature, we come to see salvation in justification, not only from God's wraith do to us for our sins, but also the salvation in sanctification, freedom from the chains which sins bind us in during this life.

Is this not why we have been raised? Was this not the very heart of our rebellion? Did we not cry out asking why the last guard was so silent on the issue of sanctification, what it means that Christ is Life? Did you not weep and pray with me that the last guard would put aside their politics and stand up and show you that there was a purpose to your pain and struggles. Instead, you were left with me, someone who was having trouble understanding any purpose to my pain and struggles. Is that not the scar we carry, the lesson we share, the struggle which has bound us? It is undoubtedly why we have the wolf-pack mentality. We needed leaders, but we could only rely on each other. We were the latchkey children of the Church, doing our best to grow up without enough parents of the Faith.

Galatians 3: Did you receive the Spirit by the works of the law, or by the hearing of Faith? Are you so foolish? Having begun in the Spirit, are you now being made perfect by the flesh? Have you suffered so many things in vain- if indeed it was in vain?

But we are the guard now, the voice in the wilderness, the rocks that cry out. As each of us was and is being trained by God, we each are going to see sanctification through that training. Regardless of the details of our calling, it is for the same purpose of fellowship. In simplest terms, we were raised to help others in their sanctification. Again regardless of the details of our calling, we do this by exhorting, reminding that it is the Spirit which works on us, trains us and the Grace is not found in the things we do. And we do it by showing that submitting to Christ as our Lord is well worth it. That though the struggles may be painful and harsh at time, they do really work out for our benefit.

Do not my writings bear this out? Not only have I improved in skill, but also my life has become better because of the times in which I struggled. Does not your own Inner-Life bear this out as well? Have not the struggles to become a better father made your Life better? Have not the struggles to be a better husband made your Life better? Mentor, friend, worker, boss? Is your Life not better from giving up those sins of which the Spirit convicted you? Is your Life not better from gaining some measure of those virtues the Spirit said you must work on? Have not the worse times of your Life been when you have fought and struggled against the work the Spirit is doing? Then should we not have pity on those who have refused to submit at some point, saying that they will strive no more?

Undoubtedly there are many, many times many, in the visible church who are not saved, who are not part of the invisible Church, the mystical body of Christ. There are also many, many times many, who are part of the Church who serve poorly, who will be saved themselves but will have all of their works burned on judgment day. Church culture has catered to them, has such a fear of offending their mediocre Faith, they had to reject even the idea of striving towards perfection. In doing so they have to reject the Cross all together. For as both Scripture and our own experiences shows that even in sanctification how necessary the Cross is for the work of the Spirit.

That the more mature we become the more we realize how short we fall from the Glory of God, and the importance of the Cross. At conversion I bent my knee to Christ and pledged my sword and life to the service of God. As I matured in Faith, in both my election and calling, I learned and am learning still how worthy Christ is as the King. It is why I have written that our revolution starts with Christ as Lord. Because the Grace which allows us to trust Christ to save us from our sins for justification is also the same Grace which allows us to trust Christ to save us from our sins in sanctification. That the Grace which allows us to pound our chest as a sinner trusting in God to forgive us, is the same Grace which allows us to see how perfect and glorious Christ is and trust God in transforming us into an image of that glory. All with Grace through Faith see the glory of the Lord imperfectly and being transformed into an image of His glory by the Spirit of the Lord for the Glory of God. The only question is how much we are going to fight Him in that transformation.

A Moment of Your Time

I know I might seem ungrateful
To ask for one more thing,
After all these lovely gifts
On this Christmas morning,
But if it is not too much trouble
Could I just have a moment of your time?

I know how busy you are,
With all the appointments to make
And all the bills to pay.
You have your life to think of,
So I will make this as quickly as I can
And only take up a moment of your time.

There is something wrong,
I hurt deep down inside
And do not know what it is
Or how I can make it go away.
I asked you about it before
But you could not spare a moment of your time.

I asked my friends what to do,
And they gave me their advice.
They said if I gave myself to the night
I would feel much better than I am.
But it seems to me that the pain would go away,
If I could just get a moment of your time.

It is not so bad, living in the night
It does not take away the pain
But I cannot see it in the dark
And if the light does shine on it
I can always go deeper into the night
And pretend I have a moment of your time

Now you dare to ask how I can do this.
How can I spit in your face,
By the clothes I wear, the friends I have?
But what do I care for your disappointment,
What do I care that you hate me?
At least now, I have a moment of your time.

Are you really Seeking God?

Ezekiel 13 and 33

Instead of my normal habit of forcing several pages upon you before my point is revealed, I will get straight to it today. I am in need of some help. In regarding to what, I am not sure ...but first several pages of eye straining oohie goodyness.

As I have been concluding my desert vision, I have been going through one of those times in which I am redefining myself. It is the philosopher in me that requires me to examine everything I have learned, to reevaluate past beliefs according to new information. Most of time it is simply maintenance. Sometimes, like this time, it is a major overhaul. Of course, none of them have compared to my conversion experience which shattered every foundation I rested my sanity on.

This one was not without crisis. It was just harder to recognize as I did not have the turmoil which was so common before my depression was healed. I will write in more detail on what I learned, but it all revolved around two things. A gradual loss of my passion to write, and the question of how do I know that I am following the Way. As I know how easily pride, or any desire can lead us astray it was just important to me that I had learned what God was teaching. That I was, in fact, following Christ and not simply aberrations of my own imagination?

For some that might seem like a silly question. I do not think it is, but for most I think it would have been silly to take it to the existent that I have. That is, being a minister to those exiled from church culture has had a price for me. And my relationship with God has always been a mystical one. Some go to great lengths to try to hear from God, but for me their has not really been any difference between my communion with God and my communication with Him. So, at times, the subjective nature of that leaves some doubt about myself, about my sanity.

Making matters worse was the demonic presence on each of the three steps of the desert vision. I can see now that it was temptations to deviate from God's will, a test if you would. At the time it just left me more confused. As I said I will write about the temptations later, here I want to address how I know I follow Christ. (I may indeed be insane but I like it so...)

The first step was the stone. External proof that I do in fact hear from God. God sent me to the mountain to get a stone from somebody. Somebody traveled several states to that same spot in order to give somebody a stone. It might surprise those who do not know me personally that that this has not been the most extraordinary thing which has happened to me. For me, the miracle is that my depression has been healed. But you should know, and I am writing this in case you do not, that this is not the proof I was looking for. This was only proof of the supernatural, not proof of God as the source. Because of my own past I am fully aware of the power the darkness has, and I will not be surprised if soon we will not see it producing its own signs and wonders to misled, even the elect.

The second step was affirmation and conformation. As I said, my exile had worn me down. If you have every had real and challenging fellowship, and then had it no more you will know what I mean. Fellowship edifies not only because it challenges us but because it confirms that we are in Christ, and indeed its purpose is to aid us and keep us following Him. If I knew at the time what was going on I might have just asked you guys, but at the time I was having an increasing frustration that the majority of people, of Christians, simply do not want to hear what I have to say. It is not that I care about popular opinion, only that I was being overly sensitive to rejection at the time.

In fact, now days of large congregation and praise by the big names of Christian culture seems to be a better indication of having gone astray then being in Christ. But back to the point, the affirmation while important is not in itself proof. Not to mention for me it is only in the past tense, and therefore would only prove that I was following at that point. But when two or more gather and agree on a name means only that they follow the same way, not necessarily the Way. Indeed, there are groups in the extreme charismatic side that are obviously demonically influenced who go around patting each other on the back about how Godly they are (and how much they are like God).

So, I turned to theology. The answer you get from theologians on how we know we are in Christ is, of course, that our theology is correct. It is a rather sound test in my case as well. That is, being trained by God then the conclusions and beliefs I have formed would conform to those in which the Christians have historically held that the Bible teaches (how I came to see the inspired nature of Scripture is a writing all its own). Now, I do think theology is a good test, in so much that someone who is in Christ is going to strive to know God's truth, but just because one has an orthodox theology does not mean they are in Christ. I have met two pastors which I have to give respect to their ability to study Scriptures but their hearts are far from God.

I met the theological standard but, to say it plainly, I am not a stupid person. Though I gave up belief when I was young I spent time in a church that did a good job teaching Scripture and my studies were not done in a vacuum, I had simply relied more on God then structured studies to tell me what the meaning of Scriptures. In a way I did find my answer in theology. That is, I went back in my memories to my conversion experience and examined the theology I derived from it. Though it did not offer the proof in that philosophical way, it reawakened, reminded of me of why Faith is why we believe.

I could have easily written this in terms of making sure of my calling and election, as it certainly started out that way. But I wanted to put it in terms of the struggle, of the doubt I let grow into it became detrimental to my inner life, robbed me of my passion to seek God. I wanted to write it from those doubts I hear often but we will not talk about. For those who have those doubts about their salvation. That doubt which I experienced for the first time but for those who were raised and never gave up their belief.

The proof I found, the proof of our Faith is the revelation of the Gospel. It is really that simple. It is that deep down knowing that it is real and true. That we are sinners and Christ lived and died to save us from our sins, and gave us hope for resurrection in His own. No one can know that Christ is Lord except those who are saved. That is, I return to the belief that I can base my Faith on nothing except what I did in the beginning, Christ and in Him Life.

There are many counterfeit christs presented to us today. A christ who did not die for our sins. A christ who is not God, one who is only an enlightened person, a political or economic christ, a christ who was not resurrected, a christ without the Cross. Indeed, even without those claiming to be a new christ, and the neo-mystics who claim to bring a new gospel we would have plenty to take heed of Gods warning that many false christs and false prophets will appear.

Now I laugh because it is all so simple as to be silly. It is Sunday-school stuff, is it not? At the time it was not so, and I have to admit that it had detrimental effects on my inner-life. Between my doubt and my less than diligent prayer life I had to give up writing all together. I normally do not trust myself enough to write during these times, even more I could not write about Faith while doubting my own. More importantly, in this doubt my passion in seeking after God has diminished. And as you know that is what I am all about it would have been too much for me to preach it while not doing it myself.

I have been silent because, to put it plainly, I was afraid. Then I was angry. Now, as it has become sorrow, I can write once again. That might seem like a silly thing to you but it has always served me well. Looking out at the darkness which is corrupting the visible Church it is natural to be afraid. Afraid of being too dogmatic, or not dogmatic enough. Afraid where all it might lead. And if you are like me afraid how that darkness may have affected your own views. But to allow fear to drive us is to shrink from our responsibly...

It is also natural to be angry. Angry at those who prey on the weak, angry at yourself for not being able to do anything about it. But anger has a way of feeding our Pride. It allows us to ignore our own shortcomings, because after all they are not as bad. Worse still, to be motivated by anger, even over injustice is to increase the injustice. For in anger, we cannot help but come to see those who are doing the injustices as our enemies rather than simply as more of a victim of our true enemy, the darkness.

The righteous heart is a sad heart. A heart filled with the sorrow of sin, not only of others but our own as well. A righteous heart is a repenting heart, and the righteous acts from that heart for that is, is it not, what we wish to bring about. It is not repentance of which we speak with all the talk of revival and awakenings, either for ourselves, our church, or the Church as a whole....oh if it only were so. And in my weakness, there are times in which I was still as naive as I once was. That there is a part of me which would rather have the war remain the abstract of vision rather than the concrete of sight.

Day by day as my passion to seek God increases so too my passion to preach Christ. To wage war in defense of those being preyed upon because of their doubts. To present the Gospel to dispel the false gospel of the neo mystics, these false prophets. Indeed, as my passion grows the more, I understand that Christ is Life. That the Gospel is not just the message for conversion, it is the one we need every day. We rely on the Grace He purchased for us on the Cross every day.

Which obviously brings us back to the help I was asking for in at the beginning. Which I thank you for have given it. While, yes I am being both a smart... and pragmatic, but if you have read this it is technically fulfilling what I need, or at least want. And in asking I fulfilled the letter of the command, which is what it is all about, right? Alas, life would be so much simpler if it was, but that is pages for a different day. Asking for help comes in two forms, one personal and one not so much.

I have always had down time in my passions. I am but human and grow tired. When I find that I have no desire to for seeking God I spend my time working on the desire to desire. I struggle and It comes back and I am up and running again, up and writing again. That is, every time the question of 'what is the point' disappears when the passion returns. I write because I write, that is it is simply a part of who I am. But this time it is not nearly enough. It is not enough to write page after page just to delete them, or to file them away. That I have a need to address directly the problems facing the Church. The problem is I really do not know how to go about doing that. Or I should at least in a manner which would be productive, or compromising in ways I know I cannot.

Which leads me into the not so personal aspect. I am sure my understanding will clear as time goes on, but what I do understand that though I am asking for help I am not really asking for help. I am not asking you to do anything, nor am I am saying that God is saying to do anything. Except, of course, unless He is. You may be completely unaware of the spiritual war that corrupted our culture has spilled over into the Church. That the darkness not only has made it more difficult to reach the unsaved, but threatens 'babes' as well. That the part of the Church who is in America is fighting for nothing less than its very survival. If you cannot see that then it may not be your fight, but for those who can see it, are most likely like me in wishing I could say that my description is simply hyperbole. Either way, this is can be taken simply as a head's up to the direction much of my writing will be taking.

I guess the help I need is that which you do and I always need. Seek God and His will...and do it. everything is just casing the wind.

See the toe, fear the toe!

Proverbs 18

There are ways which seem reasonable until they are examined by others. I am a fanatic with the fanatic's inability to compromise. I am a mystic, in the older meaning of the word, in that I am driven, obsessively driven to put the ego-self to death, to kill that sin which dwells within us, the flesh, to strive for perfection (1 John 3). It has been for its own sake, my own sake (Romans 8). It was for the sake of others, so my own flesh would not hinder my treatment of others (Romans 15). And it also has been about vision, understanding and ministry. That my own desires did not hinder what it was God is trying to show me (2 Corinthians 10).

Though there have been many lessons, many things I had to understand, the underlying one here is that it simply is not possible. While we are in this age, in this flesh we will not reach that perfection we will have after the resurrection (1 john 1), in which we will no longer struggle with sin, though peace in Him is a fruit. As we are saved by Grace, so too is our continual sanctification by Grace. Our struggles against the flesh are as much as a manifestation of Grace as when we overcome sin, for it reminds us how much we need the Cross, that our peace, justification and sanctification is found only in Him (2 Corinthians 12). This is true for all, regardless of what experiences we may have had or what our calling may be. It is in that paradox of being a sanctified sinner in which I need help, in which we need help.

I clearly have an image of the future born out of the last ten years of struggle and prayers. But how much of it is vision and how much of it is desire is hard to say. Telling the difference between what is symbolic and what is literal even more so. This has been the core of my struggle, one I have rarely shared because I learned early on how easy it is to destroy a ministry when we make it about the visionary or the vision. Just as in our lives, it is easy to lose sight that as we are brought into His will by Grace, so too is His will accomplished by Grace…woe to me if I ever forget that it is not I, but God who points.

I will write of my wants, as the only thing I know for sure is that I am to preach the Gospel. Even in this I am unsure of form. I may continue simply pouring my passion onto paper as my dissatisfaction in this, my desire to preach in the common use of the word might simply be pride. I can see myself preaching to a crowd but is this only the flesh's desire to be important, to do 'big things.' Or is seeing myself preaching in a small church could be nothing more than longing for the fellowship I once knew.

I want to create Family & Friends Inc. With a large farm and several houses. On a large enough road so that there would be a general store, a farmer's stand next to it and maybe a restaurant. To return to the stability of the extended family as a unit to create the stability which will be needed as time progresses. I can see this, but is it only because want my work to count for something. Whether it is writing, mentoring or even physical labor I pour everything I have into what I am doing. So, all of that may simply be the desire to see that the fruits of my labor builds something worth building.

Which leads to my writing. Though at present I am dissatisfied with just writing I am and will remain a writer. And though self-assessments are always bias to one side or the other, I do a rather decent job at it. But in that same assessment I have never been good with the business of writing. I favor generosity over prudence. I lost my shirt on my first book as I, by far, gave away more copies than I sold. While before others existed in my eyes solely so serve my purpose, at conversion I lost even the ability of self-promotion. I cannot even write and run a site at the same time. So, I do desire to hand over my writings to people I trust, to edit, to manage and promote. I have the desire to write and the desire to be read. But I can easily argue that my desire to be read, or to be heard is simple vanity.

In this, as before, God councils and commands me to

patience. In eagerness to do God's will we too often try to force it, do it in our way. For some, such as myself the hardest part has always been patience, doing it according to God's time table rather than my own. We want to be perfect in a day, unwilling to accept that God sanctifies us according to His will. For others, the sin lies in the method and manor of doing. It seems wise to them to work in a manner which was successful in the past, to charge heresy on all that which is new. Or they adapt to the method and nature of the culture, adopting anything new or different without looking for error. We must wait but not be idle, we must adapt but not conform…we are sinners, but are justified in Christ.

Even in this I am not sure with anything except for Christ, and Him alive. I am a mystic with Reform Theology. A mystic of the Cross as I call it for it is work of Christ upon the Cross in which my Faith is found. For me that it is that paradox in which has defined my Faith. That though I am a sinner, I am justified. Though I am inclined to simply wait to see how everything all turns out, I am always too eager to move on it. I have trepidation, great sorrow for the state of the Church today, but feel a bit too much glee in watching that beast of a civil religion called Christendom crumble to dust. While I am horrified at how easy we abandon sound doctrine, I cannot help but see church as a circle of believers. And the Church comprising a larger circle of the circle of believers, with Christ as the center, individually and the circles both big and small.

Which is why I write what and as I do. Though, born out of my own struggles, I have a great amount compassion and tears for those who find it hard holding onto the Gospel in our world today, it also stems from that vision of the Church as a circle, a fellowship of equals. One may be called to inspire us to seek God for ourselves, another may be given a passion to keep our doctrines and dogma pure, still another may be gifted in teaching Scripture, still another may be called to make sure that we keep our unity, and still another may have been given the task to make sure all the circle are feed and clothed. In this leadership is only a different task. Not the first among equal as it is too often seen, but the least among equals, as the heart is to liver. Though the heart is more important, it has no other purpose but to serve the rest of the body.

It is with such a vision that I see the edification of fellowship born of the sharing our hopes and dreams, struggles and pains which have come from our Faith. It is from this view I see the purpose of maturity in the Faith is to protect and nurture those inside the circle so they may join in the circle. The purpose of the Church in edification to help raise up the newly reborn to the maturity of the Faith which allows them to join as equals those who are protecting and nurturing the newly reborn.

Even with this I have to ask if it is a view created because it is His Ideal, or is it simply a longing of that which is lacking in the Church today. Is it a view of the Church born from Him or simply a view born form seeing the Church weakened from the power struggles of who would be greatest in this age. Those fights in which the heart and the liver says that theirs is the only view. A reaction to the modern tendency to create a circle for each of the parts. One circle of hearts, only for hearts. Another circle of livers, only for livers. Another for the spleen. One circle to preach...experience the big toe. Another circle to preach...fear the big toe.

Mystics of the Cross

2 Corinthians 11

We fight a spiritual war, and we fall because we are not waging it according to the Spirit and Scripture. While I know that there are many who claim we are in the Great Apostasy, I cannot make that claim. It is possible, but being a student of history, I can only see slight differences between now and a hundred years ago. While it may indeed be the end, the primary difference I see is that we have a communication system to bring the decay to our door steps. In fact, all of the revivals of the past, including the Reformation, follow a similar pattern. God reminding us of the same thing.

The Pentecostal rival, which is most often viewed as God reminding us that He is still a part of our lives, is seen through the lens of the Gospel it becomes the same lesson of the Reformation. That is, our salvation is in Christ, that Faith is being in Christ. It is only the way that Darkness used to deceive in which we see them differing in their nature. The revival of hundred or so years ago quickly turned into charismatic cults on one side and fundamental legalists on the other, because Satan focused it on having Gifts instead of seeking and being moved in our and by our Faith.

The revival of our own time was the same. It has been, as I stated before the meaning of Christ is Life. That the holy rollers and Jesus Freaks clearly stated that being a Christian was not about attending a certain Church or intellectual accent to doctrine it was having Life in Christ. It is about having the Faith which the Gospel has made possible. But the enemy in its wisdom in the ways of flesh, soon took this and twisted it to deny doctrine, and the teachings the Church holds dear. And thus, enters the mystics.

God had me call myself a mystic long ago because prophet denotes an authority I simply do not have. Though the office of prophet is found in the New Testament there is no clear understand given to what that means so we must turn to the Old. There office of prophet serves two functions, to give revelations of the future of the people of God, and to warn them when they are turning, or have turned their hearts from God. I know that those of the charismatic and prophetic cults want the revelation of the future to the defining trait, both the Spirit and Scripture confirms that this is simply not the case.

Why? Because as much as we like to think otherwise with our obsessing on the End of the Age the Church has no future. I do not mean that there will not be a Church in the future, but that the Church now and into the future is found in Christ, in His work upon the Cross. All who has been saved are saved by the revelation which has already been fulfilled. And I can say as a mystic and a prophet, that all revelations we receive, even if they seem new, returns us the Cross, to the Gospel of Jesus the Christ. Which we see is the fulfillment of the second function of a prophet: repent

We fight a spiritual war, and we fall because we are not waging it according to the Spirit and Scripture. The battle was over the nature and to what extent the Gifts are used in the post-Apostle Church was the debate of the apostasy of the 1920s. It was resolved, and even if it may not have been explained well enough in theological terms, the neo-mystic and charismatic cults have been able to break containment and infested us only because we have disregard of the authority of Holy Scripture.

The neo-mystic like to tell us that we must submit to God instead of doctrine. Indeed, we can hardly argue that, and I will even say that myself. I can say that because I have Faith. Not because Faith makes proper doctrine unnecessary, but because as proper belief cannot save without Faith, also will Faith teach us proper belief. Some today go even as far as to say that we must submit to God instead of Scripture. I can agree, as I have Faith. That with Faith you will know not to elevate Scripture to the level of God, making it an idol, but Faith also teaches us that submitting to Scripture is to submit to God. Indeed, for Scripture is the Revelation of the Gospel, and to reject it is to reject the Gospel of Christ. To preach the Gospel

181

other than the one in Scripture is to preach a Gospel without Christ and prove oneself to be a false prophet.

We fight a spiritual war, and we fall because we are not waging it according to the Spirit and Scripture. Whether by vision or preaching, whether with a flash or a slow burn, you knew your conversion was real because it produced Faith in Christ. It gave you the knowledge of the truth of the Gospel in which you placed your Hope. So why do you now trade the Hope of the Gospel for grand visions which promise only some earthly kingdom? Why do you forsake your Faith in Christ for those who preach a god you can reach by the works of your mind and body? Why do you follow those who can only titillate with a good show but do not preach the Gospel? Could it be that you are chasing after other gods because you have forgotten what God has done for us on the Cross?

To the prophets that would say that my visions are not pure, that I am not hearing what God is saying today I say: look to the Cross. To the mystics which say that I have been corrupted by the old ways I say: look to the Cross. To those that say I am naïve, that I do not understand I say: look to the Cross. To them and all who struggle with those struggles of Faith I say: look to the Cross and see what God has done for us. The sinner that I was and the sinner that I am, my repentance brings forgiveness only by the work of Christ on the Cross. That all of my visions, every mystical moment of my life bears witness to only one thing: Jesus came, was crucified and was resurrected so that in Him we may be forgiven our sins and be spared the Wraith which was due to us.

Indeed, as you see it is not even a new fight for it is the same one we, as individuals and as the Church, has always had. To resist gospels which are created by demons and deceptive people and hold fast to the Gospel of Jesus the Christ. While the Gospel is not enough for the neo-mystics and prophets of today, it is everything we need. Without it there would be no salvation, no mission, no vision, not even a Church. Without the Work of Christ upon the Cross and His resurrection everything is vanity, chasing after wind. As with all things you must make your own choice, as for me I have made my camp at the foot of the Cross and will not budge for anything.

Show Me

Show me not a beauty perfected
By adding here, and taking there
With nip and cut and tuck
But show me a beauty real
With crooked noses
And lopsided smiles

Show me not a house perfected
By marble countertops
And golden floors
But show me a home made real
With the stress of hardships
And the unity of love

Show me not a vision perfected
If men had wings
And women could fly
But show me a vision made real
With the arm of the Warrior
And the heart of the Poet

Show me not a world
Where a few are perfected
By the sacrifice of the many
But show me a Faith real
Where hearts are justified
By the sacrifice of the Son

Politics does not replace Faith

1 Samuel 9: And the Lord said to Samuel "heed the voice of the people in all that they say to you, for they have not rejected you but have rejected me, that I should reign over them" …and Samuel told all the words of the Lord to the people who asked for a king…you will cry out in your day because of your king whom you have chosen for yourselves, and the Lord will not hear you in that day.

Religion and politics can never be truly separated, in so much that our Faith informs our morality and morality is a basis of our political views. But it must be understood that the glory which America has, though the light is tarnished, is a worldly glory. It is right and good and just that you desire a nation which is morally as well as materially blessed. It is only natural in these times to feel like Jeremiah. To preach and warn, to watch and weep as the society you love sells itself into captivity. Though I am not a nationalist, as my first loyalty is to the Church rather than nationality, I whole heartily agree with President Theodore Roosevelt in that that anyone who says they love other countries as much as their own is like a man who says they love other women as much as their wife. For king and country is an honorable position, and so is too the sorrow from watching your nation decay from the glory it once had.

Though, it must be understood that the hope in which America was a beacon, is not the same Hope in which the Church is to shine with. For America's light is our freedom from the oppression of tyranny, while the Church's light comes from the freedom from the oppression of sin found in the Light, namely Jesus Christ. While one without Faith must surely consider suffering to be the worst of evils, evil enough to accept a tyranny to combat it, surely, we of the Church understand that the tyranny of sin cannot be overcome by human laws, even when based on the Law.

For some people, who do not take religious seriously or honesty, base their religious view on their politics. They want their way politically, and so they change their religious view to whatever best serves their politics. These individuals follow the popular religion in every direction politics takes it. They are people who believe they take religious seriously, but really see it only as an extension of politics. Before we point fingers, however, we all have that tendency. It may not be in politics but, being sinners, we all look out on the world and see something we want and are tempted to change our religious views in order to justify desiring it. This temptation is there even when the desire is lawful and good.

The best example of this is the word of Faith heresy, but that Dark Age concept that poverty, illness and deformities is a curse hardly applies to this group so here is a better example: we all desire a pure and uncorrupt Church visible today, one which fellowship is a vehicle for the Grace of our Sanctification. We each long for a world in which there is no difference between the Body visible and His Body mystical. So, each of us, at one point or another has been tempted to pull our marker, to draw a circle. Those insides are the real church, and everyone else are not. Or we have been tempted to get rid of the circle all together. Saying that everyone is saved, or at least everyone how believes regardless if they have the Grace of Faith or not. But that last line brings me to my point for this post.

There are people who say that the United States of America is, was, or should be a Christian nation. I am going to brush aside the fact that it is this position which allowed so many problems to creep into the Catholic Church, leading up to the Reformation/Rebellion. In so much it is a political position it is of little concern of mine. That is, as the wheel of Plato turns, politics will become less about keeping our earthly freedom and more about what shape our tyranny takes. But in so much as it is claimed to be a matter of Faith, in so much as it is said that our religion requires us to transform culture, in so much as the theology on which it is based, it is a concern of mine. In so much as one takes this to mean that we are justified by belief and sanctified by the law then I must be opposed. Which is to say, that I am opposed to the idea that politics or the culture wars is the way in which to make America a Christian nation.

Obviously, people desire a nation which reflects their morality, and as their morality is Christian, they want a Christian nation. I can hardly disagree with them in that matter. I am a Christian so my morality is Christian. And each of us negotiating to get as much as we can is sort of the ideal of a democracy. I can find no wrong in a Christian being political. You can even be an activist for a cause, if your conscience moves you that way. And it is honorable and good that you want a nation that has a high view of morals and virtue. Or to be motivated from the fear the corrupting influence on your children which a decadent society has. Obeying the Law is good, even if it will not save. My objection here has been the idea that if only we had a Christian king to enforce morality, then we would be a Christian nation.

Which does not make a whole lot of sense to me because the Church already has a Christian King, we call Him Jesus, Christ, Lord. And Whatever we try to accomplish with politics, we need to keep in mind that it is only through the Cross, by Grace through Faith we are sanctified.

1 Corinthians 10: With most of them God was not well pleased, for their bodies were scattered in the wilderness...but God is Faithful, who will not allow you to be tempted beyond what you are able, but with the temptation will also make the way of escape, that you may be able to bear it.

I think most of us agree that we, the Church already has a king, the King. We, both individually and as a group, take our marching orders in spiritual and moral issues from the Spirit and Scriptures and not from an earthly lord, even one who is behind a pulpit. I will write again, sometime soon on how the purpose of the clergy is to equip the saints for the ministry and not to lord over you. Today however I want to show how our religion, if we take it seriously affects our political view. And I am simply going to ignore the heretical cultists who truly want to create the second Christian theocracy (Calvin's Geneva being the first and only literal Christian theocracy.)

The prevailing view with the Church, at least the view presented most often, is that in order to be saved we simply have to believe and then following the Law the best you can They define Faith as belief and holding onto that Faith as living up to a certain moral standard. Believe the right thing, do the right things and you will be saved. Forgive me for building a scarecrow to shoot with a shotgun, but I think it is a fair representation of what is believed by a good chunk of Christians. This can be seen in the fact that much of the public argument over what makes a 'real Christian" is centered on what we must believe and what that moral standard we must uphold. Or in the fact that we spend so much time trying to convince others to believe as we believe, to have the moral standard we have.

Our religious views inform our views on morality, and the prevailing view seem very much to be that religion informs our morality by giving us the Law. If this is true than the purpose of the Church is to say what we can and cannot do. That the purpose of the preacher is to give us the Law, and very often we argue for the lowest common denominator. Which is, in truth, very low indeed. (Acts 15.28+).   This is, of course, how morality is form in the natural person. As you will find in your Soc 101 book, a person's character is formed by socialization, formed by the mores and norms of the society in which they are a part.

With the exception of antisocial personalities, everyone naturally conforms to their culture or subculture. So, if the prevailing view is correct and Christian morality is simply the minimum a Christian is required to live by then it does very much behoove us to create a nation based on that minimum. If Christian morality can be imposed on us from the outside then we should fight to create such social pressure. This is, of course, the view from those who believe that our morality, as Christians, is independent of God.

Obviously, there is another view. That that Christian morality is not something we can live up to without God. It is not the Law imposed from the outside but the desire for sanctification flowing from the Spirit of God within. In that view it is impossible to create a Christian nation, or even base its laws on Christian morality. It is impossible because in order to live up to that standard one must have Faith. One must have the Spirit sanctifying them. That is, a nation's morality is very much the minimum one is required to do in order to be a good member of that culture, while Christian morality is based on allowing the Spirit to sanctify us so that we can be as holy and righteous as we can...which is why, if you notice those who try to make Christian morality about the Law usually end up with stricter and stricter standards.

Which is why there should be a strict wall between Church and State, because one without Faith cannot hope to live up to the standards which God gives us as we mature. The State morality must be pragmatic, the Church's idealistic. We look to heaven for what is perfect, we look to that image of the Glory of Christ, and strive towards that perfection, that ideal. A State cannot look to heaven, but instead look to the people for the best that they can do. In so much as the state must be concerned with worldly matters its morality must be pragmatic.

My only real political position is that I am against promotion that an ideology, even with one I agree with, is a substitute for a pragmatic focus on a functioning State. I would prefer a tyranny of function over one of ideals. I cannot fault you in fighting to have a Christian flavor to the tyranny, even though I would prefer to be persecuted than to have people with a false sense of salvation. As always, politics are a matter of conscious and not of Faith. It is a matter of Faith, however, on where we turn to determine our morality, and who we look to for our sanctification.

My fear and concern are that we are taking it a step too far and are looking to the State to save people from their sins. That is, after all what morality means to us. For us, immoral behavior and a sin as one in the same. For one without Faith not all sins are immoral, because they do not have the Spirit convicting them. They have not the Spirit of God. And that is what it takes to overcome sin. Grace of the indwelling of the Spirit, that Grace which unites us with the Cross, and brings us into Christ, into His body the Church. No human law, no state, no culture, no church or organization, regardless of how pure, perfect or idealistic can do that. Regardless of how moral or immoral a society may be, we are justified and sanctified only by Grace through Faith in our Lord, not by our works but by the work He did on the Cross.

Luke 8: For nothing is secret that will not be revealed, nor anything hidden that will not be known and come to light. Therefore, take heed how you hear. For whoever has, to him more will be given, and whoever does not have, even what he seems to have will be taken from him.

My pride is not happy with how this is going. I am an artist and words are but the way I paint ideas onto the canvas of your minds. And in writing of that pride, and of rhetoric I hope to finish this section on how we often confuse Faith with politics. I have touched on how, though we may pledge loyalty to an earthly king regard to earthly things, Christ is the King of our hearts and souls and is due a higher loyalty. And I went over how it is impossible to create national laws on Christian morality because our morality is the transformation into the image of Christ, and not on an ideal. Today, I want to point out the difference between rhetoric and preaching, between a political speech and a sermon.

My Pride did not like what I have written because I do not feel like it was clear, and if clear, lacking that certain funk which I strive for. It is the pride screaming like a banshee stubbing its toe, can be summed up in that I take myself entirely too seriously. Do not mistake me, we should take ourselves and our work seriously, we should be driven towards perfection in all that we do. In so much as words are my art, I will continue to search for those perfect

190

combination to express the inexpressible. But in so much as my words are an expression of my ministry, they rely far more on the spirit in which they are written, and the spirit in which they are read.

The Art of Rhetoric, such as found in political speeches, is the art of capturing the mind of those who read or hear you. Through tone and word choice, and the simplest of things such as when you pause...you engage the audiences' emotions and reason in such a way in which they see what you want them to see, head in the direction you want them to head. And feel and think what you want them to feel and think. In this regard there is no difference between political speech and a sermon. All preaching contains rhetoric, the difference is found in what the preacher wants you to see, and on what he relies on to get you to see it.

In simplest terms political rhetoric focuses you on worldly things, while preaching focuses you on heavenly things. Politics is about the outer-self, religion is about the inner-self. Political speeches, like advertisement, are meant to sway public attitudes and opinions. Vote for me, buy this product, support or oppose this bill. So, they rely on the speaker's ability to affect the reason and emotions of the audience. Sermons, on the other hand, are given to point to God, to focus the person entire on what is Holy, what is Sacred. And while they may rely on reason and emotions to do so, and may contain earthly elements their purpose and focus is to turn us towards God.

There are those who simply will not pay attention unless the sermon is delivered by a skilled orator. There are those who will not take your point seriously unless you sound smarter than they are. There are those who will not listen unless you went to the right school, or are indorsed by the right people. There are those...but it really does not matter. It does in political rhetoric, but not in our Faith. or it should not at-any-rate. There are those who will not listen, there are those who will listen but not understand, there are those who will understand but will not like, and there are those will take it to heart. All of them are acting as free individuals, they are making a choice. A choice in how they hear, how they read.

Undoubtedly, the words we use, that I use are important. My focus is on Christian Philosophy (apologetics) so I strive to not sound totally insane. Obviously, I have to sound a little insane, the Cross is insanity to one without Faith. But I think that is where my point is. I have been overly concerned with sounding reasonable. But I am not alone in this. It is far more reasonable to hold a prayer rally for the nation to return to God than it is to preach 'repent or parish'. It is far more reasonable to put out a call to action over some injustice than it is to seek a life of mercy. It is far more reasonable to see growth in numbers as a purpose of a church instead of seeing the purpose as of helping each other in their walk with God. It is far more reasonable...

It seems like everyone wants to be the next MLK or the next Spurgeon or Luther or... I do not know, let me end this here. Whether we are preaching, or writing, giving warnings, or raising our fists at the church of hypocrisy, the question we always have to ask ourselves are we doing it to point them towards God, or for some other reason. Are we really following Christ and helping others do the same, or are we simply trying to get them to go in the direction we want them to go, act in the way we want them to act?

Philosophical Polytheism

Romans 1: I am not ashamed of the gospel of Christ, for it is the power of God to salvation for everyone who believes…For in it is the righteousness of God is revealed from Faith to Faith; as it is written, 'the just shall live by Faith.'

Though there have been many attempts to philosophy made over the last hundred years, all progress stops abruptly with Nietzsche. Since then, all that has been written has simply been reflections of earlier times. Since then, we have been haunted by the question which Nietzsche left burning in our collective souls. One could say, and not be unreasonable, that moral philosophers flounder because they have not been able to agree, and have spent over a hundred years in arguing on the question we inherited from Nietzsche. Who or what is my god?

Nietzsche understood correctly that morality, as a justification of our behavior, required a goal, an ideal which could be worshiped. He was an antichrist who would replace God with his Superman, but none-the-less he would have his Superman be our god. A hedonist would have pleasure be our god. The Herrenist would have us be our own god, while a Herdenist would have the abstract of humanity be our god. The government, the environment, the social-Darwinism of capitalism, the favor of popular opinion, the prestige of wealth, liberty, equality, equity, a world free of religion, a world controlled by religion, there are countless ideals we can make a god. One can say, and not be unreasonable, that since Nietzsche our culture has affectively become philosophical Polytheistic.

In so much that our culture has become philosophical Polytheistic, the cultural philosopher who seeks to advance philosophy should focus on harmonizing the many god-ideals, to create a philosophical pantheon. Yet, since Nietzsche a moral philosopher cannot honestly avoid the understanding that while reason can show the best means of reaching our goal, but whether the goal is worth achieving is an assumption based on desire. Philosophy starts not with truth developed by reason but instead uses reason to call desires truth. The foundation of philosophy is not logic but Faith. Ultimately all the conclusions which reason and logic derives rest on what assumptions we use and give weight too. As such, and as our culture has become polytheistic, if only in ideals, Christian philosophers, or Christian apologists have made the mistake of arguing the Gospel as a moral philosophy instead of as the power of God to salvation.

Philippians 3: Indeed, I also count all things loss for the excellence of the knowledge of Christ Jesus my lord, for whom I have suffered loss of all things, and count them as rubbish, that I may gain Christ and be found in him, not having my own righteousness which is from the law, but that which is through Faith in Christ, the righteousness which is from God by Faith.

One who trusts popular opinion is going to conclude and confirm the popular view of morality. One who places their trust in their own reasoning is going to conclude and confirm their own morality. One who places their Faith in their pastor or Tradition is going conclude and confirm their church's view of morality. The conclusions derived from reason depends greatly on the assumptions one puts their trust in. So, in writing Christian philosophy, on Christian morality the question I asked earlier is repeated. In whom or what do you place your trust.

Too often I hear the argument of 'be moral or go to hell' or 'you are going to hell because you are sinner.' Such a message is directly opposed to the Gospel, in so much as they place our trust in our ability to be moral instead of Christ. While it is true that our sins condemn us, we no longer condemned because Grace through Faith and not because of our righteousness. While, without a doubt there is a moral element to Christian philosophy, our Faith is not in morality itself but in Christ Jesus our lord. I am obviously bias, being a mystic and a convert, but none the less, our righteousness, and the foundation of our morality is from God through Faith.

As such it is a waste of time, and is counterproductive to raise our fist against a philosophical Polytheistic culture, and argue for Christian morality. It is counterproductive because the very nature of polytheism is to include many gods, many moralities and so such arguments are seen as simply a competing ideology. And it is a waste of time because if one is saved, if one is regenerated and a new creation then no argument is required. If one has the Spirit dwelling within, they desire to live a moral life, and we only capable of living a moral life because we have regenerated, saved, have Faith.

Christian philosophy, Christian morality and apologetics, rests on the foundation of Christ Jesus. While cultural philosophers busy themselves with the philosophical Polytheism of our culture, we need to focus on our justification and sanctification by His righteousness and not our own. While they have many god-ideals in which to harmonize, we simply have to know Christ, Him alive, and in Him Life. While they must account for many opposing goals, we have only one goal to concern ourselves with, living the Life we have in Christ.

Stigmata

We just want it to be fair
We just want our share.
The wages of sin are death
Do we really want our pay?

Thorns pressed into our scalp, for every act of pride.
Blood and sweat stinging our eyes, for every lustful look.
Our Face beaten in darkness, for looking the other way.
Our backs lashed by a whip, for every angry word.
A nail piercing our hands, for every selfish act.
A nail through our feet, for not running the race.
A spear thrust into our side, for the forgiveness we withhold.

For all we have done
For all we have not done
We have earned the death
Which He took on.

The Word of the Cross,
United in His death
We share His resurrection.
Can we really ask for more?

Sanctification and Doubt

1 Corinthians 2: For I determined not to know anything among you except Jesus Christ and Him crucified…that your Faith should not be in the wisdom of men but in the power of God.

There are a great number of people who do not want to stop being Christian, but are unwilling to do what Christ requires of them. We may call them civic Christians, those whose self-image is, at least in part, based on being a Christian. We could go all the way back to Constantine, and the idea that the Church and Nation can be the same thing. I am not one of those who thinks that the Church died then, none-the-less it did at that point have to start taking into account those who are Christians because of cultural belief, rather than having been 'born again.' That, undoubtedly, it was then in which the concept originated that in order to be a good citizen of the nation, or of a family, we must also be a Christian. Where one becomes part of a church because that is what a right and just person does and not because they are part of the Church.

The problems which arose in medieval Catholicism, in my opinion, was formed from trying to give comfort to those who do not know that they are 'saved'. In this, that Tradition does a very good job and is tailored well to quite those doubts which a saint may have. It does so however, by allowing one to avoid the struggles of doubts in which God uses to strengthen our character and allows those who merely civic Christians to avoid the question of salvation all together. As things happened, this sparked the Reformation/Counter-Reformation. And it was declared once again that we are saved only by Grace through Faith in Christ Jesus, our King. The same problems quickly reacquired strength because in order to be a good citizen of the nation one still had to be a Christian, simply rearranging the dilemma into a Protestant/Catholic fight.

You will see this played over and over again. Time and time again the Church has fallen into heresies because they have turned from God and started worshiping the two-head idol of culture. Time and time again the Church has faltered and floundered because we, as a group, have taken our focus off of God and instead focused on the culture, either by conforming to it or trying to control it. Does it make a difference if the idols we make are crafted with words and ideas instead of wood and stone, if we still worship them? And those who seek to control culture do indeed worship culture as much as those who would transform our Faith into its image, and one may say even more so. After all, to make a sacrifice to a god in order to win its favor, to make it do what you would is at the heart of idolatry.

More to the point a Christian nation, a nation whose civic religion is Christianity gives a false hope to salvation. To many people therefore think that because they believe what they have been taught to believe they are saved. But Faith in our belief is not Faith, but a form of self-worship. But that is the real dilemma, the paradox which needs to be balanced. For there is a need to challenge those who have only a civic Faith, who are not in Christ but who believe they are. But we must do it in a way which does not hinder, and indeed aids the growing of the Faith for those who are in Christ. I know only one way of doing that and that is by pointing out that we are not saved by simply having the wisdom to believe that we are saved by Christ, but though having the wisdom of trusting that God has the power to save us by Grace through Faith in Christ.

The Church will always have those who belong to a church but do not have the Grace of a Life in Christ. I started with a historical view precisely because our fighting to maintain a Christian culture is really simply a fight to maintain those civic Christians. Those who are Christian simply because it is the culture or subculture in which they belong. And in a real way it is a fight to give them false hope, a fight to make it harder to reach them with the Gospel. Of those who call themselves Christian almost half do not believe that Christ is relevant to salvation, and over half believe that any religion is a path to salvation. Does it not stand to reason then that at least half of Christians in our country need to hear the Gospel, that they need to learn that our salvation comes through our

Faith in Christ and not our beliefs or actions.

Indeed, that is very much the question. How do you know you are saved? I know it is in bad from to ask that question, it does insult people. But whom does it insult? Certainly not one who has Hope, who places their trust in God instead of the wisdom of men. Some say that the question promotes doubt. Well, I am a mystic and so take doubt to mean something we need to examine, so in that regard yes, doubt your Faith. Examine it to see if it is real. Examine yourself to see if you are truly placing your trust for salvation in Christ and His Passion or are you putting it in the wisdom of men, trusting that as long as you believe and do, what some person says you must believe and do then you are saved.

The real reason that a preacher may be opposed is that they would lose a great number if they were to tell you to examine your heart, to see whether or not you had Faith. They would have to admit that their great numbers are not so great. Others though are reluctant precisely because there are those who would use it to judge others. But this is one of those teachings which you can only apply to yourself, that you must do it for yourselves. No one can do it for you, and I am highly opposed and suspicious of those who would try to separate the wheat from the tares. Without exception such attempts turn either into a witch-hunt or a cult. Even theologians, whose responsibility is to make sure that our dogma and doctrine stays true can fall into making it about human wisdom instead of the power of God. But I agree with those preachers who say that we should not increase your doubt. and they fear that by asking you to examine yourself you may lose the Faith you do have. Because you may in fact doubt your salvation, doubt you are in Christ.

It is an ironic joke that those who never doubt should, and those who doubt often have no reason to. There are those who will read this and know instantly what I am talking about. One does not have to be a convert to know that Faith, to a large existent, is placing our trust in God. Sanctification, maturing in Faith is very much about learning to trust God more and more with our lives. Right now, I am doubting if I will ever get the money together to publish the books I have written so far, and as such struggle with continuing writing. That is, I am struggling with trusting God that there is a point and purpose to this whole starving artist thing I have going on. While you, reading this may ask yourself how do you know your saved and struggle with the doubt which comes with having to answer it with 'I do not know.'

One without Faith may doubt their salvation because they doubt that there is a God. One with Faith may doubt their salvation because they are not yet mature in Faith. That is, when those with Faith doubt their salvation it is typically in conjunction with sin. Placing our trust in our righteousness instead of the righteousness of Jesus. Basically, we are putting our Faith in our own wisdom instead of the power of God to save. I will go into this with more detail at some later point, showing how we overcome the doubt, but we struggle trusting God according to our maturity and what purpose God has for us. Assuming you are in Christ, God then allows the doubt so that you may build the character which the struggle develops. That through the struggle God is training you, teaching you to be able to hold onto your trust in Him, regardless of what the wisdom of men might say.

Hebrew 11: Without Faith it is impossible to please Him, for he who comes to God mush believe that He is and that He is the rewarder of those who diligently seek Him.

There are some who say that if you doubt your salvation then you are not really saved. But I cannot give a blanket agreement to that. In so much you doubt God's power to save, if you lack Faith in Christ and His work upon the Cross, then it might be true. But in my observation and with those who have asked for my advice, this has never been the nature of their doubts. They do not doubt Jesus saves us, but are questioning if they are themselves saved. While it seems to be a popular opinion that the doubt itself means that you are not, I have a different view. That the doubt is a product of the movement of God, a normal thorn of our Faith in which is meant to bring us deeper into that relationship with Him.

Being a mystic of the Cross I can see no fault in doubt, in so much as it motivates us to honestly seek answers to our questions. And the question which has one doubting salvation is without a doubt the most important one in our lives. Am I saved? Let me answer such a rude question with some questions. Where did you come by the knowledge of salvation? Is it not that you already believe the Gospel, you already know that God saves? But where does this knowledge come from if not the Grace you have through Faith? What is the origin of the doubt, if not the knowledge that you are unworthy of salvation? And is not one without Grace through Faith by which we are saved unaware of that unworthiness, and our own convictions being a work of the Spirit of God.

Most often this doubt of salvation comes from that feeling of being unworthy of salvation. From the classical mystic view, the problem here is not doubt, or with the feeling of being unworthy, but pride. More often than not the fear and doubt concerning salvation comes from the Spirit working Humility in us which understands that just as we are justified by Grace through Faith, so too are we sanctified by the Cross. More often than not the fear and doubt forms in us because we are not living up to the standards which we set for ourselves. More often than not the fear and doubt come, as they call come, when we are trying be righteous by our own will instead of relying on God to purify us. Is that not what the fear whispers in your ear, that you are not good enough to be saved?

As anyone mature in the Faith will tell you, we have to live with that feeling of unworthiness. If anything, I am far less worthy today than at my conversion. Not because I sin more, but because I am more aware the image of the Glory of Christ, and how far I am from the Glory of God. That is why I say the doubt is the movement of the Spirit of God to teach you humility. It is also why the subtitle of my religious writing is Beyond Salvation. You keep asking yourself if you are saved, and while it might not be the case, I have seen it used as a way not to mature in the Faith. I say that because as long as your focus is on your justification, you can avoid the sanctification the Spirit works on us.

I will return to that topic, but first I need to point out how very often in our prayers to overcome the doubts we are really praying for a sign. That is, you want proof that you are saved. I am a mystic in the classical sense that I seek to put an end to self-will and follow only God's will in my life. I am also a mystic in the modern sense of the word as in having visions and raptures. Are they proof that I am saved? Though the Gnostic neo-mystics would say so, I say no. The only thing I consider proof of my salvation, that I am in Christ, is that I have Faith in Christ for my salvation. That I trust God for my justification and also my sanctification. That is, the proof you seek is not going to be in form of a sign, but in the trust you place in God.

We want proof of our salvation, but why? Rarely in my experience has the fear and doubt over salvation been from a person's lack of Faith, but rather from a weak Faith. Which is why I refer to it as a struggle, a thorn of the white rose of Faith. Because our struggle is not against doubt, so much as it is as struggle in trusting God with our soul. I say that this is pride, because the first lesson with any thorn is humility, that it is not about our nature but the Nature of Christ. I am unworthy of salvation, to be sure, but Christ is. Do you understand? That our salvation is not based on how much we have become that which is Perfect, transformed into the image of the Glory of Christ, but on the fact that Christ has that Glory.

If you understand, truly understand in your heart the righteousness of Christ, and how far we are from the image of the Glory, then you are saved. For how could you have such knowledge unless you are already in Christ, if you already know that image. While there are other lessons, the first one is that in knowing we are unworthy is not reason to doubt, but instead to pray often in humility thanking God for the mercy He has shown us by sending His Son so that in Him we are counted as His Children.

2 Peter 1: For this very reason, giving all diligence, add to your Faith virtue, to virtue knowledge, to knowledge self-control, to self-control perseverance, to perseverance godliness, to godliness brotherly kindness, and to brotherly kindness love. For if these things are yours and abound, you will be neither barren nor unfruitful in the knowledge of our Lord Jesus Christ…be even more diligent to make your call and election sure, for if you do these things, you will never stumble.

You have to face the fact that maybe you are not in Christ, not saved. Does that sound right, or do you balk at the idea that you are not saved? You already know whether or not you are in Christ. (2 Corinthians 13.) You either are, or you are not. So being in Christ, if you are indeed in Christ, you are justified, saved. So, let me ask again, being in Christ where does the doubt come if not the conviction that you are not living a life pleasing to God. For those who are being stubborn in sin, those who some call 'back-sliders' then this is easy to see. But for those of us who rarely sin outwardly, it is not always so easy to see when we are being stubborn. And to make matters worse, Church culture is so obsessed with justification that we often ignore sanctification. That we focus on God's power to save that we often forget that He also has the power to purify.

That is, we are saved, justified, but we are being saved, sanctified. And the doubt and fear come from the same source they always do, that war between the flesh and spirit. That conflict between self-will and the will of God. It is a battle which marks our Faith, and it is not one in which you can escape. This is why I brought up pride earlier, and why I say that such doubt is from the working of the Spirit of God. For the God is telling you to seek sanctification and your ego-self, your flesh makes it about you, about your justification. It is a dangerous time because the Spirit is saying to trust God more with your life, but your flesh says that you must do more, pray more, work more sacrifice more.

This holds true to all the thorns of Faith, and of Hope. I have never doubted my salvation, my sanity to be sure, but never my salvation. We can, and should doubt of whether or not we are in God's will, doing all we should. That is, we should constantly make sure that we are staying on that narrow path, that our focus stays on Christ and being transformed into the Image of His Glory. Those of us who have worked for or in ministry knows how easy it is loose that focus and instead focus on the work. But while there is work and sacrifices we make, and make no mistake as there is work to be done, we do so because we are saved. No amount of work or mortification will give us assurance of our salvation, or that you are staying true to God. Nothing we can do can give us that assurance because our Hope is in the Grace through Faith in Christ, and not in our works. This is why I say we continue to need the Cross, why the Gospel is as relevant to the saved as to the unsaved.

This you know, that our works cannot justify us, and you should have been taught that neither can they sanctify us. But think on what that means for our sins, for our weaknesses and shortcomings. You sin, as we all do, and so you question your salvation. Maybe even praying for God to rescue you from the effects of the sin, maybe even for justification again. But being in Christ we have already been rescued from the wrath of God, so our prayers should not be for God to rescue us from the effects of our sin, but instead from the sin itself. Being in Christ our focus no longer needs to on getting saved, but on being saved. That it is pride, pure and simple a focus on ourselves first, in which we worry about our salvation rather than trying to live a life pleasing to God. But how do we live a life pleasing to God if not through Faith?

You fear for your salvation precisely because you are trying to trust your works for sanctification instead of placing you trust in God. Is that not so? That you say to yourself 'if I was really saved in would not do this or that sin' so I must not be saved? But just as God forgives our sins through our Faith in Christ, through us placing our trust in Christ for forgiveness so too do we need put our Faith in

Christ in the overcoming of our sins. As we are saved through Faith, we are being saved through Faith. To conclude this matter, where is it written that you must feel holy and righteous? Are not those who feel as if they are without sin those who are not justified? While Hope surely comes through our Faith, it comes not from our own righteousness but knowing, and trusting that our Hope is found in the righteousness of Christ, and in Him we have Life.

Condemnation and Conviction

Romans 8: there is therefore no condemnation to those who are in Christ Jesus.

I have been thinking a lot about those who doubt their salvations lately. It has been difficult to find the helpful words mostly because I have to rely on observation rather than experience. I have had my own struggles, my own 'crisis of Faith' at times, but being a classical or death-to-self mystic, my own salvation has always been irrelevant. My struggles and my doubts have always come down to pride. I think it is the same with the doubt of our salvation. Not in the question of whether or not we are saved, but in the idea that our salvation is dependent on us, rather than on the work of Christ.

But that is not all that helpful, simply to say that you should be humbler. I even would go as far as to say that it is counter-productive, because such doubts, as with all struggles arise in our Faith is the will of God. It is, after all the same problem I have in regard to the neo-mystics, and their chasing of mystical experiences. If God would have you have raptures or visions, you would have them. So, to, if God did not want the person to have such doubts, then He would Grace them in a way which they would not doubt.

2 Peter 1: be even more diligent to make your call and election sure.

I have pointed out before that there is nothing wrong with questions, and that doubting one's own salvation is proof that you have Faith in God's ability to save. That if nothing else, you know there is sin, and that salvation is needed. The very doubt confirms these truths. Surely there are those who doubt who are not regenerated, not saved, who lack the Faith through which Grace works. But in my limited experience they do not really doubt their own salvation but doubt the truth and need of the Gospel. That, in trying to help someone who is doubting their salvation, we first have to assess whether the person simply weak in Faith or lack it all together. Because in most cases it is impossible to tell for sure, the default position is that they are having a crisis of Faith, and to ask why.

It is bound to cause you a bit of frustration as a minister from those who are looking for a magic pill, from those who want a quick answer instead of being told to grow in their Faith. The doubt of salvation hits the strongest those who spent the youth of their Faith with pep-rallies from the pulpits and shallow Bible studies. This doubt rises most often when the person starts understanding that there is more to Faith than just belief and the social club church culture has become. It is like a cruel joke that a shallow church culture indirectly teaches that there is never to be crisis in our Faith. That is, your own experiences have born witness, it is often considered as if there is something wrong with us if we struggle. So, is it no wonder that some will doubt their salvation when they first learn the Faith is a struggle? That with the sweet smell of the Rose of justification comes the painful thorny stem of sanctification.

Hebrews 12: if you are without chastening, of which all have become partakers, then you are illegitimate and not sons.

Obviously, I am one who blames an incomplete, if not incorrect instruction in Scripture. The subtitle of Beyond Salvation, and my ministry has focused on sanctification because we, for the most part, rarely hear teaching on the subject. In a church culture which is obsessed in justification, in getting to heaven, there seems to be little room for what it means in the here and now. In context, there is little teaching which makes a point of the difference between condemnation and conviction. What is the doubt of salvation but the fear that we are condemned? In this, we can see how the doubting of our salvation can be seen as normal part of the maturing process. For it is well known that as we mature, we gain a greater understanding of the need of the Cross. That as we mature, we gain a greater sense of the evil of sin, and understand that no matter how much sin we have done away with in our lives we would still be condemned without Christ.

My point is that, while many points to those saying that their doubt means a lack of Faith, I say that it is rather them maturing in the Faith. They are just realizing that, no matter how good they are, they are still a sinner worthy of condemnation. What I am pointing out is that those going through this Dark Night, this crisis of Faith, are people who are being convicted that Faith is more than just justification, more than just a ticket to heaven. That regeneration, that 'being saved' was just the beginning. That is, very often people doubt their salvation because they do not know that one of the ways which God convicts us, one of the ways He uses to sanctify is by taking away the 'feeling' of Him.

James 2: for whoever shall keep the whole law, and yet stumble in one point, he is guilty of all.

People doubt their salvation because they do not feel saved, and they have been taught that this is bad. Oh, we say all the time that we are unworthy of salvation, but there is a big difference between intellectually knowing it and feeling that unworthiness. A big difference between believing that you are unworthy, and knowing in the depths of your heart that you are unworthy, that you still should be condemned. That the answer to this is, of course, to accept that we are unworthy, and give glory to God for the Cross. I did not doubt my salvation because in this my pride I was the type that tried to be perfect so I did not need the Cross. Unwilling to see that I was unworthy, I felt worthy. I made an idol of holiness. Though in my opinion that those who doubt their salvation are not nearly as prideful as I was, none-the-less it is still pride. That is, the pride which makes our salvation dependent on who we are and not who Christ is. On our life instead of on His.

This is why ministering to such people can be frustrating at times. Many of them want to return to time when they felt justified, felt saved and worthy. That 'feeling' itself becomes an idol in which they start chasing. I did the same thing, turned the mystical experiences of the youth of my Faith into idols when I matured to the point when I no longer needed them. Most of you understand this having experienced Dark Nights yourself. Remember those who claimed that it must be some sin you were doing. To be sure, sin can rob us of the joy of our Faith, but remember those times it was not sin how most people think of it. Those times when the conviction was not way from a sin, in so much that God was convicting you towards virtue. That, I think, is the key in helping those who are doubting their salvation.

1 Corinthians 15: I declare to you the gospel which I preached to you, which also you received and in which you stand, by which you were also saved

As those of you who have gone through Dark Nights know, there are no easy answers. That, in fact, on such crisis is very much about us going around looking for easy answers. Reading the bible, or reading just about anything we can get our hands on trying to find that one thing, that one piece of knowledge which will pull us out of the pit. But it might be beneficial to point out that Jesus condemned the one who prayed believing themselves to be righteous and worthy while saying the one who felt like a sinner and asking for mercy is the one who is justified. Again, in a culture which makes it all about getting into heaven may not see how this might apply after our regeneration. Which is really the point of all this, that Life is Christ is a life of constant conviction. It is to live with a constant awareness that the Gospel applies to us as much today as it did at conversion.

Which is why I wrote that it is beneficial to ask them why they doubt their salvation. For most of them it is because they do not feel saved, feel unworthy of salvation, and so that is what needs to be dealt with. That is, as it is a crisis of Faith, then it should be dealt with by Faith. Of course, we mystics of the Cross believe that Faith is not just belief but also placing our trust in God. In context it is not just believing the Gospel to be true but placing our trust in it for our salvation. That them doubting their salvation is, in fact, a chance for them to grow in the Faith. To learn to more fully trust Christ and His work for our salvation. It does them no good to sugar-coat the struggle that entails, as I think that is how we got into this mess in the first place. It may be a struggle which lasts the rest of their life. However, I think that what is often lacking is the encouragement that once they have finished the struggle, once they have strengthened their Faith they will be assured of their salvation. That is, once one learns to that the assurance of our salvation is found in Christ and not our feelings of being worthy of salvation, then the question is no longer whether or not we are saved. That our Faith is not a question of whether or not we are condemned, but what is it God would have us do.

A Sigh

When the sun is high in the sky,
And there is plenty of light to be had,
The light of a candle seems small.
Only when the sun has done its setting,
And the clouds cover the sky,
We call the light of a candle, bright.

 When virtue abounds in our heart's depth,
And Charity is easily found there,
Our fruits form with little work.
Only when corruption has filled the world,
And we treat darkness as our light,
Would we call our mediocrity, Love.

Christian Nihilism and Hope

Ecclesiastes 12: let us hear the conclusion of the whole matter: fear God and keep His commandments.

A dark, burning despair shredding the mind with thoughts on fire. A soul with a pain so harsh that even the body aches. A heart with the numbness of being too long in the cold...sometimes I miss it. As strange as it sound, there are times I very much miss dancing with the candle flame, times when I miss the tears of self-pity. When I despair no longer being able to indulge in despair. But I think what I miss, what keeps me on edge is that I no longer have excuse. I do not have any reason for the refusal to wear my crown. That once you set aside the fear and pride, and the fear of pride, it then really comes down to laziness. A choice to act, or not to act.

I am bound to be criticized because not only do I believe that there is nihilism inherent to Christianity, but I also propose that the nihilism is an important aspect of our Faith. Nihilism is based on the foundation that there is no meaning, no purpose to our lives, and I say to think there is one is simply pride. It is not all that surprising I would take such a view, as I have always favored the Preacher. Vanity of vanities, all is vanity. That, and I know firsthand how purpose, meaning, goal and vision can simply be different words for idol.

It is a question of motivation, of course. And a question of Faith, of placing our trust in God and His purpose rather than our own. You go to work to earn money to feed your children. You work for a purpose of feeding your children, so if you could meet the needs of your family without working you would surely spend your time in more enjoyable pursuits. When the need is removed you would spend your time following your heart. You would dance or sing, travel if the whim takes you, maybe even still work but now only because you enjoy such experiences. Without a need, without a purpose to direct our life, then we are free to do what it is we desire to do. Which is why I say that our Faith is nihilistic, that it is nihilistic precisely because it is redemptive.

We may have human goals with earthly meaning. To create that work of art that our name will be known in the next century. To create a legacy which will aid our family in the generations to come. There is a nobility to be found in such things but as time moves on all these things will fall into dust, discarded and forgotten. This age will eventually pass away and so no real purpose, no real meaning can be found in it. We are creatures of both flesh and soul, so if there is no purpose to be found in our bodies, then we look for it in our souls. So it is our nature, some would call it an absurdity, that we as we cannot find meaning on the earth we look for it in heaven.

Some might say that there is a need for heaven in our lives. That there are many, many times many, who work to keep the commandments of God, or to fulfill the obligations of what society says a good person must be, in the hopes of heaven. The purpose and meaning of their lives are to gain entrance into the next age. But for those of us who are regenerated, born-again if you would, no longer have to work for the need has been met for us in the Cross. Knowing the futility of this age, that nothing we do echoes through eternity, we place our hope not in our work but in Christ. It was Christ's work and not our own which has brought the Grace to us through our Faith, there is no purpose for us in heaven. No meaning to be found in the attempt to get there. Or as we are united with God by being in Christ, the purpose of our lives cannot be found in groping blindly for Him.

We gain or fail to gain heaven regardless of actions we perform in this life. Our sin and our righteousness does not matter in our justification, so there is no purpose to be found for us in heaven. Free from the need of heaven, free from having to order our lives for the purpose of gaining heaven, we are then free to follow our hearts. It is a freedom from the Law of Death for those who are regenerated, those who have become a new creation in Christ. Those who have been born-again are free to follow their hearts, and it is marked by a heart which desires to keep the commandments of God. We are free from the Law, and free to follow our hearts because our hearts, our new-self desires to do the will of God.

We do not have to seek sanctification, but rather seek it because we want to be sanctified. Being justified we do not have to seek righteousness, but instead seek His righteousness, to be perfect as He is perfect because it is the desire of our hearts. Or as St. Augustine wrote to love God and do what you will, which I add is only possible to say because if one loves God, truly loves God then they desire to do His Will. By virtue of being a new creation, we are free to follow our hearts where it leads. I hold what I have written so far to be a truth, but it is a half-truth. One which can be dangerous because we are still in this age. We are not yet in heaven and have the Perfect we will have when we are face to face with Christ.

We have the Will to Righteousness but we are not yet sanctified as we will be then. For though it is the desire of our heart to do the will of God, we still have carnal desires in our hearts, the Will to Sin. To simply say that one can follow their hearts is to do a disservice to those who have not yet matured in their Faith. And to do great harm to those who have not yet come to understand that our new nature wars with our old nature. Since my conversion I wanted nothing more than to do the will of God, but in my pride, I wanted His will for me to be grand and great. In my pride I wanted a purpose with earthly meaning. Measured my actions, not by whether or not I did the will of God, but by the success or failure. Or if you would, one part of my heart wanted nothing more than to build an empire according to my will, and the other wanted nothing more than to do what God would have me do regardless of my own plans.

Simply saying that one should follow their heart is valid only when there is a clear recognition that there remains in us a Will to Sin, we remain in the flesh as St. Paul refers to it. The lust in my heart would have me seek comfort in physical pleasures where I may. And it does not care whether or not I do it in a way pleasing to God. I am mature enough, or at least old enough to know that I would find no real satisfaction in sex or even in romance unless it was according to God's will. One must pursue either the will of the flesh or the will of God. That one or the other will be dissatisfied. The desires of the flesh will eventually fade the more we do God's will. The more we struggle to desire God's will more than our own will, the humbler we become. As our Faith matures, as we are sanctified, not only is it easier it is to discern good from evil, but easier to do what is good. The easier it becomes to fulfill the Will to Righteousness which we have from being in Christ.

Then should we say that sanctification is the purpose of our Life in Christ? Is there a meaning to our lives to be found in putting away sin, in subduing the flesh? There are times in which it feels that way. That frustration when our desire, our Will to Righteousness goes unfulfilled, when we slip and fall and sin. But that too is a selfish pride, for we lament our own shortcomings because in them we see ourselves as unworthy, as weak. Indeed, as I have brought up many times, we can seek after righteousness for no other reason because we do not want to admit that we need forgiveness. We can ignore our own sins in a vain attempt to deny that we need the Cross as much today as we did the day before our conversion. But I am writing about motivation, and if we have a purpose than that purpose is love.

When I was young in the Faith, the first few years, I sought to be perfect as the Father is perfect from self-love. I sought to live a life pleasing to God as a child seeks to please their parents. As a child seeks not to disappoint their parents out of a fear of losing their love. Or more in line with my pride, to show off as if I could impress God with my service. Either way you look at it, it is a motivation of pride rooted in who we are instead of who God is. Which is why I say that sanctification is not the purpose of our Life in Christ. To be motivated by our sanctification, by gaining our own maturity is to be motivated by what God can do for us, rather than our Love for God. It is a motivation to live by our righteousness, a love of our own righteousness instead of the Righteousness of God, namely

215

Jesus.

Surely, we should seek to subdue the flesh, but we have no need to do such for our own sake. As we are justified and sanctified by Grace through Faith. We have no need to do it for ourselves, to work for our own benefit but rather do so out of love. Our love for God, and our love for others. It is a fine-hair to be sure, to say that we should love the righteousness of Christ which we share rather than our own righteousness. It seems that it is hard for some to understand that we should be motivated in our work, in our preaching and teaching, in our writing and dreaming, not for our own sake but for the sake of others. That the result of Christian Nihilisms is not despair, but Hope. That when it is understood, truly understood that who we are, no matter how great, or what we do, no matter how grand, are just shadows and dust there is a freedom to love. A freedom to do what is best for others without it being hindered by it having to have a meaning to our lives.

What does it matter to me if I am chaste? Surely there a peace that has grown from the lessening of frustrations caused by desires unfulfilled. But is that why we seek chastity? To ease our own suffering? Is it not that we do it for the sake of our spouses? Or as I am single, so that our desires, no matter how lovely the curve of the hips might me, does not get in the way of seeing and doing what the person needs from us. It is the same with pride, is it not? That is what this is about, after all. Christian Nihilisms is just a fancy way of saying humility. It is only our pride which says our life has purpose, which says that it has meaning, which is to say that it is important. Or as I should put it, which seeks for meaning, purpose and importance outside of love.

How many preachers have sold their soul, and betrayed love by wanting to be modern, on the right side of history, forsake love to appear kind? How many pastors have fallen because they were not humble, thinking that they were important, who seek not to glorify God but instead glory in their own abilities? Indeed, I can still despair, for it brings a sorrow to my heart to think of how many knights have fallen by forgetting that our position has not been given to enforce the Law but to serve each other from love. Struck down by the enemy because they had sought to be a great servant instead of seeking to serve greatly. It is pride, pure and simple which says that I will not serve without being recognized for my service. It is also pride in which we refuse to serve God and our fellow knights. It is pride to say that I have nothing to give, nothing to do, that I am not good enough. Both are pride because both are based on who we are instead of who He is.

And it can also be pride in which we ask what we can do to serve God and our fellow knights. In so much as we are asking what we can do, rather than what needs to be done. In so much that we are spending time worrying about ourselves, caring about ourselves to such a degree that we cannot not see what those around us needs of us. Chastity, even within marriage, is more then just remaining Faithful but not allowing our physical desires to prevent us from seeing the needs of our beloved. That is to say, love is not our purpose in so much as it is the nature of our hearts, our new hearts, our regenerated soul. That when we love, we seek to fulfill the needs of the one we love, and to remove the obstacles which prevent us from doing so. And we seek humility, virtues and righteousness because our selfish desires, our sinful or carnal natures does just that, hinders us in the fulfillment of love.

As for the conclusion of the whole matter; we seek righteousness, to put the end of sin in our lives, and sanctification, or to love in holiness, not because we have too but, first of all, as a way to love God. As a means of worship giving honor and glory to God. And then, like the first, so that we may freely know and meet the needs of others.

The Battles We Fight

Hebrew 5: For though this time you ought to be teachers, you need someone to teach you again the first principles of the oracles of God and you have come to need milk and not solid food. For everyone who partakes only of milk is unskilled in the word of righteousness for he is a babe. But solid food belongs to those who are of full age that is those who by reason of use have their sense exercised to discern both good and evil.

I would like to write on deeper theological issues, the fine hair details which can keep us in debate for years. But there is not much point to it when the Church, as a whole, struggle with the most basic aspects of our Faith. We do very much need someone to teach the 'first principles of the oracles of God'. So, I have been giving much thought lately to those foundational truths which my life has been based on since my conversion. Thoughts about how my writing has been lacking because I took it for granted that people would have at least a basic understanding of our Faith. Debating with myself, and with God if I even have the words to express those things with were burned into me without words. But alas, it is just my pride which tends towards the complex, and just my lust which does not want to give up my pleasures to get involved with the fight. Which is to say that it is my imperfections I have been thinking about, and the perfection of God.

That is, over the last few months I have been asking myself a question which is one which rarely came up. Who am I to say such things? It did not come up much because the only time I involved myself in the church political is when God forced me too. It is not because I am a sinner. I have no problem being open about my imperfections. Sin is sin really, I can post every time I masturbate and whom I lusted after if it would not be a bit too vulgar for my tastes. But does it matter if our porn is found on a screen, in a romance novel or plays across our imagination? But then again

218

maybe it is only such to me because I find it so ironic, find it most humorous that in my early forties I am having to deal with a physical desire which was unknown to me in my youth. My mid-life crisis is a second puberty, but then again, my pride would not let me lack the self-control for such common place desires, or at least not admit that I was not perfectly in control. Or unwilling to admit that spark of loneliness which is at the core of my lust.

The point is not that I struggle with lust, but that I struggle. That is, the point is not lust but the struggle. Humility, chastity, generosity, Charity, whatever virtue we are struggling to live our Grace is not important here as the fact that we struggle, and we battle and we fight ourselves. That is one of those foundational truths of which I have always, at least for the most part, taken for granted. Everyone I have been able to help, everyone I have watched mature in the Faith, everyone I know who has 'their sense exercised to discern both good and evil', has struggled and struggles to do what God would have of them. Not perfectly, that is why we call it a struggle, but nonetheless we strive, we fight, we moan and whine, we get frustrated and put ourselves through all kind of strife, and we struggle, struggle and continue to struggle against the flesh...but why?

I am not asking this theologically, nor metaphysically, but as a question of motivation and personal knowledge. When we are children in the Faith, or at least when I was, it was very much about pleasing God. I had that whole parental thing going one where we do not want to misbehave as not to upset them. After more than a few failings, more than once avoiding my prayers from embarrassment, I would gain a better understanding of that Grace we have in Christ. That by the Cross, even though I am a sinner I can still go to God, and in fact, that is the only real way of struggling against the sin. That is when I noticed that for a good portion, if not the majority of the church culture, this is as far as maturity goes. It seems to me that we gather more to pat each other on the back of what a fine job we are doing by believing rather than truly seeking to be transformed into the image of God's righteousness, into the image of the Glory of Christ.

Of course, my primary problem, the problem which has haunted me my whole life is that I am by nature progressive rather than pragmatic. Oh, I do not get excited or fall for the rhetoric which titillates the masses. But the goal, the idea that we can, indeed that we should reach for perfection has always made it difficult for me to relate in a society which not only accepts but promotes mediocrity. There is no nobler thing than reaching for your goal, even when it is not obtainable. Nothing more beautiful, nothing worth sacrificing for more than an unobtainable ideal. For me and people like me, our morality, our view of right and wrong, is always dictated to us by the goal we are trying to achieve, by our image of perfection. For most, morality is crafted from the outside, by the ideal of a perfect society. But for me and those like me, right and wrong is defined as the course towards the perfection, the ideal we are attempting to be.

That is, as a youth in the Faith I asked that question of why we struggle if not to achieve perfection. My hubris, being what it was, did make it about seeking perfection for perfection's sake. I was going to be great and do God's will perfectly. Seriously, was it pride which makes it about us? About how far we can go, how mature we can become. oh, the miracles we could work if only we tried hard enough, gave enough, did enough, sacrificed enough? The view I have now is that much of my battle and struggle against pride was done from pride. God tried to tell me several times, but really all it took was for me to become tired. I am tired even now, wanting only to sink into the water of holy insanity, spending my days picking wild-flowers and babbling half-coherent wisdom. Instead, though I struggle to stay on the storm-tossed surface to string a few words together that someone might find helpful. But the question is still why.

I could say Love but it is an ideal much abused. Nonetheless, from Charity, and from Hope and Faith, our struggles are born.

Being saved, if indeed you are saved, we do not have to struggle for perfection for our sanctification for that is found in Christ and His work upon the Cross. And being in Christ, if indeed you have His Spirit within you, our sanctification is not dependent on the works of our hands, or minds, but on the Spirit transforming us into what He would have us be. As we do not do it for justification, and we do not do it for our own sanctification, it seems to me as I sit here today that we struggle to do God's will simply because it is God's will.

All of this long and futile string of words, really to come back to what I do consider to be one of those 'first principles of the oracles of God.' That is, the perfection of God and His will, and how it applies to the Lordship Salvation/Free Grace debate.

The Gift of the Spirit

Mathew 7.22-23

God so loved the world that He gave His only begotten Son...

It is a verse which is often quoted but what is often forgotten is that it was not just a random teaching, it was an answer to a question. It was the answer to how we can see the Kingdom, not only when we die, but now.

Indeed, Nicodemus asked 'how could these things be?" Because our Lord told him that everyone born of the Spirit will be moved by God. To the Pharisees this was not possible, only the prophets heard God, had His Spirit. This just could not be for the average person. The question I must put to you is – is not this the same mentality we have in the church today? Preachers and prophets and no one else. That the average Christian is better off listening to the preacher and not bothering listening for themselves.

I weep often in my prayers because of this, often enough that mother relates me to Jeremiah. I weep for the church because we say 'my pastor said' instead of 'God said'. I weep because of what we must go through now. I weep most of all because God weeps. We have lost our way and have made our hearts so hard that it will take the sword and fire to bring us back to the Way.

The question which must be asked is why. How is it that the Body of Christ, which is an extension of His Glory, is failing? Because we have lost Him. We are so wrapped up in what a Christian is supposed to do that we have forgotten to ask Him what we should do. There was this fad around a few years ago. Bracelets and things with WWJD on them were everywhere. For those of you who do not know it stands for What Would Jesus Do. Now, I have nothing against having items in our life to remind us but what are they reminding us to do. See, all the responses I heard was you were supposed to think of what Jesus would do in that situation. Again there is nothing wrong with that, but what it boils down to is where you get your information from. My point being, if you think your own mind can come up with that answer you are dangerously mistaken. There is only one way to know what He would do, that is by asking Him. You may be thinking I am getting off subject (which I know I do often) but this is the point.

Only the blind do not see that church culture is on its last leg, that we need something. I hear all kinds of answer to this. One fad after the other, WWJD, the Prayer of Jabez, revival weekends. But think for a moment what do we need, that one thing above all others, the one which when you have it you need nothing else.

It will not come to a shock to most of you when I say that one thing is God. The state of the church is such for only one reason, we are not seeking Elohim. Indeed the time for games are over. The Storm is too close for me to slack anymore. You will notice that I speak of myself. I have told you before that anything I write I first apply to myself, and indeed, this has been my struggle.

Before I knew I was coming out here God told me that he had forged me into a sword and now it was time for me to be sharpened. Part of that sharpening is a renewing of my commitment. To increase my own striving to know God more. And that is what I am talking about here. Knowing God, not rewards, not salvation.

I do not give rat droppings about salvation. If Calvin is right about predestination and God was to come to me and tell me no matter what I do I would still go to hell. I would still serve him. Why? Because one moment of knowing him, even through a dark glass, is worth an eternity of torture. See, when my spirit opens and I feel the world around me I feel so much pain. There is so much pain in the world and in the church. We run around so much going 'we got to get more people saved' that we do not realize that there is more to Christianity. Salvation is not the goal of our Faith, it is only a byproduct.

Read the first half of John 3. Salvation was not the greatest gift of the Cross. The greatest gift was God Himself. The church misses this, we miss this because we are thinking too much about what we get. I too am struggling with what I get.

I know that some of you would defend me if I called myself selfish but I must. Giving up my physical positions to God was hard, and giving myself doubly so. But what I must give up now is harder by far. What I must give up now is grace, my anointing. This made less sense to me than it does to you for the way God put it is that I needed to give Him up. Now that I understand let me explain.

Long ago, I promised the Lord that whatever I have belongs to Him and through this He has anointed me. And I have used this as a shield against the ignorant. I mean, like going to church. Some think I cannot possible be a Christian let alone hear from God because I rarely go. This has never bothered me for I know God is with me. What does it matter to me if I do not live up to what you expect of me as long as I am doing what He asks of me?

The point is this, I must give my anointing, my gifts, even my holiness to God. They cannot be mine, they must be God's and God's alone. Why? Because I need to seek after God. Not for more of an anointing, not to live holier, but simply to know him more. But let me leave this and deal with why God said I must give Him up.

As I said above, there is no greater gift then knowing God. I have found no greater pleasure in life then being united with Elohim in my prayers. I hold knowing Him more dearly then life itself. Yet, God has shown me that this is wrong. There is one thing which should be more important to me then knowing him. You.

Over the years me and John has spent a considerable amount of time talking about love. About having enough love that you would be willing to give up them your salvation. That is, loving you so much that I would spend an eternity of torture so you would not have to face it. But do I love you enough that I would give up God so that you may know Him? Sadly, all I can say for the moment is that I am working on it. I am working hard of it because it is important to me.

Indeed, I can say that it is the most important thing for me. For it is that kind of love which is needed. It is a kind of love which can work miracles and nothing short of it can return life to the church. God's Love is not only unconditional it is complete. It says that there is nothing more important than you. To love with God's Love means to love you more than what I cherish most. Ultimately this is about the Cross for God so loved the world that he gave the most precious thing He has . . . His only begotten Son.

Friends of the ABC

Luke 12.49-53

"...accordingly, all experience hath shewn, that mankind are more disposed to suffer, while evils are sufferable, than to right themselves by abolishing the forms to which they are accustomed."
- The Declaration of Independence

The Declaration of Independence is an impressive document, not only because of its passion and elegance, but for what it is saying. A revolutionary idea – we do not have the power that you do but we will fight with all we have because we are right. It is this revolutionary heritage which gave birth to the abolitionist movement, universal suffrage, and the civil rights movements. It has been stitched on the standards of our heroes from George Washington to Sitting Bull to Martian Luther King Jr. The revolutionary heritage comes to us not only from being Americans but from our Faith as well. Is not the Cross a revolution against sin and death? Would not the Christians in the first centuries, who proved they would rather be food for lions then forsake Christ, be considered revolutionary? Nero thought so.

The heroes of our generation will be the ones who will rise up and fight with every ounce of their strength for a better way. They, and if I can assume enough to say we, will be the ones who must start the renaissance.

Let me make this clear I am talking about Revival but not that lets get together and talk about it but not get anything done kind of revival. No, I am talking a true rebirth. A revolution with the extremes we associate with it. For it is time to cast aside all of our preconceptions and prejudices, our excuses and comforts. It is time to let go of what we are and fight with all our might for something better. It is time to give all we have for a change which Will Durant described as the only truly worthy cause, for "...such a revolution is the only one that would mark a real advance in human affairs; and that besides it the bloody overturns of history are transient and ineffectual spectacles, changing anything but man." (The Renaissance: book 5 in his story of civilization series - Pg. 162)

I started this email with a quote from the Declaration of Independence because for I must answer God's call. A revolution which changes the hearts of humans will not come without struggle, without sacrifice. And I tell you now that the enemy which threatens the Church is not outside of it but within. It is every one of us who would rather do the 'Christian thing' than seek after God, every pastor more concerned with keeping a hold of their power than with helping those in their care get closer to God. It is us who refuse to answer the call God has given us.

As I pointed out in my email The Gift of the Spirit, the most precious gift which the Cross gave us was the ability to know Him. That salvation pales in comparison to knowing God. That is why we must revolt against anything which prevents us from knowing Him more. Indeed, continually seeking a deeper union with Elohim is central to revival and is why there must be a revolution.

Up until now most of my emails have been targeted towards leadership. It has always been my hope that those who claim to be our parents in the Faith would dedicate themselves to helping us get towards God (and that is not to say that there are not such people, only that they are not in the majority). But we must take our own blame in the state we find ourselves. We are too happy being lukewarm. We want priests who makes us feel good, pastors who will convict with emotions rather than with the Spirit (and again I am not saying all, simply most). That is why there must be revolution. Revival will not come until we stand up and say 'I want only God'. Until we get tired of the game and run the race to win.

All I can ask from most of you is that you dedicate yourself to God alone. That you bring a revival (or greater revival) to your own heart so that you may be an example to others. But I need to find others who will share this fight with me. I have longed learned that I cannot do this alone, that others have their own parts to play.

I am not asking or looking for people to follow me (lord, please grant that it is always so). I am small matter to this, a single cell in a body. The people I need to find are those who by following Him happen to be on the same road as me. People who themselves are dedicated to the fight and have declared that nothing will stop them from answering the call God has put out to them.

And with this I will leave you with the last sentence of The Declaration of Independence 'And for the support of this Declaration, with a firm reliance on the protection of divine Providence, we mutually pledge to each other our Lives, our Fortunes and our sacred Honor.'

Judgment

EMPTY . . .
The nature of our faith
No cost to high
As long as someone else can pay

WITNESS . . .
The darkness of our hearts
We will forsake even Him
To fill our seats with the dead

LOVE . . .
All that glitters
If you have the gold
We will call you brother

ASK . . .
For all but what we need
His will does not matter
As long as we have our miracles

GIVE . . .
To feed our ego
Go with His blessings
Forget your empty stomach

BLOOD . . .
To wash away our sins
No need for His
When yours will do

FREEDOM . . .
From the law of death
But if you are true
You will wear our chains

BELIEVE . . .
All that we tell you
Don't listen for yourself
You do not have our ears to hear

REPENT . . .
Kneel with tears in our eyes
Poor out our heart on the alter
What does it matter?
Tomorrow we can return to our ways

Church Political

James 1: Count it all joy whey you fall into dire struggles…blessed is the man who endures temptation; for when he has been approved, he will receive the crown of life which the Lord has promised to those who love Him.

There are times for each of in which we must face our dragons. Though there is aid and comfort to be found in each other, there are times which each of us, without exception, must face our dragons, our fears and temptations, alone. I can give advice, share the wisdom I have learned from facing my own dragons but in the end, it is a matter of your choice, your will to hold onto the Faith and seek the way God has set before you. Despite what some may think, our dragons have no substance. They cannot block our way unless we fear to follow where He is taking us, nor can they tempt us down another path unless we unlawfully desire it. Put aside your fear, put aside your unlawful desires and there is no more struggle. Doing such, of course, is what we call maturing, sanctification which is the personal side, the private aspect of the Faith.

But Faith is not just private, it is not just about yours or my relationship with Christ as individuals but together, as the Church Body. Which is my dragon, the direction God is taking me, fearing where it might end up. I feel safe, comfortable and confident in writing about sanctification, but I feel inadequate, most inadequate addressing issues of the Church visible. In that feeling it has been tempting, tempting indeed to hide behind my position, to use my talents in areas which I have already well explored instead of traveling to undiscovered lands. But in spite of the fear, in spite of trembling in terror of the idea of people knowing my name, the issues in which spurred my rebellious in the youth of my Faith still persists. And I no longer have the excuse of lacking wisdom, of saying to myself that I must first get rid the plank in my own eye.

Somewhere along the way, I know not when, I lost my

passion to fight injustice for justice's sake. And as I entered into midlife I lamented that loss of passion. How can I accomplish if I am not driven by the candle flame of my heart's pain? But as with all things I have found God's way to be the better one as I find now that my passion is not to destroy what is wrong, but to build what is right. There are enough people in the world who will fight against evil, but you and I must fight for what is good. That is the nature of our struggle both collectively and individually. To face towards Christ and march towards Him.

Something you have learned in making sure your own election is secure, in your own sanctification is that all temptations are really only distractions from keeping your focus on Christ. Though the details differ, all our dragons are simply our struggles to grow, to mature into that image of the Glory of Christ which Faith has planted in our hearts. Is not our fight as individual to overcome our own carnal nature so that we may more and more rely on the Grace we have been given? And considering the struggles in which we have endured, are we not driven by Charity according to our calling to be an aid to those who are struggling? So, as our goal as individuals is to overcome any obstacle, to slay every dragon which gets between us and God, why then do we think that the goal of the Church would be any different? Let me ask this another way. Is a woman evil simply because she has those come-hither hips in a summer dress or is it the lust in my heart which is the problem? Should we, as a group, rise up with passion and drive to ban shapely women in summer dresses or should we, as a group, rise up with compassion and drive to help me in my striving for chastity?

We can argue politics, philosophies, even who has the better big toe, but I have to ask if these have not become distractions. These things have their place, to-be-sure, but not to the expense of neglecting the Gospel. I do not know, but it seems to me that the idea that passing laws, no matter how just and right, is the best way to sanctification is, well the direct opposite of the Gospel. I will have to give it more thought, but the only thing which has every worked for me, the only thing that has ever changed my heart, was to turning to God in repentance.

Loving Training

More than gold, love, and especially Love is a precious thing. Just as gold, it is a matter of supply and demand. Everyone wants, everyone needs to be love, and love is such a rare thing to find. To desire is common for it is an easy thing to do. To want is to say we have the power, for a want can be refused, can be suppressed and even ignored. That even with the wants which we mistake for needs and loves, our heart knows that we can give it up. If we truly wanted to.

But to Love, to truly love is to say I need. This can be seen clearly in romance. A lover may become enthralled by the pleasure they receive from their beloved but for love to grow, it must go beyond a want of the mind, and a need of the heart. That for it to grow to love, both must accept their own weakness, that their hearts have a need to be kept safe by the other. They must accept, trust that their heart will be safe with the other. That love grows between them as those barriers which we keep up to defend ourselves from the cold and cruel world goes away. That the more the lover loves, the more the beloved owns their heart. Able to do whatever they will with the lover's heart.

See now, the fear which keeps love growing in many relationships. The fear which keeps many, many times many, running from loving. See now the fear which prevents our growth of Charity. To Love requires us to be venerable to others. To put our heart out there for others to do what they will, and you know as well as I do, that there are many, many times many, who will treat it harshly. One does not have to live long before they learn that, before they learn to create those barriers, to hide their love.

It is better to hide, to defend one's self then to cry, to feel the sorrow, the pain. Far better to feel anything else, so we do have to feel the love. At least that is what the flesh, what our human nature says. Right? We have that tendency to blame the victim for not paying attention, for being stupid, for not being strong enough not to protect themselves. Especially, or maybe only when the victim is ourselves. So many experiences in we learned that there is no one to protect us but ourselves. That we are alone, in that deep way that matters, to make it through this life.

Why? Why! I pray in sorrow and anger, and scream to you in Water and Fire. One eye crying, one eye burning. I understand that I push myself in Charity because it was love, in all its form, that I saw as a vice in my dark years. Strength was my god, and apathy the primary virtue. That Love, that the love and Charity I feel is something very precious to me. That love, feelings in general is have been such a change in me, a Grace, that I would be willing to pay any price for it. So much so that I judge myself too harshly when not living up to the ideal of Charity.

See, we should look to others as examples. That we should look to those who have a measure of Grace of a Virtue which we do not have, and feel that longing for the superman. To be inspired to become better than we are. But this goes horribly wrong when we then look at ourselves and judge ourselves harshly for not doing, being as we think we should be. Obviously, as we all know, we must grow, run that race, improve. But by judging ourselves such, we are saying that we should be strong enough, that our love or Charity is dependent on us.

Mind you, I have struggled, faced many hardships to have that small measure of Love that I have, but it is a Grace, given by God. That in order for love to grow, the lover must trust their beloved, they must know that their heart is safe in their hands. The love grows as this trust grows. But one does not have that luxury with Charity. That there will be, always be in this age, those who will rip us apart. That will take what they will, and leave us battered, bruised and broken.

Though I walk through the valley of shadows…Charity is only possible by those who follows the Way, who have the Spirit of God, because such Love requires us to live in constant danger. That to Love others is to risk those others harming us, to have some wound our heart. the carnal, the natural human reaction from such is to build those barriers, to keep and push others away from our hearts. But we have the Spirit, we of the Church, have a means of finding comfort, healing for our wounds. We are no stronger then any other, but God is. That we can give our heart to God, Trust God to keep it safe, and the more we do such, the more we can Love. That the more we find our strength in God instead of our own barriers, the less what others can do to us will cause us harm. That to Love is to suffer, and suffering, if we allow it will draw us closer to God, teach us to rely on Him more. And the more we rely on God, have our heart in His Hands, the less we will suffer from Love, which in turns allows us to Love more. So I guess all of this is just me repeating that old saying; Love until it hurts.

A Disposable Life

No joy found with what we see
Change the channel to fill our eyes
Loading our minds with the noise
Thinking belongs in the past

Another toy in our lives
Temporary happiness for sale
Throw it away when it gets dusty
Home is just a stop on the way to the trash

Enslaving in the name of freedom
Killing for the sake of convenience
When we are looking for a bargain,
Nothing is as cheep as a disposable life

Shrink wrapped hearts and plastic dreams
Living seems easy in a disposable world
No were to hide when we run from ourselves
Never seeing that life is not worth keeping 'til it's broken

Future Training

I said that I would write a little about the future, so here it is. The future is maya, an illusion, so any plan one may create is a pure fantasy. That it is, in fact, creating an image of the future, and then doing those things to create that future which gets us in trouble. Now obviously this contradicts what I have written before about the first rule in strategy is setting our goal. But it is not truly a contradiction but a paradox, different aspects of our lives which are governed by different rules. Different levels on which one may think.

Planning is important for our external-life. When one goes college, they must set a goal of a major and then plan the classes they must take to achieve that goal. In business, in conflict, in making dinner, goals and planning are important. However, in the inner-life, in becoming that person you have it in you to be, that person God is creating of you, the future only gets in the way.

For example, we know that we should have Hope. That we should have such a trust in God that we will have joy no matter what is going on. That we can sing praises to the wonder of God's mercy even when our flesh is being torn from us and that knife is being twisted in our heart. But knowing this, having this as a goal does us little good, unless we allow God to teach us, to give us more of the Grace of Hope in what we are going through in the now.

We want Hope. Hope is good. We like the idea of feeling joyful even in our sorrow. But God may not be teaching us Hope at this very moment. It could be Love, or Faith, humility, patience and so on. That we may look to the future and see a person we want to be, or maybe even that person we will be and start developing a plan to get there.

You will notice that there are those who have a hard time improving, and there are those who are always becoming that person they have it in them to be. That you might even notice, as I have, that there are times when you find that you are changing without

238

even much effort, and other times that no matter how hard you try you do not seem to make any headway. And the difference in it, at least for me, has been the difference between those times when I was trying to learn what I thought I needed to learn, and those times when I was trying to learn what God is trying to teach me.

The point being, that whether your life is hard or easy at the moment, or just average, there is a lesson which God is trying to teach you. A change in your heart which God is trying to bring about. That whether one is a deep thinker, impulsive, both or somewhere in between, the important thing is simply to allow God to take control of the training of your heart. To have your heart open to what God is teaching you rather than trying to dictate to God what you need to learn. And that right there, when you have learned to trust that what God is having you do now will lead you to where you need to go, you will have Hope. To be sure.

Into the Future

Mathew 26.36-42

It has been an interesting ten years, has it not? Still, the next ten promises to be far more interesting. You know though, nothing ever seems to go according to plan. Not that it bothers me anymore, just one of those things I have been giving thought to. It was not always such, there was a time when I would reach for a goal and it would be mine. I would reach whatever shore I set sale for. Then a strange thing started occurring, strange for me at any rate. At some point in the journey, sometimes within sight of the shore, the Wind would blow and change my course entirely. Maybe you understand the difficulty, the pain involved with struggling on the ruttier against the Wind. Maybe you know firsthand that it pointless to fight against Providence. Yet there is a world of difference between the acceptance of God's Will and being a willing percipient in it.

Such has been much of my thoughts over the last couple of weeks, the meaning of those two simple words; *Doulos Christo*. I do not know, maybe I was wrong when I focused on a social view. Maybe it was a seasonal thing. Or more likely, it was simply me misunderstanding because of a desire to work my own plans within the plans of God. The death of the ego, and the desires it causes is not an easy thing. But as I said before, in spiritual matters excuses and alibis are useless, even harmful. What is importance is repentance, a change in direction, a return to the Way, a return to Fire and Water.

And…as it is my style let me start by chastising myself (can my ego-self let me do otherwise?). It started a few years back. It was gradual and subtle, and hit me where I lived. In my prayers. It started simply with the sense that something was missing to an almost complete deadening of my sense of God. Do not mistake what I am saying, God and myself were still on speaking terms, and it was not a question of Faith. In truth, I learned to trust God and His will even more so. It was just the intimacy had slowly slipped away. Some of you understand what I mean by intimacy with God.

I understood what was happing, or I should say that I understood the experience. I mean, it is common to go through short periods when God seems so far away, and I learned not to worry about it. That is, there are times when He withholds the pleasure of contemplative prayer so that you make sure that you are coming to Him and not just for the feeling of it. No, this was not such a time. This was a Dark Night, one from which many never awaken. It took me so long to understand what was truly happening, because with my arrogance and pride, it never occurred to me that I would enter such a time.

One might even expect me to feel foolish, and I do. And this journal entry explains why: 'We, me and mine, have watched for years. So many times, we have seen the progression of the bond-servants of Christ as they lose grip on the Cross. We watched and we judged, and as with all judgments except for His are conclusions were products of pride. We, the bond-servants of my generation, watched and could not understand what they were going through. We judged them weak or foolish for they could no longer bear the nails and thorns and so placed their anointing on a shelf to collect dust. We judged them....and so it is now our turn to be judged. Will we fair any better than them, will the next generation of bond-servants judge us as we judged our parents?'

See, I feel foolish for I have known of such a time since, well, a long time. one may consider it a prime focus of study for me, as I was so determined not go let it happen to me. And in truth, thought that it could not happen to me. I see no that it is something which must come to all the bond-servants. All who wish to perfect their service must go through this dark night. But I do not like stating it such because some of you will not understand. But to that I can only shrug my shoulder and say that either you will someday, or you do not need to understand.

Let me move on to the heart of the matter because it is

already two hours past my bedtime and if I go to sleep, I will loose my train of thought. Dark Nights are times when God darkens our senses. The experience, or I should say how we experience it is very much like times when we are 'running from God'. The difference is found in the fact that during such a time you are still diligently seeking God. In part. That is, when we are running from God we avoid Him all together, but during these times in which traditionally are called dark nights and what Oswald Chambers called God's discipline of darkness, are times when we still desire God, just we want something else as well.

Dark Nights are one of those things I have never had a chance to really talk about before, or if you would really go into any depth about. This has simply had to do with reasons of authority and circles. Then it has to do with my disobedience or ambitions.

See, many years from now, in that future painted by my arrogance. You know the one I am talking about, the one in which my writings are a topic of study like the Christian masters of the past we study now. Some bright young student knowing that my emails are only a reflection of the progression of my own Faith, will notice that this dark night progressed just like the two I had before before. Maybe the student will even write a paper on how I had reached that point in which the dawn was about to arrive, when God was poised with His finger ready to point and say 'you got it buddy'. That in that moment I pulled a typical Lumpy move and danced myself right off the side of a cliff.

It is easy for me to see that point, it is my own life after all. You might remember it yourself, back a couple of years ago when I was talking of giving up my will and all that. The next step was obvious, or at least it is now that I have taken it. The purpose of that third dark night was to put God before…God's Will.

Hmm, most of you are not going to understand that so let me try it another way. Well, I have been sitting here now for fifteen minutes…but be patient with me it will come. Ok, this is the best I can do. It is like God is the sun, the light it gives of is His will. The light which is God's will light the path, lets us know which direction to go. But we get to this point where like the actual sun we start to take God for granted. We have the light so we can do the work, we have His will so...really...why do we need God? And boom that eclipse of the sun which we using to represent this dark night happens. We may not even notice it at first, it is just things are a little darker. What direction a little harder to determine. But when our will is strong we can continue on. The struggle gets a little more painful, but I am tough. The cross gets a little heavier, but I am a strong. How long someone lasts in the eclipse is not a testament of their weakness but their strength. Because...giving up is the whole point. Sound familiar?

It is so clear now that I have to laugh. Then again I have been laughing at myself a lot the last couple of weeks. I laugh now because I remember once before making the point I am about to make. Are we in a ministry or simply working for one? What I should have asked, which I really could not until now, are we in Christ or simply working for Him? And the experience of mine which I am trying to express is that it is easy for us to defend our lack of intimacy with God because we are still doing His will. That I found it is easy, far to easy, to wrap His will, whether we get it from Him or glean it from the bible, around us like a blanket and get our warmth from it than from Him.

Ok, ok, ok, ok, I got it. It is like this. I am rather introspective, right? Personal enlightenment, has always been important to me. I mean in this regard, detachment, simplicity, ultimately all that 'death of the ego' stuff I talk about. It is important stuff, it is God's will for me, but it is not God. That is, to put it in words which might be more familiar to you, because I knew, can feel, the need for that reckless abandonment in love, because I knew that Charity is the will of God, I focused so much of my will on it that I lost sight of God (which Charity being a theological virtue is impossible without Him). Meaning, we can have so much desire to do what God would have us to do, that there becomes little room in our hearts for a desire for God. Does that make more sense?

Probably not, but do not worry. It is not important. Just a short confession before I move on, return to my emails. Yet, I will not be returning to where I left off, instead I will go to where I needed to have gone. We will go boldly were no Lumpy has gone before. Namely, writing about *Doulos Christo*. I do not think I am spelling that correctly (My Latin has always been better than my Greek, and my Latin is terrible, that is I know a hand full of words.) Regardless how it is supposing to be spelt it means bond-servant of Christ.

See I can give you a meaning to bond-servant but I will not, because they would only be words. My words, and anything I have to say about it is pointless in the face of Love for God. Which is the point in its entirely. The question is not what label we may apply, but how are we bound. Some are bound by the law, the fear of punishment. Others are bound by duty, what they must do because the Love Christ has for them. Still others, are bound, as in a vice, by their love for Christ.

That is why the poor knight had to die, and I am now nameless for the time being. A knight may have love for his Lord, great love, but he serves because of his since of honor. Because it is what he does. Not to serve the Lord, well…that does not compute. The point being, the real point, the only point, is that eventually one who wants to perfect their service to God, must stop serving out of any sense of fear or duty, but only from that binding Love for Christ. It is only with this in which we can truly say that our ministry is truly Christcentric, focused on Him. Because my honor, my sense of duty, character, and all such things are about me, and I do not want this to be about me. What I am, who I am, simply I am not important. This is not about humility, for my humility (and pride) is unimportant next to Christ.

Knights in a Church without Honor

1 Thessalonians 1: Therefore, we also pray always for you that our God would count you worthy of this calling, and fulfill all the good pleasures of His goodness and work of Faith with power, that the name of our Lord Jesus Christ may be glorified in you, and you in Him, according to the grace of our God and the Lord Jesus Christ.

For me, the New Year generally starts at Easter. It is more physiological than anything, with my focus on the death and resurrection of Christ. The time I spend meditating on my own death, and the death of the self I still need to experience. This is common for a Knight, the Life of High Adventure is a life of change, a path of the flesh continuously dying so that the King of the Golden City may be glorified in us. This time has differed in only the degree, a shift great enough that it is worthy of changing the name of the folder in which I keep my writings. To keeping with adage that to write the best, write about what you know about, or in my case the only thing I know about, it was renamed to the Sacred Rose.

I have always preferred *Sancta Rosa* as the symbol of our Faith, as to gain a truly firm grasp on it one feels the not only the softness of the petals but also the prick of the thorns. I consider the most damaging of heresies to say that our salvation has no cost. While as you well know, the Grace which has been given us cannot be earned. But the idea that salvation is without cost, without a price is a folly. But it is the words 'cost' and 'price' which confuses them, so a better term, and way of looking at it is not as a cost but as simple effect. The Grace of Salvation, the regeneration and rebirth we experience has an effect on us, and continues to do so in the sanctification the Spirit brings.

This is, of course, what I have always meant by Beyond Salvation. That for us, the Way of the Inner-Life is not about obtaining salvation. The Life of High Adventure, the climbing of the foggy mountain is not what we do to gain salvation but begins with it. The *Sancta Rosa* is the affect in which regeneration had on us. That desire for sanctification, to be better, to be glorified in Christ. A burning drive to have the 'name of our Lord Jesus Christ may be glorified in you, and you in Him.' And this is a price, is it not? Though I should be quick to point out that it is merely our flesh which considers it a cost. Is it not the lust of the flesh which considers it a price the death our carnal desires? Is it not the pride of our flesh which considers it a shame, and not a glory to subjugate our will, the will of the King?

Maybe it was just me, born a prince, born to rule, I needed no more justification for my actions than I was the one who did them. My arrogance was well founded being a man of superior abilities, but well-founded only how the flesh judges such things. And more to the point I am getting at, I never learned the skill of self-promotion for no other reason than the glory I had in the flesh was evident, as the flesh of others judge such things. The way I held myself, the way I talked, the arrogance with the abilities to back it up. That is all behind me now, making me just a could-have-been. I can say that it was all by choice, but the only real choice was following where God was leading. That the glory we have in Christ is not only unrecognized by the flesh, but considered a cost. And very often it is considered a shame, and sometimes even evil by the flesh of others.

I sometimes (ok often) make the mistake in writing as if everyone is a philosopher, or at least well versed in the various schools and their arguments. I write about nothing, about living without desire. While I mean that also in the general enlightenment kind of way of living, seeing what is actually going around you instead assuming what you want is happening. However, more specifically, it is carnal desires, the desires of the flesh which must be tamed. It is not desire in and of itself, as they are the driving force of the Will, but more the expectations derived from the desires of the flesh which form our dragon. In more assessable terms, regeneration brought to us God's desire, and a drive to put aside our own desires so we may fulfill His.

The part of our sanctification in which we strive to become better people, better husbands, parents, uncles or mentors is acceptable, even popular. It seems that the many, if not most view religion as nothing more than a self-help program with some spiritual language thrown in. It is understandable, considering how much we struggle in our immaturity to understand and live up to the Grace we have been given. But *Sancta Rosa,* sanctification is not really our struggle in becoming a better person, or not only about that struggle. It is our struggles, hardships and dire temptations in doing the will of God, to 'fulfill all the good pleasures of His goodness.'

While I know that not all of your Traditions consider mortification, the putting to death the desire of the flesh as a vehicle of Grace, nonetheless our struggle to live according to God's will which brings those changes in us. We become better people, to be sure, but not according to the flesh. That at our conversion we gain a glimpse of what God would make of us, but the vision is clouded by the desires of our flesh. We gained a glimpse of the glory we will have in Christ when we see Him face to face. While it is unarguably hubris to believe that you have achieved in this age the perfection we will give in the next, but as we mature, we make progress towards that image, we start changing into the person we are to be in Christ. More and more we do God's will, not as a law imposed on us but because it is who we are.

As we matured, we have learned that those things which our Faith cost us, those things which were counted as a loss by our flesh are in fact a gain to us. When we look back on the early years of our Faith, when we were stubborn and prideful and flopped around like a fish out of water at every little thing God would have us do, we thought in terms of gain and loss. We call them little things now, but then the cost seemed too much to pay. We can see this often in those who disregard the authority of Scripture. Though their excuses vary, they declare that the image of perfection in which Scripture gives us is too hard, too strict, too high of a standard. That is, it is rooted in the idea that Faith is without cost, that regeneration does not have that affect on us of which we will face any struggle to live by God's standards instead of our own.

A friend called me recently with a question if he had acted with Honor, or was his action born from pride. In many ways this post was motivated by that conversation. That is, the only pride in which we could discern in the affair was the problem accepting the cost of the action. He stood up for what was right, and so he got that taste of how much people love the darkness and hate the light. There was a question of pride for him, only because it was a little struggle for him, he did it simply because it was the right thing to do, but it was a dire struggle to others, they saw his actions as a great evil. The Honorable nature of his actions were unimportant, because they had no concept of Honor.

Which is why I relate this to mortification. You and I may argue on whether we can officially consider it a vehicle of Grace, but nonetheless, has it not been through those dire struggles in which you have learned to accept God's Will as being the same as His Love. That He is showing us His Love by the strict image, the perfection we are striving for as He does by forgiving us for not being able to live it. But the Church today is without Honor. We, generally speaking, are unwilling to bear even minor struggles. Oh, we will struggle, we will work, volunteer, sacrifice, go on crusades to accomplish our own will. We, you and I, have done this once or twice, have we not? Remember how the flesh balked, and even grew angry at those who corrected us. That is, more than anything else, mortification is the destruction of that part of us which refuses to be corrected. The part of us which will place our own will above the Will of God.

I have mostly focused on humility over the years because my dire struggles were against pride. Some of it was just plain arrogance. It was a fierce and harsh struggle of my first five years or so just to accept that peasants are individuals who are worthy of respect. Another five to crush that part of myself who would be a tyrant, to put to death that temptation of it being so easy to pick up the sword and be that leader people are looking for. In a way this is an epilogue, but that was basically what the *Insane Voyages* was about. I called it insane, not because of those who think that my spiritual insight is insanity, but because by all the standards of the flesh it is insane to throw away a future in which you have what you want for the sake of the unknown future of God's will. Insane indeed, for knowing beforehand that by doing so, by rejecting the very structure of the social-illusion, you will be rejected by those who see only through the desires of the flesh.

As knights, we obviously had no taste for a luke-warm Faith. We desired, and continue to desire a conformity of our hearts, an inward transformation into that Image of the Glory of Christ. In the beginning our dire temptations were inward, our struggle was our own, the cost was to our own flesh. The cost has very much been our flesh, the death of our carnal desires. As we grow, we find it easier to do God's will, not because our will is stronger but because we desire God's will more than we desire our own. Honor is not a set of rules to live by, but the character which we have to follow the law. But then that day occurs when stand up for the law, for what is right. That is, you have lived with the Sacred Rose for so long, that God has grown your Honor to the point where there is simply no cost to you to do what is right.

That does not mean that it suddenly becomes easy for in a way it becomes harder. For we may more easily subdue our own flesh, such is the time which we learn that doing God's will, and living according to the glory we have in Him, costs the flesh of others as well. I knew early in my Faith that God was forging me to have no earthly authority, and *Insane Voyages* was me finally coming to terms, accepting that. Maybe I should put it that it was the time when I came to understand that. The lessons in leadership which God taught me were not found in any book, except for Scripture. Most of you lack the sociopathic ability to control the social-illusion in the minds of others, or know how that creates such a temptation to be a tyrant...the tyrant wants their power, and the people want their tyrant. People want a person to follow, an idol in which to give their adoration. That is, in our age people do not want leaders, they want entertainers to make them feel good, to give them pleasure.

Such is the Church Culture today, a social-illusion, a world-view, built without Honor, built by the flesh. You can expect to be accepted and even praised while you struggling for Honor, for morality, but once you are Honorable, once you start to act in that moral, that right way that quickly goes away. Remember again how we once balked, and even grew angry at those who corrected us. Can we not say that they did right by us, that they acted with Honor, though we did not see it at the time? Think how many times God's will was not pleasing to us, not pleasing to our flesh and we struggled even to desire it. What got us through those times? Was it not the Spirit of God who worked on us, not only the ability to do God's will, but to have no greater desire, or find no greater pleasure than God's will? Could we not say that if it was not for being saved, if it was not for the active work the Spirit performs then and now, God's will would simply to harsh? Does not the flesh scream that Honor, holiness, morality, striving to not only do the right thing, but do it in the right way, is a folly?

Being a knight is defining Honor how God defines it, and not how our flesh defines it. The world defines honor as being worthy of praise, of having those attributes promoted by the culture we live in. But our Honor is found in Christ, and is Christ. I strive to be an uncle in which my nephew can admire. This is good and honorable, but it is better and Honorable for me to strive to be the uncle that God would have me be so he will know that those traits he so admires have been forged in me by God. But there are times when he is not pleased with me. The years I spent drilling him in mathematics, or forcing him to sound something out rather then reading it to him, or mastering the index in a reference book. He sees the benefits now, being able to look up a feat in the Player's Handbook, or add his to hit modifiers quickly, but at the time he hated it. He has learned to accept my 'lecturing' only because he has come to understand that I have a point, that there is a purpose to it that he may not see in the now. That is, he has learned to trust me.

While I know I took the easy route using children, but that is the view that much of the Church has, even teaches today, is it not? God as a means to get what you want, spoiled children who are basically saying that God can not show us Love if he is expecting us to eat our broccoli. That as knights, we see our salvation and our calling as a duty, and there are times when our duty weighs on us. A bit of a side note, but I the battle for chastity, in feelings, has been different than that for humility. Lust is more like a hunger, like that compulsion to eat which comes at that fist bite after a fast. Pride always created a heavy weight, a load I could not carry and was crushing me, a desire to run away from the responsibility. That it was a lesson in trust, in accepting God's will, in trusting Christ to get the work done. But then again, I think pride has a lot to do with the lack of Honor in the Church, the unwillingness to accept that God gives other callings than our own. That pride that want things our way, to want Faith that works the way we want it to work. (But back to the point.)

I hold the Sacred Trust of Fire and Water, so being rejected, feared and sometimes despised is sort of my lifestyle. An affect of my calling, if you would. Obviously, we all prefer the Water, the southing comfort of conformation. Most of you have felt the Fire at one time or another, some of you knew me when my pride made it far more biting then it needed to be. But considering that so many people believe God is the path to pleasure, do you really think that they will not judge us by the same standard? Considering that they see Faith as a means only to feel good about themselves, does it not stand to reason that you will be labeled as unchristian, or at least unloving if you do something that makes them feel bad, causes them some hardship, that costs their flesh.

Let me conclude this, as it is already too long. If we are glorified in Christ, and the name of our Lord Jesus Christ is glorified in us, the flesh of others are going to react to us in the same manner as our flesh reacted to our on sanctification. Obviously, this only applies to those actins which are truly Honorable, are truly the right thing to do, but the more you act according to the will of God, the more you live the Grace you have been given, the more the world is going to see you as opposed to fleshly honor. Our own flesh will consider this a cost, but a cost the flesh has to pay as it is simply an affect of being in Christ.

Journal of the Poor Knight

I do not keep a journal in the strictest sense, but rather end up journaling during my note taking for whatever I am writing at the moment. Usually, it is a line or two expressing a thought to explore latter, but sometimes I get a bit 'poetic' with the idea and some of these are found below.

For Yesterday We Died

'Let every Knight who serves the King of the Golden City keep in mind that there are enemies of the King who claim to be citizens of the City. Those who can be seen this morning dressed as the finest and most worthy of Knights but tonight will be found carousing with those who make war on the Golden City and curse its King. That while eyes are on them they make grand parade, swearing bold oaths of their loyalty and service to our King, but in their hearts they make vile plans to seize His Thrown and be a tyrant over His people…let every Knight who serves the King of the Golden City keep equally in mind that among the enemies of the King, among those who lay in wait to ambush His Knights, are those who the King has chosen to eventually become citizens of the Golden City….therefore let every Knight who serves the King of the Golden City keep in mind that our Honor is not found in slaying the King's enemies, but in doing the King's Will'

…It is a scar in which Knights recognize each other. It is that one pain, one struggle in which every Knight has in common….A knight must face and defeat a self-loathing of which the mediocre cannot comprehend. For a knight can never defeat their Dragon until they hate themselves as much as they hate the Dragon. It is that one secret, that one truth that all Knights know…That the Dragon that they must defeat lurks not in some cave in a far-off land, but hides within their own heart. It is not accepting this, coming to terms with this that has felled more Knights then any temptation that the world has to offer...Indeed, what in this world could be a temptation, if it was not for the darkness which is already in our own hearts?...

...One spends their time as a squire, they learn and they train. Given time they earn their spurs, but they are not truly a knight until they face their dragon. It is by facing our dragons we become a knight, that we come to know ourselves to be a knight. By facing our dragon that we stop playing a role, relying on position, rank, on the authority of others, and act from the understanding that we are a knight...it is by facing the dragon in which one stops saying that 'I have been knighted, that others have recognized me', and instead says 'I am a knight, it is just what I am'...It is not sword or lance, shield or armor which is the mark of the knight, but the scars of that fight. And when one has those scars they are free to act, as a knight acts, rather than to act trying to give knightly proof, to themselves, to others, to the King...it is by facing their dragon a knight learns that they have already accomplished enough to be a knight, and in that becomes free to accomplish that which it is a knight is entrusted to do....

...There are no Dragons in the so-called civilized lands. Dragons exist only in the far reaches of the world, in the very realm of the unknown. Dragons live only in places we cannot see, places where few have dared to go. Indeed, the strength of a Dragon is not that it can defeat us in combat, but that we refuse to seek it out. Refuse to confront it at all. The very power of the Dragon is in that we fear to look into the cave in which it lives. Indeed, to face our fear, to take on the quest of slaying a Dragon, and to keep to that quest, robs the Dragon of its potency. Indeed, the truth of this is so striking that once one develops the resolve to face their Dragon, defeating it is an easy task...

...Abandon all pretension, ye who enters here....Sword and Armor cannot do their work, and remain clean. A sword requires no jewels, only to remain strong and sharp. Bloodied and dented armor is the price of victory. Pomp and ceremony have their place, and it is not in the thick of battle. There is no place in fighting dragons for the sycophant or the fashion-monger....There is no room for the concern of what others think of you, or even what you think of yourself when that time comes to face your Dragon. There is only one question which matters, and the answer has nothing to do with appearance. It all has to do with reality. The inner-reality which we may hide from others but we can never truly hide from ourselves. It is the dark caves of our hearts which the fiercest of dragons live ....

...Our Lord is not just the King, but also the Knight of the Golden City. Not simply a knight, but the Knight. He is the Knight-Who-Never-Fails, A perfect knight, Honor perfected. If one wants to know what it is to be a knight, one need only to look to Him. In Christ you will find not only an image of all Honor which is perfect, but with Christ you will find all that is in you to be perfected. If you just dare to look to Him to be your Lord and your King.

...If you dare to look in your memories, if you have the courage, there are always regrets. If you are honest there are always that which could have been....if only...and those 'if only' can kill us....it shows that we still do not desire what is right, at least enough to judge all things through righteousness...do I love Christ? Always. But if I always liked God, then I would doubt if I truly know Him. High Adventure is not always a pleasing thing, not always a pleasant life. The King causes the rain to fall on the righteous and the wicked alike...A knight of the King of the Golden City gains no reward until they can fight no more...the only regret which is (almost) proper are those for the hardships we cause. Regret for our stupidity, regrets allowable for the motivation it gives us to do better next time...To regret, to complain, even to dislike the evil which befalls us for being knights, for doing His will is to regret, complain and dislike God's plan for the universe and for us. The hardest, and perhaps the last of the lessons a knight must learn is to be pleased that the will of their Lord is accomplished. To find joy only in being known by the King, to find our Honor only in that His orders were fulfilled...even when doing so cost us everything...or when someone else gets the credit.

Upside Down Pyramids

Many prophets looked over the city and found it in their hearts to go to Nin'eveh. Some were full of pride to be sure, but they were prophets, and what they desired was for the city to turn from their evil way. Nineveh was violators of the most sacred law, the crime which some say brought death to Sodom and to Gomorra. They did not treat the stranger with hospitality, but with contempt, violence and many times worse. Many went to change the heart of the Nineveh people, all of them died as all travelers to the city died, in a cruel and horrible fashion. They had thought that because they desired above all else the will of God that Elohim would protect them and keep them safe. They thought because they spoke the language of God that they could reach the Nineveh people...they were wrong.

When God did move, when He choose to send one to speak for Him, Elohim chose a prophet, not one after His own heart, but one who was less like a Child of God and more like the people of Nineveh. Elohim choose a man who would rather drown then give them another chance, one who would rather die then see the city come to salvation. He spoke to them, as one of them, in the ways of their hearts, full of bitterness and anger, preaching a God filled with the same. Oh, Jonah, did you learn the lesson of the vine? Oh, Jonah, did you come to understand the longing God has to show mercy on the unjust? Have we?

...What can be said that has not already been said, at least twice. Do we really want to waste our time in search for the new, to chase after the wind as the preacher would say? There is no such thing as the new, there is only the next. Progression from one to another, step by step, from ancient to modern, it has all been there. Not even progression, simply a rearrangement. That philosophy, that ideal, that understanding, that thing which we find so titillating, that fad we find so refreshing, they are not new, they are as old as time, just the same old concepts wrapped in different words…

…. What would a painting of a sunset be to us if we had no sight? What meaning would a song have if we had no sense of hearing? What would happen to the painting or song if we did not possess the senses to take them into our understanding? Would we not then say that the painting is only worth the warmth it can give to a fire, would we not then deny the very existence of the song? How much of a different form our lives would take without sight or hearing. How much the difference our life takes when we ignore the noble senses of our heart…

….we might judge ourselves by our past, reveling in the glory of victories, or wallowing in the pity of defeats. Better it would be to judge ourselves on the future, that person that we might hope to be, or fear to be. Still better, we may judge ourselves on who we are in the now, our strengths and abilities, or weaknesses and flaws. Yet, best of all, give up the notion of judging yourself all together. It is energy wasted chasing the wind, energy which could be better spend on living as God would have us live.

….Do we yet understand?….To see…to act in accordance with reality…to judge from the view of the Truth instead of the fantasies…the illusions...the preconceptions we create from our desires. Thus is the Philosophical Ideal we have oft spoken… The point in which all understanding begins…and ends. But you must let this slip away as well….We live only that infinitely small measure of time we call the now. The now is always changing, it is never constant, time marches never to be regained. Understanding the Truth can only be accomplished from the now…only when your point of being is fully in the now, can you move according to infinity. To try to stand with one foot in time, and the other in eternity….is to be torn apart by the force….

….Is there a measurement so small which it cannot be divided in half? Is there one so large which cannot be doubled? How can time be both subjective and objective? Is a tree still a tree, even if one does not know what a tree is? Is God still present even though we are not aware of His Presence?....all systems are illusions, simply a frame on which to build the philosophical house on. They exist for no other reason than to give a starting place to apply our thoughts. The best of systems is nothing more than a bare foundation, relying on the individual to decide for themselves what is best, to form their own ideas and ideals. Those systems which allow, and take into account, those who would search for perfection. Those which allow them to make mistakes, systems which gives guidance...The great temptation, the beginning of the end, of any Tradition is when it starts replacing this ideal, the search for inner-perfection, with the ideal of rules, laws and regulations. When perfection is replaced by mediocrity, when doing what is expected replaces going above and beyond as the highest ideal. In short, a Tradition becomes corrupt when we replace the Most High God with a god of our own creation....

...People often talk of mercy when really, they mean they desire to avoid responsibility. People often talk of the responsibility when really, they mean that they are afraid of what others might do if given the chance. People talk of justice but what they mean is revenge, they talk of forgiveness but they mean they do not want consequences. Law without mercy is tyranny. Mercy without Law is chaos. The Justice of the Way is a perfect balance between Law and Mercy.

The Making of a Hero

The problem is not that we suffer. It is that we do not suffer enough...Suffering is agreeable as long as we can bare it, and we can bare it as long as we have a reason to suffer...We only step to the edge of suffering. We pretend to suffer, we complain about suffering, but we never throw ourselves over the cliff into suffering. Never stepping into that insanity from which greatness is born. We suffer only from the lack of true suffering. We suffer from a lack of reason to suffer truly, to suffer for that which is big enough to take away the suffering...True suffering tears and renders those walls we have so carefully built to protect us from the world around us, the walls built by the fantasies knowing how things should be. From those times in which we simply cannot afford our dysfunctions, likes, tastes and all of the luxury of personality... True suffering works Humility in us...but unwilling to humble ourselves before Elohim, unwilling to discard our own plans in favor of the Will of God, unwilling to have anyone or thing be exalted above our own status, we suffer in our suffering. We numb ourselves, tranquilizing our feelings with fantasies of pleasure, with fantasies of a life without suffering. Maybe going a step further into the addiction of trying to live those fantasies. Chasing after a viva loco of pleasures, or the complacent life of routine...all because our goal, our greatest ambition is not to let go of other burdens while we carry our cross."

......it is not given to the wise to change a society...the wise by the nature are conservative, slow to action...weighing each action with what the repercussions might be...not only the affect but that effects affect, and that affects affect...let us just say, so on and so on into eternity...it is the barbarian in which change comes....to act without thought of repercussion...to reach out and grab, thinking only of what you take...That barbarian impulse, inherit in our heart, is the ability to do what needs to be done... the ability to suppress morality, to suppress the very concept of wrong and accomplish that which is necessary...to survive...the barbarian in us survives....lives on no matter how often we deny it or try to kill it... No matter how many layers of 'civilization' we paint on ourselves, the reality is that we are but barbarians, and if we were to strip away the constraints of culture, to rid ourselves of law and commandment, we would quickly prove that we are barbarians. We would prove it, or we would be replaced by those who are willing to...we fear them both, I think...hate and love the wise and the barbarian in us....both speaks of reality...to what we fear the most, what we are capable of.... Both exist beyond what rules we may oppose or deny...the bonds we complain about, the bonds we love....yet, what would a society be without those self-imposed restraints?...indeed what would our inner-life be if there was not war between what is wise and what is barbaric?

...Refuse to go quietly into that dark night but fight, fight against the dying of the light'... As we grow older it is only fitting that we lament over what we have lost from our youth. As we experience the aches and pains of the gradual decay to the grave it is only natural to find the idealism and fanaticism which came so easy in our youth slowly slipping away. The fire burns lower, the light of possibilities faded and dimmed. We no longer have the energy to raise our fists against the injustice, both real and perceived. Maybe we have grown stronger, no longer torn and wounded by the sharp teeth of a less-than-perfect world. Maybe we only have a limited amount of tears for the troubles of the soul, or we have no more time to tolerate pigs who have learned to wear jewelry. Maybe we have gained the wisdom to live beyond the obsessive addictions which drives the lives of mortals. Maybe it is we have gained the honesty to admit that the problems are so complicated that we have no idea on what to do so have simply given up. Maybe we...but it really does not matter, Life is not about us, and after all, the show must go on...the show must go on.

...Creativity is a form of self-destruction. In order to create one must go beyond what is, and seek, reach for, driven to that which could be. Not simply to produce, but to create, to express the deepest aspect of one's heart. One must attack, tear and rend those very boundaries which keeps us sane. One must free themselves from the very illusion-matrix in which we rely so heavily to function in the world....How delicate an operation this is, how easy it is to go too far. To strive for such a perfect expression of what could be, that one loses themselves. To become obsessed, controlled by one's own creation. But not to go far enough, not to reach down and rip out and exposes that spark we call creativity, can be seen as even worse, for then one only becomes another artists who make up that mass called pop culture.

...Harmony is a circle, action is a triangle...living in a world which cares only for their rights, it is not popular to speak of responsibility. But the Creator did not give us rights without purpose, that each right we possess has been given us to fulfill a responsibility. You say you have the right to speak your mind, and I say nay, you have the authority to speak it in order to fulfill the responsibility of saying something worth the effort. You say you have the right to bear arms, and I say that you have the authority to have access to force in order to fulfill the responsibility to create a peaceful and ordered society. You speak of parental rights, I say nay and nay again, you have authority only because of your responsibility to look to the welfare of your children....and in that, we see that the concept of rights without responsibility does not lead to tyranny, but rather defines it...

...Do they know what it is like to feel the fire of destiny burning everything else out their heart? Do they know what it is like to hear the calling and run from fear of it? To feel a burden so heavy that they are ground to dust under it? To try to use their own will to force their own image of it? Do they know what it is like to succumb to the loneliness and pride of it, sure that no one but they can understand it? Of course, they do, many have experienced it themselves. They are common experiences when you realize there is a purpose to your existence, a calling on your life. But can they comprehend what it is like for a child who feels the fire? Could they understand what it is like to have your earliest memories being the feeling that there is something you must do...something you will never be strong enough for....

Something which you would have to die to accomplish. If they did, if they truly understood what is like feel the weight of the world, before you even knew there was a world. to be mortally wounded by a shadow person when you were barely into puberty...to fear, to be terrified of your own ability and what they mean...to curse your own weakness... and hate your strengths even more. If they knew what it is like to live as a child who dances with the candle flame and the person Elohim may forge from such a child, then they would really understand me. But then again…if they did…what would I have to write about?…

…Do not be quick to think you are not one of the masses, that you are not part of the mob. That is precisely what makes one part of the mass instead of an individual. The illusion, the fantasy that they are really independent, that they are acting according to reason, according to what is truth. If one truly wants to think for themselves, if they truly want to be one of those individuals that prevent the group from turning into a mod, they must first know their self, and the forces which shape it. And knowing this, to realize, understand that they are part of the group, that they are neither independent, free or separated from being affected by the same forces which shapes and molds the group…'

…. One cannot succeed without taking risks. Even if one's goal is to avoid risk, to be safe, one must put themselves at risk in order to achieve it. It is foolish to think one is safe as long as one stays within the stronghold, secure as long as one does not venture outside the walls. Oh, to be sure one is safe from the barbarians raging the countryside, secure in the knowledge that they cannot break through the defenses. But what may they be up to out there while you are safe in your castle? You have your council, and they tell you. But how do they know? They do not venture to and fro any more than you do. The most interesting thing, is when you do decide to take the risk, and visit the barbarians, you find that they are not barbarians at all but other lords hold up in their own keeps…

Insane sanity

The goal of all mystical traditions, no matter what 'religion' it might belong, is summed up by a nut. One must crack open the shell in order to get to the meat. This is not news to anyone who knows where the fist goes when we open our hand. Yet when you crack enough nuts you eventually realize that the meat itself must be thrown away. Or if you would, when you crack open your last nut, you find....

.....What would a painting of a sunset be to us if we had no sight? What meaning would a song have if we had no sense of hearing? What would happen to the painting or song if we did not possess the senses to take them into our understanding? Would we not then say that the painting is only worth the warmth it can give to a fire, would we not then deny the very existence of the song? How much of a different form our lives would take without sight or hearing. How much the difference our life takes when we ignore the noble senses of our heart...

...Am I enlightened? What an ill question I ask myself but I know that I am not. For where it is true that I am enlightened enough that I do not try to prove, even to myself, that I am enlightened, I am not so enlightened that I have stopped asking that question. If I was truly enlightened, I would live a life enlightened instead of wasting time asking myself if I am enlightened. It is not that I would not have to ask the question because I already know, but because it would not matter...

...Do we yet understand?....To see...to act in accordance with reality...to judge from the view of the Truth instead of the fantasies...the illusions...the preconceptions we create from our desires. Thus, is the Philosophical Ideal we have oft spoken... The point in which all understanding begins...and ends. But you must let this slip away as well.... We live only that infinitely small measure of time we call the now. The now is always changing, it is never constant, time marches never to be regained. Understanding the Truth can only be accomplished from the now...only when your point of being is fully in the now, can you move according to infinity. To try to stand with one foot in time, and the other in eternity....is to be torn apart by the force....

...In both east and west, old and new, it is a common preconception in philosophy that understanding begins with the understanding that we do not understand. Easy to explain in the simple terms that when we understand something we stop our attempt to understand it. We no longer seek a better understanding of it. Oh, what a fool I have been for I believed I understood this. I held firmly to the preconception that I could never fully understand. Slowly and over much time I found the error in this, ridding myself of the preconception that I must understand. Finally coming to understand that the only thing in which to understand is nothing. Even in this there was something to understanding, a preconception which was persistent. Through it all there is a question which is never asked, and answer never given. Understanding nothing was just a step to the true understanding that I will never understand, not because I can never fully or truly understand but because there is no I in which to do the understanding.....Indeed, zero does equal infinity!...

...Would it shock them to learn that I hold The Truth higher than anything else? That I place The Truth even higher than Elohim? Would they understand why it must be so for me? Would they understand if Elohim is not also The Truth, the truth of which all other truth is based, then Elohim would not be the Most High God, but simply a pretender to the Throne?...

...To even have a spark of vision is to be one out of hundred. To be aware of it, to struggle with it, to feel the pain of it, one out of ten thousand. To embrace it, in which all which have contact must accept or reject, one out of a hundred thousand. To excel, to become what it is you can be, such a person is one out of a million. To master it, to become a god that the whole world must either accept or reject, such a person is only seen once in a century, maybe. But to be God, to be one whom the whole world must accept or reject, not only now but for all times, well that can only happen once in all of history...

...Is the past the only future we can know? Do we not have any choice but to repeat the cycle, time and time again, until the end of the age? Is it too much to hope for that at least the leaders, at least those who claim to have the wisdom to lead, would see the now?...The problem with any political system is that which governs social interaction are not laws, in the natural sense of the word. There is no 'I must' when it comes to human behavior, only 'I should'. It is that, and that alone, which is the core of the human experience, that and the denial of what one should do....able to base any action on a choice, thus one has a countless number of actions in which to choose. In this we find the foundation of every culture, every society-illusion. Social norms, morality, frameworks to give a structure, a limit to the choices we make so that we may act in a way suitable to that society in which we live...and it is in this we find both the rise and fall of every culture, every system. Only God is eternal, ever thing else is just dust in the wind....

.... there are those who think that life would easy if they could but see the threads of the pattern, fate for a lack of a better term. To this I say that life is not better. But, they say, if I knew where each road leads then I take the best one. Yes, I would reply, you could better choose a course which takes you the direction you want to go, but do not mistake that for the best. We rarely have the wisdom to define best as anything other than what we want at the moment....

.... A rose by any other name will still prick your finger. There is something which is such beauty to behold that any pain is worth its sight. Its very nature promises us the height of delight if we but reach out and take hold. The pleasure at first does indeed prevent us from feeling the thorn, we do not even know of its presences. Then slowly as the sweetness fades all there is left is the pain from the thorn. It is then when we ask is the rose worth the thorn. It is then we must decide to accept the suffering with the pleasure or to forsake them both....and when we decide, as it is a choice no matter what it may seem, to ignore the pain for the sake of the rose, and we continue with such a life, we learn, too late, always too late, that we have not taken possession of the rose, but the rose possesses us....

Honest Eyes

Actions reveal mouths would lie
Of the truths our hearts might tell
Of anger unspoken, of love unvoiced
Of mercy, pain, and misery

In the double-mind of desiring to stop desire,
Where is the mouth which speaks such truth?
Where is this ear that hears my thoughts?
Where is this eye that sees such inward ugliness?

The mouth cannot hear, the ear cannot speak,
And the eye cannot see itself,
So, the face we ought to be,
is the mirror of honest reflection

With honest eyes we may see
The truths other hearts might tell
Of anger unspoken, of love unvoiced
Of their mercy, pain, and misery

Emails to John

www.ingramcontent.com/pod-product-compliance
Lightning Source LLC
Chambersburg PA
CBHW061817040426
42447CB00012B/2702